Cherry Simmonds was born and raised in Merseyside, the youngest of nine children. She is married to her childhood sweetheart, Eric, who was born in the same street as her. They have three sons and two miniature Schnauzers, all now living in New Zealand.

Being of a versatile nature, Cherry has had many jobs, including cleaning lady, Real Estate Agent and Project Manager building a retirement village. Her hobbies are gardening and opera, her passion is writing, especially for radio, while her obsession is building or renovating houses (nineteen to date).

NOBODY IN PARTICULAR

Cherry Simmonds

BANTAM BOOKS

LONDON · NEW YORK · TORONTO · SYDNEY · AUCKLAND

NOBODY IN PARTICULAR
A BANTAM BOOK : 0 553 81528 8

Originally published in 2000 by Acclaim Publishing Limited (NZ)
First publication in Great Britain

PRINTING HISTORY
Bantam edition published 2003

1 3 5 7 9 10 8 6 4 2

Set in 11/12¼pt Times by
Kestrel Data, Exeter, Devon.

Bantam Books are published by Transworld Publishers,
61–63 Uxbridge Road, London W5 5SA,
a division of The Random House Group Ltd,
in Australia by Random House Australia (Pty) Ltd,
20 Alfred Street, Milsons Point, Sydney, NSW 2061, Australia,
in New Zealand by Random House New Zealand Ltd,
18 Poland Road, Glenfield, Auckland 10, New Zealand
and in South Africa by Random House (Pty) Ltd,
Endulini, 5a Jubilee Road, Parktown 2193, South Africa.

Printed and bound in Great Britain by
Clays Ltd, St Ives plc.

This book is dedicated to my husband Eric, with love.
His unwavering love and support helped me
become the whole person I am today.

With very special thanks to Steve Danby, Drama Producer, National Radio, in New Zealand for his insight and encouragement. His advice has been invaluable.

With gratitude to Marion Gilhooley who sifted through and typed the manuscript.

'In Heaven even an angel is nobody in particular'

George Bernard Shaw
Man and Superman, 1903

The triumphs and tragedies of the Faulkner Family. A true story full of laughter and tears:

Cherry was born during the blitz on Merseyside. Even though she was the last in a family of eleven she was a solitary kid, who from necessity soon learnt to be streetwise and gutsy, with the power to make her own luck as she waited to be adopted by someone – anyone!

Mam was menopausal and depressed. Always saving for a divorce from 'the bloody reptile' or 'her own business', whichever came cheaper.

Dad whiled away the hours in the backyard lavvy, playing his banjo while waiting for the pub to open.

The Family was made up of five boys and four girls: two died and three got married, which according to Mam amounted to the same thing. National Service would take care of the rest.

The House was distinguished by the battleship grey paint-work. All guests were unwelcome especially the crawling and scurrying kind.

The Shop was mostly a labour of love, occasionally became a labour of hate but was one place Cherry could hold down an honest job (or almost honest). Striving for acceptance into the local business community is fraught with disaster and bewilderment as the family contends with the local council, police, power cuts and each other.

Merseyside was booming, put on the map by the Beatles, rock and roll and industrial strikes. Liverpool Football Club won the FA Cup for the first time. It was OK to talk with a thick nasal accent; it was more than OK.

The Story of nobody in particular, whose lifelong search for identity was dramatically revealed and changed by a mousetrap.

This is a true story, however some of the names have been changed – but only to protect the guilty!

1

We'd got another set of twins in our street, born just a few months ago. A girl called Victoria Edwina and a boy, Victor Edward. Their dad was a sailor during the war and he was so glad to be back in one piece that he named his kids after VE day. My dad said it was a bloody good job we won the war, as he might have called the kids Adolf and Eva.

VE day was the very best day of my life. I was fit to burst with happiness. The road had been barricaded with oil drums to stop the traffic from getting through because we were having our very own 'Victory V' street party. Everyone was happy and my mam was even talking and laughing with the snotty neighbours who were sitting in chairs placed into groups outside open front doors. The street became alive with families gathered round the crumbled front walls; kids playing marbles and flipping milk bottle tops in the gutter. Little squares of dyed rags sewn onto string to look like flags were strung across from bedroom windows and wrapped around lamp-posts. Some patriotic soul had carefully saved silver paper from his fag packets and had stuck on pictures of the Royal Family, Winston Churchill and of course, Montgomery. Pity it rained a bit as all the crêpe paper flowers and decorations we'd been making for weeks got wet and the red dye ran in patches over the bed sheets that were used for tablecloths – it looked like someone had been slaughtered on the table.

Everywhere around the country, other street parties were being held. Of course ours was the best, with my Patty working at the Co-op shop. Normally we'd get a dividend on everything we bought but we missed out on the 'divvy' because Patty had been sneaking stuff out of the door for weeks.

Old Mrs Tiplady up the road showed me how to make blancmange and junket. Patty made dozens of jellies in paper cups with a dolly mixture on top for decoration. We used up all our sugar coupons in the ration book because Patty couldn't smuggle enough from the Co-op in time to make the toffee apples. I'd been collecting lolly-ice sticks from the gutters, parks and rubbish bins, and Mam boiled them in a pan to get the muck off. The bruised apples called penny fades came from Mrs Reid at the greengrocer's shop.

I was black and blue after collecting wood for weeks with the local scruffs then piling it on the bomb-site that was once Mr Roberts's house before the Germans blew it up and killed his parrot.

I had a very important job and that was to stop any dogs piddling on the table and chair legs by sprinkling pepper; if they crouched to poo anywhere I'd been told to kick them up the arse. I stood guard amazed at the spread of grub on the table in spite of rationing. I poked under pan lids covering plates to see what was underneath them. Wow! Hovis bread with sardine and tomato paste, potted beef and cucumber, and even jam butties. After today, my mam said, we'd be starving for bread for ages as we had used up all our bread units.

When the party started our street had proper music and all, as one of the neighbours wheeled the old pump organ from out of the local church hall – and my dad played the banjo. The kids shouted to be heard over the grown-ups' sing-songs.

14

At night the grown-ups lit the bonfire. Dogs howled, scared to death by searchlights flashing across the sky, and all the boats on the River Mersey tooted as church bells put in their two penn'orth. And to top it all off we even had fireworks, and not just sparklers, but big buggers that splattered the sky. There was a deep sense of community spirit, hugs, hard sloppy kisses and handshakes. And cheers for the local blokes back from overseas making jokes of their war wounds, some crying like babies, probably because they'd survived. I hoped the day would last for ever.

Of course, Mam just had to cry and spoil things.

'What's up chuck?' my dad asked, putting his arms around her shoulders.

'Bloody Churchill,' she sobbed.

'Well what about bloody Churchill?' My dad had a cob on now.

'All those young men never comin' back. What a waste, he's got a lot to answer for, mark my words.'

I groped for a hanky in the leg of my knickers and passed it to her. 'Here you are Mam,' I gulped in my throat. 'Why do you 'ave to go an' cry and spoil things? Oh, please don't cry.'

Blinking through the rain of tears she muttered, 'Are you still up, young lady? It's long past yer bedtime, now get in the house and up them stairs, there's a good girl.'

I didn't have to get a wash for bed. Mam said I was 'done in' and could have a strip wash tomorrer. I smelt dead good. I smelt of smoke, and didn't want to wash off the memories of standing next to the lighted bonfire and throwing bricks at Guy Fawkes perched on top, or it may have been Hitler, as someone had painted a little black moustache on him.

Mam wiped her eyes and blew her nose before tucking my hanky down the front of her pinny, then she farted around the tables retrieving the family cutlery, well identified by her wrapping red wool round all the handles before we were allowed to take it out of the house. Mam was proud of our cutlery, with real bone handles, made in Sheffield.

'Are you still hangin' around, young lady? I thought I told you to scram.'

I lay in bed too exhausted to sleep. I could still hear the laughter and shouting in the street – my street with the flattened houses, uprooted gardens, and collapsed walls. The bomb-sites became a wonderland for a day.

Why did the day have to end?

Looking back, being the youngest of nine children and a change-of-life baby conceived and born on Merseyside during the war, was probably not the best start for my mam or me.

I learnt to be a survivor at a very young age, following instincts instead of common sense. My first instinct was to keep a low profile and refrain from prattling on, especially around my mam, who repeatedly declared, 'I curse the day I ever 'ad you. I should've put you in a home when I 'ad the chance.'

I always hated the way my family labelled me 'The Baby', 'The Gypsy', 'The Curse'. The crime of silence blighted my childhood. I didn't know that we were poor, as there was nothing I could compare poverty with. Towards the end of the war, when I was five, bombed houses, ration books, endless food and clothes shortages were all I knew.

My mam called Dad 'The Bloody Reptile'. We'd got so used to it that it sounded OK, even raising a laugh sometimes, but never from my dad. She must have really loved him, though, because she was always knitting him cable and Fair Isle jumpers with two- and three-ply wool on skinny needles. She also endlessly scoured the shops looking for Dad's supper treats, something I dreaded, usually some obscene part of an animal's anatomy, such

16

as cow's heels, pig's trotters, tripe or sheep's brains. They all went down well after the pub shut when my dad roared for his supper. Blindly I was unaware that I indulged in this disgusting ritual when I shared what I thought to be Spam butties. I was actually relishing tongue, pressed between the bread, until Teddy teased, 'I wouldn't eat that if I were you, it's been in someone else's mouth.'

'What do you mean?'

'It's the leftover of a cow's pimply black tongue. Didn't you know?'

What a torment he was, but I wouldn't eat it any more, just in case he was right, which was unlikely because sliced tongue was sold at the corner shop to nicely dressed people.

Dad was a bit of a romantic. Fancied himself as another George Formby. So much so that he was learning to play the banjo (seemed like he'd been forever learning). He foolishly expected to soften my mam's dark moods that he'd caused after tanking up on Guinness or Black Draft every Sunday dinner time. His pathetic rendition of 'When I'm Cleaning Windows' appeared to fall on deaf ears as his gnarled fingers twanged and thumped. But she was listening all right. With the aid of the bread knife the 'silly ol' sod' and his banjo were hastily despatched to the confines of the backyard lavvy.

Unfortunately Mam didn't always win. She often wore the results of the battles of previous weeks – after she'd either been thrown down the stairs or given a fat lip (or both!)

They occasionally observed the Sabbath by staying home on a Sunday night – they'd got pissed at midday instead. It was different on these occasions, when he allowed her to join him at the local alehouse for a 'Sunday tipple'. She would tolerate his overtures and smile coyly, sometimes even kissing him on his craggy cheek. Then when she thought no-one was looking she

17

would glance in the mirror, spit on her fingers and push her eyebrows into an arch.

After Sunday dinner at about three o'clock they legged it up the stairs for 'forty winks'.

I hated Sunday dinners.

Apart from my dad (Paddy) and my mam (Lil) there were only seven of us Faulkners at home now. There used to be eleven. Patrick the first-born died of scarletina and Elizabeth died of abscess poisoning, both only babies. Then followed Dolly and then Joey who were both married and safely out of harm's way, Patty and the lads, Jacky nearly grown-up, and George and Teddy the terrible un-identical twins. And me, usually referred to as 'The Baby', but my given name is Cherry. The lads said Mam got the name off a jam jar after she'd run out of names.

'Did you really?' I asked my mam one day.

'No, I got the name from the Cherry Blossom shoe polish tin.'

The Faulkners were of Irish descent – Catholics, at least my dad, brothers and sisters were. My mam proudly stated that she was High Church, whatever that was. My dad only laughed at her, saying, 'They call it that because it's on a bloody hill.'

My earliest recollection of the Catholic Church was of disappointment and mistrust. Dad and my mam feared the local priest who hovered over us like a big mean black crow; my dad took the mickey out of him when he came collecting for the poor. 'Always on the friggin' ear'ole them buggers.'

I was rarely acknowledged during the priest's visits, as I was never considered one of his flock. The Catholic school was too far away for me to walk there on my own and buses didn't go that way, even if we could have afforded the fare. I was duly enrolled at the Protestant primary school that was much closer – just over a mile away (which I had to walk four times a day: there was no

18

way I was allowed to stay for school dinners at one shilling and sixpence a week).

Today, Father Francis was here for the second time this week, collecting for the missionaries and black babies. The old sod of a priest grabbed at me with his bony fingers gripping my shoulders, his watery eyes piercing mine, and announced, 'I've got a grand present for you.'

Surprised he had acknowledged my existence for once and even bought a present, I was confused. I looked to my mam for a sign of approval.

'Can I 'ave it, Mam?' She nodded, benignly.

'Go on me darlin', take it, take it,' the priest said, 'it won't bite.'

He handed me a brown envelope. I carefully opened it. My eyes were riveted on twelve calendar postcards of beautiful, fat, cuddly black babies with straight white teeth and shiny faces. I was gagged. I looked from my mam to the priest.

'I've never seen a proper black baby. They're smashin'.' I couldn't take my eyes off the pictures.

'Go on, choose one, and then I want you to save your pennies for the poor unfortunate orphans that don't have a loving mammy and daddy like you. You pick the one you like best, but don't you forget you must save hard,' he said, patting my cheek.

I sorted through the twelve cards. April was my birthday month, and the black baby for April was my favourite, a lovely smiley-faced girl.

'Is it OK to 'ave this little girl?'

'Sure.'

'To keep?'

Stretching his scraggy neck out of his dog collar, the priest ran his fingers round the stiff part attached to his shirt before answering. 'Oh yes lovey, whatever pleases you. I will leave you the tin and when it's full I will come by and collect it.'

I ran after him shouting, 'Can I name her Topsy?'

19

'To be sure. Any name you like me darlin'.'

She was duly named Topsy. I knew when Topsy came to live in our house I wouldn't be called 'The Baby' any more. Having another girl in the house would be dead good. She would love me because I saved up for her. Maybe I could even be popular at school and everyone would want to be my friend.

Now talking at the tea table was never tolerated. We knew to keep our gobs shut except when we were shovelling in grub, but I was bursting with the news. I risked getting knocked over the chair backwards by my father's long reach for being impudent, but I took the risk.

'I'm gettin' a real black baby off Father Francis when I've saved enough money. I'm goin' to to call her Topsy.'

My father nearly choked. Georgie and Teddy, the twins, six years older than me, shouted in unison, 'Silly bitch.'

'Don't be daft, where will you expect to get a black baby? They're all in Africa,' said my big brother Jacky.

'Off the priest. He promised me, see! And he wouldn't lie or he would burn in hell if God heard him.' So that was telling him.

I started to save for my black baby. Only getting sixpence a week pocket money and sometimes not even that (it depended on my dad's mood), I just had to find a way of making some faster money. Horseshit, that was always good for a threepenny bit. Early mornings before school I followed the clip-clop of the Co-op milk horse round the streets. When it did a golden dollop, I was ready with my shovel and bucket to collect the steaming mass before it even cooled.

In the wake of the war my buckets of manure were like manna from heaven to the men with their allotments in Central Park, who were desperately trying to provide their families with fresh vegetables. I could see no point, even at my tender age I knew full well that their precious

20

vegetables would be nicked just as they were about to mature. Some of the better-off gardners had little shacks at the end of the allotments and they slept in them for the last couple of nights of the growing season. Even so, some lucky light-fingered bugger always managed to clean them out.

The cocky nightwatchman at the end of the road was my friend and I hated taking money from him. He had a hut with an oil drum lit up close to the door so he could throw taties on to cook while he guarded the roadworks. Sometimes they were shared with us kids who in return swapped him jam or sugar butties. My trick was to sneak him something better. I took him bread and dripping scrape. The scrape was very tasty, being juices and fat left in the roasting tin when the Sunday meat was cooked. Only one problem – there were mice at the back of our oven and I had to scrape off the feet imprints, scratches and mouse shit first. Well, what he didn't know, I figured, wouldn't hurt him; and I deserved the threepenny bit for my trouble.

The savings lark was taking longer than I expected, even though I changed my earnings into pennies and ha'pennies which filled the tin quicker – besides weighing heavier.

Why wasn't everyone as excited as me? Risking another thick ear, I pestered over and over, 'When are we gettin' me black baby?'

My dad smiled, 'Maybe some day soon, just wait and see.'

I'm glad I didn't know he was taking the mickey out of me with his drunken pals at the local alehouse (the Brighton) with stories of my naivety.

By far the easiest money I made was by sitting on the pub steps at chucking-out time on a Sunday afternoon when the regulars staggered out with a skinful, looking forward to their Sunday dinner, which by tradition was a roast with mushy peas. The drunks were good for at least a tanner to this little street urchin looking lost, fretting, waiting for her mam and dad to come out and take her home. After the pay off I legged it home before my mam and dad caught me begging.

My big brother Jacky was the know-all in our family and twelve years older than I was. Mam often said about him, 'Know-all knows sod all.' But it was Jacky who wised me up about Topsy. Even at such a young age I should have known better, as my family hated blacks as well as Jews, gypsies, midgets, all foreigners and of course Germans.

'Conned by a bloody priest, if that don't beat all,' he scoffed. 'Yer only helpin' the missionaries feed the black babies. You don't get given one, you silly bitch. Any'ow, why would me mam want another mouth to feed? You know you were her last mistake, doesn't she keep tellin' you?'

'You soddin' liar. I'm tellin' me dad,' I yelled at him, but Dad just said, 'Take no notice of our Jacky, he knows nowt. You may get one some day when yer a big girl.' He ruffled my hair and patted my back in a hopeless effort to console me. Pity forgotten over a Guinness, the tale was relayed to the Brighton cronies and from then on I was nicknamed Topsy.

I didn't understand but I knew by painful experience that 'one day' never came – to me anyway, so they'd let me believe in a lie. As my mam said often enough, I got the shitty end of the stick. Well, that bloody tin saw no more of my hard-earned money. After several weeks the priest took the tin away, without a 'by your leave or kiss my arse or bugger me'. He replaced it with a cardboard box. On it was a painting of St Joey's Church and in the front in bold words was printed:

ALL DONATIONS FOR THE REPAIR
OF ST JOSEPH'S ROOF.

(The local yobs had stripped off all the lead.) We knew how to fix that lot from the church. Teddy and I nicked the savings and filled the box full of nails. Even when my dad told us off I didn't care because I could see his laughing eyes.

My Patty was my second sister and the oldest still at home. It was her turn to take the brunt of the violence and verbal abuse after my big sister Dolly was married and got the hell out of the place. Mam seemed to dislike Patty even more than she did me. I wished Patty were my real mam instead of my big sister. I loved her to death. She protected me best she could. But just being a girl Patty didn't have any real standing with the rest of the family and hardly ever got to voice her feelings. No point anyway, it never changed anything.

Patty passing the eleven-plus exam was seen as wilfully putting extra pressure on the family finances. Uniforms had to be paid for and what was the point. Working-class girls didn't look for a career. They laboured until they got married. It was decided: working at the Co-op grocery store was the best place for the likes of her.

And that was that.

So Patty was a 'curse' and a 'burden', even though she handed her wages over every week and was indispensable with her cleaning, scrubbing and ironing on her time off, especially on Sundays. Patty's most hated chore began after we finished dinner. With a flat iron on the stove and another in use until it cooled, she cursed and waded through the stack of clean washing that covered the old sideboard stacked almost to the top of the kitchen door. Often she was too tired to go out with her pals when she'd done. Patty vowed no man of hers would wear union work shirts, so big and heavy and so hard to get rid of the ingrained sweat and muck.

But it never got her down. Patty always looked on the bright side. She made me laugh with her stories about

23

the Yanks that she dated. Music was her passion so she learnt to be a good whistler, much to Mam's annoyance, because it was unlucky to whistle in a good Catholic house, everyone knew that.

Mam called her 'The Wall-eyed Bitch' because Patty had a defiant spirit and could kill you stone dead with just one of her looks – at least it seemed like that to me. When she felt brave she would sneak Mam one of them looks, but if she was caught all hell would break loose when Mam got a shitty on her and Patty would get a bloody good hammering whilst all the furniture would be thrown around the place.

Why did God have to make Sundays? Always a roast-dinner ritual, so silent and difficult – with tension in the air, fearing that one of us would earn a clout after being set off laughing. Our Sunday-best tablecloth stinking of vinegar as my dad attempted to scoop pickles from the jar with his gnarled fat fingers.

2

Come Christmas I pestered Santa for a black doll. I was getting craftier by the year. I knew that when my request went via Patty to Santa I had a much better chance of getting my own way. This request was more cunning than anyone realized. Around November every year, my dolly disappeared and reappeared Christmas Day with a new wig, a set of new crocheted clothes and the odd arm or leg replaced. I figured if I asked Santa for a black doll this time it would be hard for him to give me back the same bloody doll. You can't trust priests or Santa. I had learnt that much already.

Topsy duly arrived on Christmas Day. From now on, anything I owned that was black was going to be called Topsy: golliwogs, dolls, cats, whatever. Yes, that was a good name. Her eyes and hair were only painted on celluloid but so what? At least I had my own piccaninny. That was a name I learnt from my dad and I knew it wasn't a swear word by the way he said it.

At school, the special treat for the last fifteen minutes of each day was story time. That was if all the free milk had been drunk, we tidied our desks and sat up straight. One week of the twins' latest rat terror tales, the teacher's story was the Pied Piper. It filled me with dread and disgust. To my mind it never had a happy ending and left me with a feeling that it could all really happen. Perhaps in our very own street, perhaps even in our own house where the mice and rat situation was already getting out of hand.

Patty and me were bludgeoned with horror stories from the twins. Then Jacky put in his two penn'orth, about rats eating babies' faces off when they were asleep in their cots.

'The smell of the milk draws them. Never corner a rat,' we were warned, 'it will go for yer throat and you'll go mad and die of rabies.'

Finally we had to get a cat when the house became overrun with vermin. Poor little bugger didn't last long; didn't have a chance – the rats were bigger than the cat. So, like a trail of other non-functional pets, our cat Lucky met a terrible fate. Despite my pleas he was drowned in the backyard tub. Course, the drowning cat didn't entertain the lads like the Christmas duck that ran around the yard after my dad chopped its head off. How the little sods laughed as they chased it. Finally the twins caught it and hung it by its feet in the corner of the backyard so that its blood would drain straight into the dustbin. Some rotten sod pinched it before it made it to the dinner table. (Or so they thought!)

I was glad. I couldn't bear to eat Donald – he was my friend. The only part of Donald left was his feet, which I discovered, much to my horror, in my school satchel – just before I wet my knickers! Anyhow the binman told my dad that when he emptied the bin into the cart last Friday, he discovered the remains of a headless stinking duck! Nobody had noticed that the string had been cut and more rubbish got piled on top of the corpse for nearly a week before the bin was emptied.

Mam played merry hell. 'You useless daft buggers, you couldn't 'ave tied the string tight enough, which is why it fell in the soddin' bin. No bastard pinched it.'

* * *

Mam and Dad's nightly excursions to the pub were something Patty and me looked forward to.

'Be a good girl and get yerself a strip wash,' Patty would say, 'and let me check yer neck and ears for potatoes growin' in them before you put yer nightie on.'

Bossy cow – but I loved her fussing over me really. We would listen to the radio playing Joe Loss, Frank Sinatra, Dick Haymes and the Andrew Sisters.

'I'll show you how to jitterbug if you don't tell Mam, 'cos she thinks I'm fillin' yer 'ead and won't like it.'

We laughed at my antics; I wasn't born to dance.

Patty said, 'Yer like a scalded cat but you'll be OK. I'll help yer, just relax.'

I fell on the floor laughing, my asthma leaving me gasping for breath. I couldn't let Patty see though; she'd be concerned and not let me do it any more.

Our house was in the bombed-out end of the street and was dark, cold and threadbare. The kitchen had a big bolt on the inside of the door and we would build up the fire with the potato peelings saved from teatime to make the room cosy. Up until half past ten, with the boys out running the streets until midnight, we had the place to ourselves and the nightly routine never changed. Nine o'clock was the time for the real treat – coffee made with milk boiled in a pan. No-one else in our house knew of this special treat. Coffee was still scarcer than hens' teeth. Patty sometimes worked in the storeroom at the Co-op filling bags with sugar, coffee, tea, etc., so occasionally she'd be able to pinch some extra scoops and after wrapping them in greaseproof paper she'd smuggle them out in her brassiere.

If we timed it right, when the front door banged at half past ten announcing Mam and Dad's return, we legged it up the stairs so as not to get involved in the violence and rows that nearly always followed. We would hide behind closed doors holding our hands over our ears to shut out the horrible wounding words being exchanged.

27

The whole house shook with their orgy of violence; sometimes the rows were so bad that the furniture got smashed.

Wednesday nights were extra special. Patty nudged me at the table. 'Hey kid, guess what? It's Wednesday.'

'Smashin'.' I knew what she meant.

Curtain Up was on the radio, with Valentine Dyall, usually playing the villain. Always these mystery plays had you hanging off your chair. We so looked forward to Wednesdays, even though it scared the hell out of me. Patty was a grown-up so I bet she didn't have nightmares like I did. I was smart enough not to tell her though; otherwise she would have put me to bed earlier.

One Wednesday was different. After nine o'clock the radio was on loud, but not loud enough to drown out a mysterious clump . . . clump . . . clump . . . on the stairs. Terrified, Patty checked the bolt was secure before putting a chair under the doorknob.

'Shush, someone's on the stairs,' she stammered. 'Shurup and stop that whinin'.'

Me chest squeaked with each laboured breath. I was half expecting someone to burst through the door any second. Nothing happened. We stayed in the kitchen and waited for Mam and Dad to come home. Both of us started jabbering at once when they arrived.

'Someone's in the house, honest. You must check under the beds and in the wardrobes please Daddy,' I sobbed. (I always called him Daddy when I wanted a favour.)

'It's our Patty,' my mam yelled at my dad, 'fillin' the baby's head full of bloody nonsense with what they listen to on the radio. You'll 'ave to put a stop to it.' Mam was already giving Patty the silent treatment – hadn't spoken to her for nearly a week. It seemed she wouldn't believe Patty hadn't been pinching the carbolic soap out of the bathroom and flogging it to her friends. Mam replaced it with scrubbing soap to show she meant business but that disappeared as well.

My dad was unconcerned. 'Silly buggers. Serves them right if they want to listen to that racket and frighten themselves, that's up to them.'

For weeks afterwards night-time was nerve-wracking. Regularly we heard the clump, clump, clump coming down the stairs and always at night and always when the house was quiet and we were alone – paralysed and defenceless.

Our imaginations ran riot – we thought it must be a murderer or maybe a one-legged ghost or a skeleton, or even a monster with one leg from the noise it made. With bated breath we huddled together on a chair waiting until Mam and Dad came home; at least they would fill the house with noise and the clump, clump, clump would stop.

Then one fateful night when Patty and me were alone locked in the kitchen, the heavy clump, clump, clump became leaden. We were in danger.

'Shush, keep quiet, the one-legged thing is outside the door and I can hear scratchin',' stammered Patty. We stood uncertainly. What should we do?

All my worst nightmares were coming true. I couldn't breathe – another asthma attack starting, and my medicine was upstairs, neither of us capable of getting it. I held my shaking hand tightly across my mouth to prevent myself from being sick.

Then the sound of an almighty crash – I almost fainted.

Frantically Patty threw back the bolt on the kitchen door.

'Quick, run!' she yelled. 'Someone's kicked the hall door down.'

We ran into the street. Patty was screaming blue murder, squawking and trembling. All the lights came on in the front rooms of the neighbours' houses. Someone took Patty by the shoulders and shook her before sending to the Brighton for my mam and dad – five minutes away down the back of the alleyway. Patty begged anyone to go for my medicine before I needed an ambulance. Dad raced home (concerned that it had to be important for the neighbours to fetch him from the pub), to find Teddy and George had also arrived home and half the nosy street was out hovering round our front door. A clutch of gossipy women parted to let the family procession through. Teddy and George ran past and instigated a search. After only minutes, Teddy was the hero. He'd found our one-legged perpetrator . . . so how come he was laughing?

'Friggin' hell, come and look at this,' he yelled from the hallway.

'I'm not bloody goin' back in that house. Not for nothin',' whimpered Patty.

I pushed my way through everyone's legs to get a better look. I was brave now my dad was home. They were gathered under the stairs by the gas meter where we kept the kitchen cabinet. The cutlery drawer was on the floor with all the cutlery and cooking tools scattered everywhere.

'Well bugger me,' roared my dad, slapping his thighs, 'come look at all this, Lil.'

The back of the drawer had been eaten away by rats trying to get to the food in the cupboard. Behind the kitchen cabinet was a rat's nest built just like a dinky igloo out of the missing carbolic soap. Months and months of soap supplies protected a nest of baby rats. Dad unashamedly then announced to all the neighbours that not only did we have the smartest rats in the street, but also the cleanest.

We learnt that what we thought was the one-legged man clump, clump, clumping down towards us was really the rats pushing the soap down the oilcloth-covered stairs. The Sanitary Inspector from the Council sent the rat catcher. What a fearful-looking rodent-faced man he was, with a long pointed nose and beady black eyes like two pips in an apple.

'He looks like a rat to me, Dad,' I giggled.

Even my mam laughed at that and said I was a bloody comedian.

Traps were set under the stairs and in the bathroom. One night desperate for a pee I headed for the toilet, which was down a dark flight of stairs on a landing. When I opened the toilet door and turned on the light I was rooted to the spot with fright. Blood was spattered every-where; on the walls, the floor, and even inside the lavvy. A huge rat that had been caught in the trap by its front legs was set going again when the light went on. It was frenzied, trying to gnaw its legs off in an effort to free itself. The squealing noise coming from the rodent as the trap was flung from one side of the room to the other in the violent tangle of its death throes chilled me to the marrow.

Terror paralysed me. I don't know how long I stood frozen before grasping the doorknob and slamming the door shut. I went back to bed shivering with fright, or cold. I wasn't sure which.

The cold woke me and I was still enveloped in misery, shivering uncontrollably in the putrid darkness, cold, wet and frightened. Patty, still fast asleep alongside me, was soaked.

I'd wet the bed.

Easter, 'Black Friday' and my birthday. According to my family it was known as Black Friday because I was born on that day. I couldn't for the life of me figure how everyone else knew about it when they didn't even know me. It was only later I found out that the Friday before Easter was called Black Friday because of the Crucifixion. Until then I thought that Jesus Christ was just a swear word I'd copied from my elders.

My dad took me out once every year, always on Easter

31

Sunday. This year I'd been presented with a new pair of black patent leather shoes with a buckle on the side, as well as a pair of full, pull-up-to-the-knees white socks. Not for playing out in, just for Sunday best. I felt so special when he walked beside me, telling me his wonderful Irish stories.

We always strolled along Egremont Promenade to New Brighton. The River Mersey was sometimes rough and the incoming tide would lash in over the sea wall. We played tag as close to the railings as possible and dared the waves to crash over us while doing our damnedest to stay dry. Never for a minute did we consider the dangers of being washed out to sea as others had in the past. The oily smell of the Mersey was familiar, pleasant and always comforting.

My dad pointed out the various ships, mostly Cunard liners being piloted to Gladstone, Huskisson or Canada Dock in Liverpool for loading or unloading. Our docks, sprawled along the north bank of the River Mersey, were once believed to be the longest in the whole wide world.

Even Hitler must have thought so – he made them the target of his bombers. After the ships were bombed the kids in our neighbourhood waited in anticipation for the hidden treasures amongst the debris that eventually reached the shore. I never found anything dead good except once an apple and a coconut. Even then my mam wouldn't let me keep them, as a couple of ships had recently docked from Singapore and there was talk of smallpox on board. Thousands of people were given a jab, thankfully not me – though lousy pity about the coconut.

We sat for a few minutes while my dad got his puff back. We watched the blue and black ferry boats called *The Royal Iris* and *The Royal Daffodil*, criss-crossing the mouth of the Mersey taking the posh people to New Brighton in style, as well as linking Birkenhead, the peninsula of Wallasey and New Brighton to Liverpool.

My dad couldn't understand why I always scurried right past the red-and-white striped kiosk on the beach with the battling Punch and Judy show being enacted like gruesome real life. Punch yelling at Judy, arguing over a baby, policemen called, and animals beaten with sticks. Fascinated children sat cross-legged on the sands delighted at the antics, but not me. It was too much of a reminder of home for my liking.

After our donkey rides, soft, dripping ice cream was always the treat on our annual outing to New Brighton. Usually we found the tantalizing cart just by the old Mariners' Home, where we could also hire deckchairs for a tanner and buy a 'Kiss-Me-Quick' hat. I liked the walk home best. That was when the candyfloss man arrived around twelve o'clock.

'How in the hell do you manage it? Bloody candyfloss all over you, even in yer hair. Yer mam won't be chuffed.'

I didn't care what my mam said – I was just so proud of being with my dad. He always wore his trilby that he doffed to anyone who looked our way, and always pinned a rose in his buttonhole. Who could question why locals called him 'The Dandy'?

We made a good team, my dad and me. He even took me to work with him one day when I was too poorly with my asthma to walk to school. I got to wear my 'bib and brace' overalls so I could really be Dad's little helper. My dad was the big boss, a foreman asphalter for the Trinidad Lake Asphalt Company. Everyone called him Paddy at work and he only told them once how he wanted a job done and that was it. Nobody mucked Paddy Faulkner about – him being built like a tank and just as subtle.

Standing next to the machine spewing out hot tar, I proudly watched my dad, with pads on his elbows and knees, crouching in the thick, hot mixture and spreading it with a wooden trowel, making it nice and smooth. I was grown-up enough to drink thick, brown, sweet tea out of his brown-stained enamel billycan. I had some of his grown-ups' butties too – real corned beef (not Spam) with pickle. I decided I might work for him when I left school. I'd seen how it was done . . . dead easy. The men who worked with my dad and carried the hot filled buckets spoilt me rotten. When the asphalt was nearly set, they made me marbles by rolling the tar around in their hands, and spitting on it to cool it. At the end of the day I looked into the bag, I had enough marbles to last at least a month. Sitting in the middle of the road all day watching the asphalt being laid was great fun. I couldn't think why my dad came home tired every night, saying he needed a drink for his parched tubes.

I paid the price from the twins for getting the special attention from my dad. Georgie and Teddy started a new wave of torment: this time little creatures, mice, moths, worms and flies were pinned to a board, while a magnifying glass was held to the sun until the helpless victim ignited or burst with the heat. If I dared to shut my eyes or turn away my hand was forced under the glass and held there just to teach me not to be a crybaby. So I was forced to watch. I cried in anguish each time that I saw them with a bicycle pump, as it was used on frogs' arses to pump them up until they exploded. Kittens were tied in sacks so the twins could watch their demented efforts trying to escape. Dogs had rubber bands cut from bicycle inner tubes tied round their mouths, so that they became frantic when food was put in front of them.

My position was hardly better than the miserable animals – constant humiliation, both mental and physical. I was tormented then tortured into submission. My crime was being a girl and such a weakling. But unlike the animals I was able to survive by using my wits. Every effort was made to avoid the twins so that there would be no conflict, but my terror was constant. Sometimes my heart hurt so much that I wished I was dead.

3

Billy Graham came to the Liverpool Town Hall. He was having a Christian Revival Crusade for anyone who wanted to know Jesus. My friend Joan Baxter said she would come with me. We sat for hours and hours waiting but we never saw Billy Graham – only heard him telling us through loudspeakers that Jesus loved us. We could wipe the slate clean. God knew our minds. We could start all over again without sin. All sins were not only forgiven but also forgotten. I held back because I couldn't tell all my sins, only the little ones, in case He stopped loving me.

I was too ashamed of telling that I had read the dirty bits in the Hank Janson books my mam had in her room, that I played doctors with the Bannister brothers and let them look down my knickers. (I thought a bit about pinching and thieving but decided it was OK – everyone did that.)

Anyway what's the point in telling everything if He already knew? If, like the minister said, Jesus was the only one who could wipe my slate clean, then I definitely needed Him on my side.

I got saved!

I knew I was saved proper because they gave me a brand new Bible. I could never have been expected to read it but it was good to press flowers between the pages. Being pleased with my 'new' self I started going to Sunday school at Brighton Street Methodist – I still didn't trust them Catholics. My dad seemed pleased that I was going and always gave me a shilling for collection. I only ever put sixpence in. The rest I used as my commission to buy gobstoppers on the way home.

There were announcements about rehearsals for Sunday school choir. I had to be in that because you got to go on coach trips to Blackpool and Wales for competitions. The choirmaster listened to our voices and moved our positions according to the tone and pitch. Even though I was only pint-sized I was pushed to the far back. I was sure he couldn't hear me and I knew for sure that he couldn't see me.

I stood on a chair. 'Hey mister, why am I shoved at the back?' I yelled.

'Because dear child, you sing like Jerry Lewis.'

'I do?' I yelled, all pleased that I sounded like someone I'd heard of, someone famous. 'Oh that's OK, I thought for a minute you didn't like me singin'.'

It was getting near Christmas and I was all excited. I'd asked for a real budgie in a cage. 'Fat chance!' I was told, but I lived in hope.

I was still a bit confused about Christmas. When Teddy told me that my dad was Father Christmas, of course I didn't believe him. Dad didn't have the time or money to make toys for the kids around the world.

'Hey Georgie, my dad's not the real Father Christmas is he?' I asked.

'Cross me heart and hope to die. It's true,' he smirked.

Well, I was going to have to watch my dad now for any giveaway signs. I wasn't born yesterday. How come if he was the real Father Christmas I kept getting bloody dolls and never a red bike?

My big brothers, Joey and Jacky, were spending more time together. Jacky bought a fretsaw. They were building a doll's house and had been working on it for ages. Dinky little windows and doors, as well as real carpet bits in the rooms and the furniture so detailed. It even had trees with tiddly little plants lining the green-dyed coconut gardens. It was for Joey and his wife's kid – if they ever got one.

One day I was going to live in a house like that, I vowed. I'd kill to own it. I'd never seen the likes. (I hated that unborn, rotten, lucky kid.) I was sure this doll's house would be worth millions of pounds some day.

I was standing in the backyard for the umpteenth time in a few days. 'Where's it gone?' I cried. 'Who's nicked yer 'ouse, Joey?'

'I've put it away for safe keepin'.'

'Please Joey, just give us another gawk,' I pleaded, wanting a last look at my fantasy home.

'Sorry kid, it's gone into storage.'

Christmas morning I crept downstairs, shivering in the dark. The shock brought on another asthma attack. I couldn't breathe. The beautiful doll's house was there. It was just for me. My eyes misted as I held my throat. It was true, my dad really was Father Christmas and my big brothers must be his helpers: I was gagged, crying with joy. Fancy, I even got a real live budgie in a cage as well. It only had one leg. (The pet-shop man had let it go for half-price.) I named it Joey after my big brother because I loved him best of all my brothers. Joey, my budgie, managed OK with just one leg, except when he fell asleep he sometimes fell off his perch. I think I loved this budgie because he needed me to take extra care of him, especially since our Georgie threatened to nail his foot to the perch.

Teddy and Georgie were a bit friendlier these days but I knew I couldn't trust them. I still had to stay on my guard. I liked their friend. The one nicknamed Simmo but his real name was Eric Simmonds. He wasn't the usual ragbag our lads hung around with. I didn't know really why he spent time with Teddy – they were so different. For starters Simmo used Brylcreem but you could expect that coming from the posh end of the street. Simmo was allowed in our house – even right into the kitchen. He didn't tell rude jokes or swear. The lads told jokes but they were usually about me so I always covered my ears. Every time Eric Simmonds looked at me I blushed, expecting the boys told him I wet the bed.

'Why don't you go up the road and play with me sister Dotty? She's about yer age.'

How did Simmo know how old I was? I was so small for my age that I couldn't even get into the matinees at the local fleapit without a grown-up taking me in.

My asthma had been worse the past couple of years since I started school. Some nights I struggled and gasped, believing every breath to be my last. Patty would nurse me on her knee and rub my chest with lard, garlic and onion, as she rocked me to sleep. When I felt too weak to be bothered sitting up to eat she often spent more than she could afford on special treats such as a pear or an orange, just to tempt my appetite.

I suppose it was understandable that I wasn't popular at school, stinking of pee as well as garlic and onion rub. I wasn't too badly off, just ignored and alone. Not important to anyone, except when I was poorly. Mam bought a paraffin heater from the junk shop and if Patty stayed with me it could be lit in the bathroom for our Saturday night baths.

Patty chuckled when she handed me a bar of scented soap, 'I expect you think yer've really died and gone to heaven.' It was sheer luxury to be so spoilt.

Our kitchen always looked so cosy on the Sunday nights that the family got together and played whist. The fire was lit and the Sunday-best plastic tablecloth announced the occasion. Mam was cheerful – she was very lucky and sometimes won as much as a pound. The early evenings were best, lots of jokes, and a kind sort of swearing. The Guinness and milk stout seemed to soften everyone's mood.

I wasn't old enough to play cards even though I was seven – well nearly – but I was allowed to watch.

'Only if she keeps her gob shut,' grumbled our Georgie.

Often I was sent to the Brighton to get more bottles of stout; the money usually came from the winner and I was sometimes allowed to keep the change.

Of course I lived up to my name, 'The Curse'. Shoved from one player to the next, staying only as long as it took for my next victim to realize my presence before pushing me away. I soon learnt to profit from my so-called jinxing ability, and offered my services to the one with the most winnings to jinx their opponent. Some Sundays I cleared two bob. But my new-found occupation was short-lived when the game was changed to canasta. This was on a more intellectual level and everyone soon got bored and it was back to the Brighton pub.

My dad was clever with words, as was Teddy, so they started taking an interest in crosswords. *The Times* crossword was a challenge. They finished it most weeks and sometimes even wrote samples of crosswords for *The Times*. Political history, art and Greek mythology were argued at length, and it confirmed in my heart that my bog-Irish dad was not really as 'thick as pig shit' as I'd heard said. On the other hand my mam never found the need to talk much at the best of times, except for the odd comments between the news and *Take Your Pick*.

My sister Dolly and brother Joey both had a 'queer one'. Now why in-laws in our family were always referred to as the 'queer one', I could never figure out. Naturally I thought this was the name for anyone's extended family, not just ours.

Our Joey came to live in our street with his 'queer one'.

Her proper name was Eileen. We lived in the scruffy end of the street but Joey and the 'queer one' lived in the posh end (as did Simmo). We had more bombed houses by us: that was why it was called the scruffy end. Well that was what Teddy said anyhow, when I heard him telling Georgie that some of the boys in the top end were sissies and they even used real snot-rags. And wore underpants. I was proud we lived at the scruffy end – we were much tougher.

Our Joey's 'queer one' limped quite badly and she didn't have a proper job – she worked from home making endless bloody socks and gloves on a Remploy knitting machine supplied by the Government for the disabled. My dad said Eileen was unlucky. I thought my dad must be right so I stayed clear of her. They didn't have any kids and she stared at me a lot. She tried to be friendly by letting me pick marigolds out of their back-yard and she made me some warm socks and mittens on her machine.

'Would you like to go to the pictures with me to see *Mother Riley*?' Eileen asked.

I didn't answer for a minute. No-one had ever taken me to the 'proper' pictures before, only the local fleapit for a Saturday morning matinee where after the singalong there was a Flash Gordon serial and a Hopalong Cassidy or Lone Ranger film.

I was in a quandary. My dad (the 'Bloody Reptile') insisted Eileen was bad luck, so I didn't want her making me any more of a jinx than I already was.

Joey lost his temper with me. 'Answer the poor woman. Yer bloody well ungrateful. She's made you a pair of woollen socks and some mitts. Considerin' she's disabled Eileen works friggin' hard to make ends meet. She only earns a pittance.'

'What's disabled mean, Joey?'

'She's got a friggin' sore leg or can't you see?' he snarled.

I thought about it for a moment. 'OK,' I said to Eileen, 'if you show us yer sore leg I'll come with you. Anyhow, why 'ave you got a sore leg?'

'I was run over by a tram, sweetheart. Best I don't show you or you might cry.'

'No, no, you're wrong,' I argued. 'I never cry, honest. Even when Teddy twists me skin and gives me the Chinese burn I don't ever let him see me cry. And when me mam threw a pan of boilin' sprouts at me and then battered me for spoilin' the Sunday dinner, I didn't cry then either. Honest to God! Please, please. I'll be yer best friend. Give us a gawk at yer sore leg.'

Well, we sat in the kitchen, my eyes transfixed on the 'queer one's' leg. She carefully undid the laces on the built-up shoe, removed the thick lisle stocking and unscrewed a wooden leg from above the knee, revealing what was left – a stump like a wrinkled polony.

Hell! I was off crying and wailing like a banshee. The 'Bloody Reptile' wasn't wrong, Eileen was unlucky all right, and worse off than me – I only wet the bed and had asthma.

In time I slowly got used to the idea of Eileen's leg being missing and started to hang around Joey's house once more, especially at mealtimes. After all, it was somewhere to get away from everyone having a go at me. The 'queer one' was really kind so I never mentioned her sore leg again. Besides, finishing any meal without my dad finding an excuse to swipe me over the back of the chair was a bonus. If I could just eat at home without Teddy or Georgie mimicking my dad behind his back and making me laugh; it would make life a lot easier. As it was, each time they mimicked, a little snigger would start inside me. Sometimes I managed to stop it before it reached a laugh, sometimes I didn't, then the more I laughed the more swipes I got.

I had a smashing idea! Why hadn't I thought of it before? Joey and the 'queer one' could adopt me. I would put it to them with a few strong hints. They needed someone like me around to liven the place up.

I did their messages to get around them; talked for hours to keep Eileen company in the school holidays; listened as she played her three sodding records over and over and over again, 'Paper Doll', 'Donkey Serenade' and 'The Laughing Policeman'. When the record slowed down I would jump up, wind the handle and set it going again. Then I'd clean the fluff that came from the wool used to make the socks off the mantelpiece and the sideboard.

In anticipation I waited, hoping for them to one day say to me, 'Will you be our little girl?' I would pretend to be overcome with surprise.

It never looked like happening. I got bored trying to be good so I went back to being the baby at the scruffy end of the street. But I had planted the seed in their minds.

Patty was engrossed in something. I didn't know what she was up to but she even looked different somehow. For some reason I felt very threatened. She'd now got a wart thing on her face.

'What's that black thing?'

'It's a beauty spot,' she told me, 'just like Margaret Lockwood's.'

She had boot polish on her eyelashes to make them darker – it looked like she was peering through the park railings every time it rained. Apart from that I thought she looked gorgeous, like Cinderella. Not all her attempts at self-improvement were successful. Like the time she put gravy browning on her legs because she couldn't afford stockings and her mate's dog licked one leg clean.

Finally Patty confessed she was in love. Mam shook her finger at her. 'Mark my words, yer ridin' for a fall.' Patty didn't care. She brazenly whistled, and Mam threatened her once and for all. It was unlucky to whistle in the house but Patty just went on whistling, as hard-faced as ever. Mam would kill her if she kept getting Mam's dander up. Patty banged the door behind her and was off for the night. I made meself scarce in case I copped it instead.

Patty didn't seem to care about me any more. I thought I was her very best friend, but I knew what she was up to. I decided not to talk to her, give her the evil eye for a change, then she'd come to her senses.

But she didn't. No matter what I tried Patty seemed indestructible. She had a new boldness. My heart ached knowing I could be losing her.

I remember the first time I met her rotten boyfriend. Patty had been watching the clock. 'Seven forty, sod it,' she said. Mam and Dad were always at the pub at this time. For as long as I could remember the house was always clear by seven thirty.

'Just my soddin' luck on the one night I want them out,' Patty whispered. 'John's due here any minute. Oh, thank heaven for that,' she said as she heard the back door banged shut.

After several minutes Patty had a tidy round, put fags on the table and chocolate on the sideboard and drew the curtains to make the room look more inviting.

'Get the coffee out of me bag.'

'Like hell!' I protested, 'that's our special coffee, not for outsiders. Our own special little treat.'

'Look kid, you'll like my John, he's dyin' to meet you. Please be nice. We're just havin' some supper and listenin' to the wireless. Promise me you won't give me away. You know Dad'll skin me alive if he finds out.'

Her true love arrived. He kissed her full on the mouth. Yuk! How could she? He talked funny – probably because he was from Birkenhead. Cheeky sod started bossing Patty and she didn't even notice. I didn't like him.

Busy in the kitchen making our coffee for him, she

whispered, 'You do like him don't you?' She nudged me coyly.

'No, I hate him,' I cried and slammed the door shut, before running up the stairs chanting curses and trying to wish him away.

I cried myself to sleep. Now I had lost everything.

4

Before long Patty was engaged to John Roberts and said she couldn't wait to get the hell out of the place. She tried to make it up to me by taking me out on dates with her and John. I would've enjoyed these treats more but he kept putting his hands all over her and kissing her, laughing and resisting my efforts to slap his mucky mitts away. Later I was to learn that she didn't like leaving me at home on my own because she knew I was as terrified of the twins as I was of the dark.

Tension built at home between Patty and Mam. Patty was so cocky now and Mam watched her every move. Mam was only waiting for an excuse to give her a hammering. Patty said that she could take it. She was answerable to no-one since the wedding was planned for March. The local Co-op Hall was duly booked for the wedding breakfast. Patty was sure of collecting her dividend bonus points that way. She said, 'The divvy comes in handy even when the Co-op do yer marryin' as well as buryin'.'

'It amounts to the same thing anyway,' my mam said under her breath.

Patty's bottom-drawer collection was stacked to the bedroom ceiling. Candy-striped pillowcases, sheets, towels, dishes and even a knitted tea cosy with two fluffy bobbins on the side. Her home seemed destined to be a little palace. John's sister said John and Patty could live in her front room until they got enough points towards a council house.

'Please Patty take me away when you go,' I begged on one of our returns from Birkenhead, which was miles away and took three buses to get there.

'Please don't leave me. I promise to be a good girl, and even to like John. Please Patty, don't leave me with them.' I wailed, panic sweeping through me at the very thought.

She smiled reassuringly. 'We'll see.'

School was half an hour's walk away from home and I only got an hour and a quarter for a dinner break. On a good day I ran home, ate a hurried meal and ran back wheezing – finding it so hard to breathe. But I couldn't tell them lot at home. I was getting too old for their dreaded remedy chest rubs that left me stinking of onion and garlic that would make even the sturdiest of vampires back off, let alone anyone I wanted to sit next to.

One day a couple of weeks before Patty's wedding I arrived home to find the kitchen was a war zone. It happened with alarming frequency when Mam had one of her funny turns. Patty had the remains of her lunch in her hair and sliding down her back. She'd made the grave mistake of sniffing the meal. Mam had the excuse she had been waiting for and was in full Armageddon mode, yelling and crying from our bedroom. I hid behind the wardrobe and looked on helplessly. Out of the bedroom window went Patty's wedding dress. In the backyard were broken canisters, towels, cutlery and most of her bottom-drawer collection. All the things Patty had so lovingly collected and carefully stored since the engagement.

Patty in her usual miserable acceptance of such situations whispered to me, 'I hope the old cow doesn't find me bloody fags. She'll kill me after her collectin' and rollin' dog-ends all this time.'

Since the war Patty had been using her stash of fags to trade for items for her bottom drawer. Mam's rage subsided; I heard a thump as she collapsed to the floor in a faint. Patty picked her up gently, cradling her in her arms and smoothing back her hair. Tears ran down my face as I tried to salvage Patty's treasures.

'It's OK love, just leave them,' she whispered, 'Mam's 'ad one of her spells; only a problem with the menopause. All women get like that. She doesn't mean anythin' – except she's depressed. Do me a favour chuck, put the kettle on.'

The house was peaceful after that for a while. My mam's expression became blank and empty and she didn't speak much at all, especially to Dad.

The dinner time sprints to and from home were a real problem with my asthma – but if I complained I knew I'd get walloped. So all by myself I came up with a scheme to fund a return ride on the bus. The bus only took ten minutes as opposed to my running and taking thirty minutes, which gave me an extra forty minutes to make the price of the bus fare.

There were a few houses in the neighbourhood that got used as betting agencies. Often Mam got me to run down the back alleyway to one of the houses to put her sixpenny Yankee on or sometimes a treble bet. Who could suspect this innocent runt of a child of being a bookie's runner, running round the streets in my dinner time putting bets on for the local gamblers?

The best part of course was taking the lucky punters their winnings. They nearly always gave me a tanner for my trouble. Being trusted to keep my gob shut was crucial, as taking bets was still illegal.

In no time I built up a thriving little sideline and my tin golliwog money box was getting fuller and fuller. It was a good feeling putting the coin in the metal hand, pressing the lever on the back shoulder that raised the arm and sending the plunder down the tinny gaping throat.

I didn't start my business career just to pay bus fares. Oh no, I had a great scheme under way. After unscrewing the back of my money box and checking the coins that I couldn't get out with the bread knife, I counted twelve shillings and fourpence, nearly enough to buy an old boneshaker bike. And then I could *run away in style*. When Patty married John I would become their little girl. It was all coming together nicely. Maybe John wasn't really so bad after all.

In fact, life was on the up and up. I was going to get a new posh frock made of green taffeta for when I was Patty's bridesmaid. My hair would be put in rags to make ringlets, but they insisted I had to wear a bloody liberty bodice because my mam said that March has a biting wind. No-one would know – I'd still look like Cinderella even if I felt like Old Mother Riley.

My big sister Dolly and the family were coming from Wales for the wedding. I was looking forward to it with great excitement even though I wasn't sure she took to me. What with her being the eldest and me the youngest, a generation gap of twenty years made me look on her as an auntie almost; there was only a couple of years in age between Dolly's first-born, Dorothy, and me. Dorothy and me got on well – after she got to know her place. I was after all her auntie, and I reminded her constantly of this.

To her credit, Dorothy was always happy to fit in with her elders. I expect Dorothy probably thought I was very grown-up, and why shouldn't she? Auntie Cherry could show her everything, including the best places to scrumpy apples, how not to get your knees cut open by the broken milk bottles cemented on top of the yard walls to keep the robbers out. And after the gaslighter had been round on his bike, Auntie Cherry was always the one who shimmied up the post to turn the light out. And it was me who figured on whose door we could play knock and run without getting caught. (Dorothy didn't know you had to pick the old geezers because by the time they hobbled to the door we were away on our toes.) We played house and I could pretend to be the big sister and not the baby. I didn't want her to go back home to Wales, ever.

The two groups of relatives at the wedding were like fighting cocks. My dad said John was common because he was from Birkenhead. I agreed with my dad. I didn't know what common meant but I knew my dad was smart. John's lot obviously didn't think much of us either. Our families were seated on either side of the church, each taking stock of their neighbours' clothes. The Practical Club, a kind of Friendly Society, had rigged out nearly everyone on our side. The tallyman called every Friday for his money and marked it off in the Club book. It would take fifty-two weeks to pay for the clobber that wouldn't last that long – well, that was what my Auntie Nellie said. In my green taffeta posh frock after I was bathed and scrubbed, I looked just like a fairy princess oozing eight-year-old sophistication.

'The 'am salad went down well. Can I 'ave some more?'

Jacky slapped the back of my legs. 'I've warned yer, stop pesterin'.'

'Why's it called weddin' breakfast when it's after dinner?'

'Shut yer gob.'

Jacky didn't know nowt.

The room was cleared for dancing. Again the 'queer one's' family were on one side of the hall and our lot on the other. The sherry for the toast and then the pale ale and Guinness loosened everyone up as they shouted over the noise of the oldies doing the Lambeth Walk. Everyone was talking louder by the minute, lumbering around slopping their drinks. I stood well away from the smoke and boozy chatter, I didn't want my bridesmaid's dress spoiled with ale.

I thought John's sister Mabel was smashing. As we stood outside the Co-op Hall beside the big posh car, she leaned over and said, 'You're welcome any time you like at our 'ouse.'

Now that was a funny thing for her to say. Didn't she know I'd be living there with Patty after today?

Patty drove off with John in the posh car – she'd forgotten to take me, gone without me. I stood staring after the car, desolate, wondering that to do next. I felt the sting of tears welling in my eyes. My Patty leaving me behind seemed unthinkable. Hastily I tried to dry my eyes with the back of my hand, not wanting them lot to see me cry. But I couldn't hold the tears back; disintegrating before everyone, I was left with a sense of unutterable loneliness.

'Come on chuck, let's get yer home, it's been a long day,' my dad whispered from behind me.

I put my arms round my dad and pressed my head tight against his belly. 'There now Topsy, don't cry – come on. Come on.'

'No! No! She'll come back for me soon,' I snivelled, 'so I'm not movin' off these steps!' And I didn't either.

Sitting outside on the steps, hearing everyone inside having a good time, I got chilled through to the bone. They were all singing and laughing. Why did booze make everyone sloppy?

It was getting dark when my mam took charge. 'Come on chuck, it's no good yer sulkin' here on yer own, after all, yer a big girl now. Big enough to be takin' Patty's place now she's wed.'

My mind was frantic. I hadn't thought of myself as being enslaved as Patty's replacement – at least not until then. Toiling over the ironing, scrubbing and cleaning, and emptying my dad's pisspot with the occasional clobbering for good measure if a spilt a drop. I wasn't going to stand for that. I always knew that I was better off being the baby. Being ignored was better than facing the clobberings that Patty got. The time had finally come to kill myself. That would show them all!

I'd heard about hanging when Auntie Nellie bought a house dead cheap. It was an unlucky house, the neighbours said. It had been empty for years, as the lodger of the previous owner had hanged himself. They found his body swinging from the coat hook behind the kitchen door.

I practised squeezing myself round the neck with my hands just to get the feel of what it was like. It didn't feel too bad. I'd teach them all a lesson, most of all Patty. She'd be sorry she betrayed me.

Well, I gave them fair warning. 'I'm goin' to kill meself,' I announced to them all the previous teatime.

'The sooner the better,' was the only comment made by my dad, who didn't even look up from reading his *Liverpool Echo*. 'One less mouth to feed.'

I decided to hang myself from the banisters at half past ten the next night. That way they would find me when they came home from the Brighton. (Go on Cherry, lay it on thick as usual.) I scrubbed my face, combed my hair and put on a clean frock so as to look nice in heaven. The belt off my dressing gown was the longest, strongest thing I could find. Not as coarse as rope, I reasoned, so it wouldn't scratch my neck.

It was difficult tying a proper knot. It kept coming undone. I looked at the clock. Time was running out. They'd be back soon. I mounted the threadbare stairs. I placed the cord round my neck and, in case it hurt too much, gingerly I lowered myself onto the next stair waiting for unconsciousness.

Sod it! That hurt! It hurt more than I had expected it to. I must have done it wrong? The choking and coughing made my eyes and nose run. Bloody Nora, now I would just have to think of another way to shock them.

Georgie and Teddy were through the door first.

'Why are you still up, Curse? Shouldn't you be in bed?' one of them growled.

'I stayed up to hang meself, smart-arse!'

'So why didn't yer?' George spat. 'Too bad yer didn't.'

Over a cup of tea Teddy joked about the condemned man whose last request before being hung was, 'Will yer put the rope round me waist 'cos I've got a boil on me neck.'

It was over a week since Patty had deserted me. Things weren't going as badly as I first expected. Today was St Patrick's Day so my dad would be in a smashing mood. He always wore a shamrock in his buttonhole as well as his best shirt with the stiff plastic collar and studs. His green dicky bow wrapped in tissue paper was removed from the sideboard drawer and handled with reverence. I was so proud of my dad when he was seriously poshed up. No wonder some of his pals called Paddy Faulkner 'The Toff'. Mam said it was because he was free with his money at the Brighton, and admiration from one of his muckers was always good for a few bevvies.

There was a roaring fire in the kitchen but the rest of the house was freezing. After shouting at each other, it was not the usual St Patrick's Day mood I was seeing from my mam or dad. Making myself scarce, I knew what to expect. The twins braved it out. They didn't want to move away from the heat. The air was thick with abuse since my dad had just discovered his green dicky bow all grubby and greasy. He needed to wear it today. It was unthinkable not to wear it today of all days. Mam was indifferent, giving him the silent treatment. Dad's face broke into a smile, chuffed with an idea to show he wasn't beaten. He elbowed Mam away from the kitchen sink and washed his dicky bow with Sunlight soap. 'Came up like new,' he boasted. He put the dicky bow over the end of the toasting fork and held it in front of the fire to dry. Getting impatient, wasting good drinking time, he moved closer to the heat and crouching over the fire with the toasting fork, he whistled 'Danny Boy' just to annoy my mam.

Suddenly the twins legged it past me through the house into the backyard, laughing, tears streaming down their cheeks. 'The old git has dropped his dicky bow into the fire and it's incinerated.'

I hid in my bedroom until the door banged. He was in a killing mood.

Soon it was my birthday. As there were a lot of whisperings and sly looks, I knew I was getting something extra special this time. I just knew it. I heard Mam confiding in Jacky, 'It's too big to hide, so I've left it up the road in Mrs Tiplady's front parlour for safe keepin'.'

It must have been expensive because Mam was buying it from the tallyman and for half a crown a week.

'Please God let it be a red bike with a basket on the front and a bell on the handlebars. Oh, by the way God, can I have a dynamo as well so I can ride round the streets in the dark?'

It was no surprise they were being so good to me since I kept the house spotless, using the Cardinal red polish on the steps and window sills every Sunday. Truth was, I always picked my moment to do that as everyone who passed the door made comments like 'What a good little girl you are. I bet yer mam's proud of you,' or 'My, a proper little muvver you are.'

April 8th and me not being able to sleep with excitement, I was up dead early standing in the kitchen before Dad went to work. My mam stood beside me smiling, probably not wanting to miss seeing me overflowing with joy and gratitude when I clapped eyes on my new bike.

'That's it? That's all? Oh, Mam, I can't believe it!' My voice wobbled. 'It's a mattress!'

Disappointment unnoticed, Mam rabbited on, 'It's a proper spring interior,' obviously overjoyed with her

53

surprise. 'We can throw that stinkin', saggin' old horse-hair one away. Yer a young lady now so no need to wet the bed anymore, hey chuck?' She hugged me and rubbed my back. 'A new beginnin', that's what it is, well worth a few bob on the never-never. Can't 'ave me baby sleepin' on wet beds, not with yer asthma and bronchitis. Yer'll be as snug as a bug in a rug.'

I was numb. My mam had lovingly called me her very own baby. My mind was racing. I knew this was the worst birthday I'd ever had but I couldn't disappoint her. By bedtime, I'd decided I had to spend the rest of my nights sleeping on the floor so I could keep this mattress looking like new. Sulkily, I tested the bed. It bounced all right but I couldn't dare risk an accident. I wanted them all to be proud of me – I wanted to show that I could be grown-up and trusted. I'd sort out a bike some time later when I needed it to run away.

April turned biting cold, no warmer than the previous months. 'Brass monkey weather' my dad said. Now, tired of fitful sleeping on the floor night after night, I gave in, crawling wearily into my old, iron hospital bed with the spanking new warm sprung interior mattress. Sleepily I huddled between the sheets. Lovely and clean, warm, dry bedding which only stank of nicotine and stale cigarette smoke. The airing rack hung from the kitchen ceiling over the fireplace. Unfortunately my mam's favourite chair was positioned under the drying washing where she sat chain-smoking, sometimes having one cigarette burning in the ashtray while puffing on another one. She said she smoked so much because she was saving the coupons for an anniversary clock with brass balls. My dad said she would be better off saving for an iron lung.

Mam once backed a horse she said was named after her, called 'Fag-ash Lil' ridden by Lester Piggott (better known as 'The Pig'). It won and paid seventeen and sixpence . . .

It was beautiful, back in my warm bed with the new

mattress embracing and enveloping me. I pretended I was staying at the Adelphi Hotel. Sleep descended like a warm cloud. I was so knackered in no time it felt as if I was soaring above my body like an eagle. There I was, floating, floating away.

Certainly I was floating all right; I was floating in pee. I'd wet the bed. Shuddering with revulsion, once more I wished that I were dead. How will I be punished this time, I wondered? Mam would put me in that home for sure, like she theatened. Her words reverberated in my head: 'I curse the day I ever had you. I'm goin' to put you into a home.' Braving the fearful bathroom in the middle of the night I got the carbolic soap for the stain, then pulling the covers over the top I prayed no-one would notice.

They noticed all right. The overpowering stench of carbolic coming from my room gave the game away. Just to make things worse, the old bedsprings left rusty marks on the bottom of the new mattress.

Her face was set hard with contempt
Me mam could hardly bear to look at me.

5

As my stature increased so did my workload, to the point that it seemed all chores, school and bed. Most weekends seemed just chores and bed. Putting a high polish on worn threadbare lino, scrubbing the drains and steps, dirty dishes piled over the sink and a mountain of pans. Mam did stacks of endless washing and ironing, said I was useless at ironing – thank God. She sometimes made Teddy help with the dishes, but after him inducing me to hold my hands under the scalding water to see if I could be brave and test my threshold of pain, more often than not I volunteered to take on the task of washing all the dishes on my own. The point of the cleaning was lost on me as the house, with the stinking damp patches and all the rats and cockroaches, never looked any better anyway.

Eventually with enough money saved I bought an old bike from the rag-and-bone man. More use than the gasping bloody goldfish he handed out after swapping our junk and cast-off clothes. (They always floated belly up after a day.) He was pushing his wheelbarrow down the back alleyway and it was on top of the rags when I spotted it . . . a black, sit-up-and-beg bike. We argued before settling on fourteen bob. It was a done deal. For me any possible hope for escape had to be a bargain, even at fourteen bob.

Knowing nothing about spokes, brakes, pedals, or how anything worked, I spent weeks cleaning, polishing and tarting up paintwork.

Hiding the bike in the wash-house, I pleaded with the twins not to tell anyone.

After all, I hadn't told Mam that the twins had an air-gun and shot milk tops that they lined up along the mantelpiece. (Fancy, no-one ever questioned why the chimney breast was pitted with holes.) Those boys got away with murder. They even had a dartboard, which they hung behind the kitchen door when Mam and Dad were out. And that was another thing, how come the smooth circle on the door surrounded by dart holes went unnoticed? Even the floor looked like it had a severe case of woodworm to the unsuspecting eye.

I was happy that the twins' attention was occupied with these amusements, as their most recent acquisition had been a potato gun, with me and the local animals constantly fearing the pain of its sting at close range. That was when they weren't inventing new devices or tortures to fill me with dread. Jacky, on the other hand, turned more to creativity, spending his spare time building model planes from balsa wood and tissue paper. He even put little engines in that turned the propeller round a couple of times, just before the plane smashed to the ground.

'Someone's pinched me friggin' bike,' I wailed one Sunday morning, as I ran through the house. All my escape plans were in ruins.

The old git didn't blink an eye. 'I gave it to the rag-and-bone man. He's left you four goldfish, they're in a bucket in the yard.'

Betrayed again. 'Why did yer 'ave to do that? It was me own money, you 'ad no right,' I cried bravely.

'I've been a bloody road asphalter all me life and I've seen more kids comin' off decent bikes endin' up dead, let alone on bloody old boneshakers like that thing in the

57

shed. It was a death trap. I don't want to 'ear another word on the subject, understand?'

Turmoil again. Even though my boneshaker had gone, my dad must love me because he was worried about my safety. It was all very confusing – I dried my runny nose and eyes with the back of my sleeve and made a hasty exit, slamming the door for good measure.

One Sunday night when the house was empty, I put all my possessions in a crocheted bag my granny had given me: my Noddy clock and pyjamas, my Bible with a few flowers pressed between the pages, Topsy, who was pretty battered by now, and a few clothes. I didn't leave a note, it was better to let them worry. Now my begrudged entrance into the family would finally be avenged and the twins would have to help more with the chores.

Two hours and three buses later I arrived at Patty's. She and John still lived in his sister Mabel's parlour, sharing the kitchen and the outside lavvy. Her face dropped while she stammered her excuses.

'There's just no room here chuck, I'll 'ave to take yer back tomorrer. One day when we get a place of our own, it'll be different then – you'll see.'

Going back to the house at Littledale Road was very crushing for me. It proved that even my beloved Patty didn't want me. The kitchen was full with the rest of the family. No-one looked up as I slithered through the door.

'Can I please come home Mam?'

'Fifty-eight, fifty-nine, sixty.' She counted the stitches as she dragged them across the needles.

'Mam. Can I please come home?'

'What are you on about? Why, where 'ave you been?' She said without even raising her head or tearing her eyes away from the yellow-coloured square she was busily knitting.

Sod it, they hadn't even noticed I'd gone – run away – or was it another of their mind games? I was just starting to cotton on to mind torture. I'd been a bit young and naive up to then.

Another week of silence. No meals made for me. Doors slammed at every opportunity when anyone left the room. More empty days and miserable nights.

I wished I knew what it felt like to be loved. Despite our big family I suffered incredible loneliness. Teddy for instance had refused to speak directly to me for the last four years. Seemed I had once used his own special gold-plated Jublilee fork that was given to him and Georgie by the Mayor for having the good fortune to be born in Jubilee year. Even though Teddy's anger had worn off some time ago, he still used sign language to communicate with me if a third party wasn't around to help out.

Many was the time Teddy handed me a note to run messages for him to the local sweetshop for a bottle of pop, chocolate and a tube of Smarties. The Smarties would be mine, but only if I got back before he counted up to five thousand. How naive I was. Time after time, for almost a year I would race to the shop trying to beat his time barrier. Just as I'd almost collapse breathless on the kitchen chair, Teddy would be saying 'five thousand and six, five thousand and seven', or anything over five thousand. Then I'd watch him throw the Smarties on the back of the fire for my failure, never realizing the reward must always elude me. As everyone else knew, he only started counting after I burst through the door.

It was the dares that frightened me the most. Like the time I was told I could have the two-bob piece at the bottom of the enamel bucket filled with water if I didn't mind getting my hand wet. When I plunged my hand in the bucket to get the money, my arm shook and tingled painfully. Georgie had wired the bucket to an electric current.

For a little while when I was about nine I had a friend

called Joan Baxter who lived down the back alleyway. Having had scarlet fever as a kid she was left with a limp as well as a bad heart. Her gaping mouth seemed to hang permanently open.

'Please Mam, when me new friend Joan comes to play, can she wait in the house for a change? Her mam lets me in her house.'

Mam's attitude was that no-one who called at our house was allowed in past the front door. 'Don't want half the soddin' street runnin' through this place mindin' our business! Never encourage neighbours – they're like dog muck, always on yer doorstep.'

Surprisingly, when Joan did come to visit Mam relented. Joan was allowed inside out of the cold, but only in the hall, mind. I worked hard to finish my jobs, knowing Joan was waiting. When I opened the door she was gone. The twins had got to her first.

'Stop a minute would you girl? Did you know our Cherry got 'er name off a jam jar? How many flies a day do you collect in yer gob? Hey, we can cure yer limp – come outside.'

And there they were, pretending concern and showing her how to walk with one leg in the gutter and the other on the pavement.

'See, no limp, it's easy. You just 'ave to walk up the road on one side and down the other, unless you fancy walkin' backwards.'

Joan never came back to our house.

I was used to my own company and had learnt to live in a make-believe world. I played for hours amongst the old bombed houses, never considering the danger as I walked the rafters and ceiling joists beneath the collapsing roofs, balancing precariously and hovering from room to room. I built pretend furniture out of bricks and derelict wood. I had a pretend oven, and tin cans and jam jars became my pots and pans. The most delicious pretend meals were made from coloured broken glass,

60

which I ground between two bricks and matched with the colour of vegetables. Broken concrete was stacked to mark out rooms, windows and doorways. I never bothered going home to get changed out of my school clothes because I would be given a job and wouldn't get time to play in the street. Sometimes I forgot the time and went home after dark. Nobody seemed to give a damn anyway.

I hadn't finished telling my dad about the kind man who followed me home from school and gave me sweeties. And how he said that I was cute and laughed while showing me a pink torch thing under his coat. I added for good measure 'And *he* likes me 'ouse . . .'

My mam was grabbing at my dad. 'Paddy, get the bloody bobby,' she yelled.

What was all the fuss? Why did the local bobby ask all those daft questions? What had I done now? Had he heard I'd been nicking pop bottles from behind the chip shop?

'What 'ave you been told about talkin' to strange men? I've told yer till I'm blue in the face,' Dad shouted, shaking me until my teeth rattled.

Now Dad and the bobby said I was a wicked girl and couldn't play on the 'bomby' any more, I'd got to come straight home from school.

'You, now Dad, yer've gone and spoilt everythin',' I sobbed. 'You shouldn't 'ave told the bobby. You 'ad no right, that was me own 'ouse.'

The bobby surveyed me with a long, penetrating glare as I squirmed miserably. Then he poked me in the shoulder saying, 'You've had a lucky escape my girl, mark my words.' He turned away nodding his head and muttering, 'Innocence, absolute innocence.'

Even growing up in a house full of men who were crude, yes, but modest about their bodies (our 'rude parts' were never discussed, and certainly never exposed), I only realized years later what a lucky escape I'd

61

had from a man flashing his willy. How could I know? I had never seen a man's willy.

'Please Mam, can I go to me granny's after school?'

'No. Yer dad told you to come straight home.'

'I won't go to the bomb-site, honest. Oh, please. Cross me heart and hope to die.'

'No. Be told – it's not safe for you to be out on the streets on yer own.'

'But you never take me to Granny's any more. P-l-e-a-s-e.' I whined on and on, risking a thick ear.

She eventually gave in; she said she was past caring and I was getting on her nerves.

It wasn't very far to Liscard where Granny lived; only fifteen minutes if I ran my fastest all the way. Granny lived in the back room of my Uncle Harry's house. Even though it was ages since my mam had taken me there the memories were comfortingly vivid. Lead-lighted windows with diamond-shaped inserts of coloured glass – painted cardboard replaced the missing pieces that Hitler blew out. The backyard was a patchwork of broken paving stones my Uncle Harry nicked from the Council yard. Several death-defying weeds struggled up through the roughly cemented cracks, standing out against the freshly whitewashed yard walls.

I entered the respectable, carbolic-smelling house through the back alleyway. I hammered on the shiny brass door knocker. Uncle Harry stood at the kitchen door, his crossed arms over his chest.

'What do you want?'

'Hiya Uncle Harry. I've come to see me granny.'

'Does yer mam know yer 'ere?'

I stood squirming in front of him with downcast eyes and just nodded.

'Go on in but don't you talk her to death. She's old and gets very tired. Are you listenin' to me, girl?'

I could see why my dad said Uncle Harry was 'up

himself' after being made a sergeant in the Home Guard during the war.

Bloody old fool!

As I entered the silent room my heart swelled with love when I saw her, the quaint sleeping beauty, almost hidden on the bed amongst an assortment of crocheted cushions. Liky a tiny clockwork doll, she came to life before regarding me with an air of sleepy curiosity.

'Hiya, Granny, it's me.' I bent to shout into her good ear.

'Why it's little Cherry. Come in dear, let me get a proper look at you,' she said with a little quiver in her voice. She painstakingly eased herself up, gripping the old iron bedstead for support.

'Well sit yourself down. I'll brew us some tea.'

Each time she spoke her face was only inches from mine, as if checking I was still in the room and not part of her wanderings.

She mumbled to herself while she collected the tea things together. 'Little Cherry. Fancy that, little Cherry has come to visit me.' I didn't know if she was talking to my dead granddad or me.

I had no memory of Granddad, since he was burned to death before I was born. Some families have two lots of grandparents. I never knew why we missed out. Maybe the other lot were somewhere in Ireland – or heaven.

Little hairline cracks patterned the two rooster-shaped eggcups Granny handed me. Elastoplast held together the parts of a broken tail and the beaks were chipped off.

'We will have a nice chucky egg for our tea and perhaps if you're a good girl I may be able to find an orange we can share. How does that sound? Little Cherry, fancy that. Little Cherry has come to visit me,' she was again telling herself as she smiled and nodded.

Whatever she understood me to say didn't make any difference, as she went about the task of preparing tea. For years Granny had eaten, slept and cooked in the small, dark, solitary room in the back of Uncle Harry's house. She did all her cooking on the open fire, and a big black iron pot was brought out from a cobwebby corner of the room. Cheeky bloody spiders taking advantage of Granny's tired old eyes.

'Be a good girl, go to the wash-house down the yard and fill this pot with water. My eyes are not as good as they used to be so I'm afraid I might fall.'

Couldn't imagine my Granny falling. She shuffled everywhere. You could just catch the tips of her tiny lace-up boots peeping out from under the layers of her long black skirts. The twins said that like all the nuns Granny had wheels instead of feet. There was a time I would have believed them.

Everything, including water for tea and washing dishes, was heated on the open fire by screwing the big black pot into the middle of the dim embers. Occasionally she would stab at the fire, causing hot cinders to spew over the already singed clippie mat in front of the fender. It was a wonder she didn't go up in flames like my dead granddad.

Exhaused by her efforts of preparing the banquet of boiled eggs, Granny rested in the rickety old chair and rocked contentedly. I watched her doze off again. Her hair was like a new Brillo pad. It was then that I thought my precious old granny was really my mam's mam. How come they were so different? Funny that. Soon I got bored; the room was so silent. Was she still breathing, I wondered?

'Granny, Granny, talk to me,' I whispered prayer-like.

Suddenly, her false teeth dropped into her open mouth. I panicked, thinking she was dead, until she pushed them back into place with her tongue. Seemingly sustained after her forty winks, Granny opened her eyes and continued the conversation where she had left off. '. . . And are you still a good little girl? Your mam's little treasure? I'm sure you are.'

My eyes started to burn with sad old tears, as I thought of the unlikelihood of being 'me mam's little treasure'. I was 'The Curse' and I believed the only reason I wasn't in a children's home was because they didn't really know of any.

I thought for a moment of asking my granny to adopt me, but I changed my mind when I considered the cramped dark space she existed in.

'Now, will you read to me, little Cherry?' Granny handed me a folded newspaper. It was yellow and worn. I squinted at the words, long since faded. 'Use this, don't strain your eyes,' she said, as she passed me a magnifying glass as big as a saucer with a broken pencil for a handle. That was what my granny always used to find lost things. She swore that, if she'd used something like that when she was younger, she wouldn't have the problems with her vision she had now. Bless her. After all she was over eighty-five.

After the reading, Granny burrowed under mountains of linen at the bottom of a battered mahogany dresser, finding the prized orange wrapped in a tea towel. Like everything else in the room it smelled of mothballs. She might have been old, but Granny peeled that orange so expertly the trailing skin was over a yard long without a single break. I bet it took years of practice. I vowed to learn that trick one day when I was rich enough to afford my own oranges.

The ugly mantle clock groaned seven just as Uncle Harry marched into the room and placed a newly filled oil lamp on the table next to the waxed flowers.

'Haven't you got 'lectricity yet? Me dad says you's was old-fashioned.'

'Better get goin' now. Yer Granny is tired, and it's gettin' dark. Go on now, bugger off, there's a good girl.'

I nodded reluctantly. I didn't want to leave this cosy room – the room that never failed to cheer me. Granny struggled to her feet. I hurled myself at her, wrapping my arms around her. Granny held the door casings with both hands to steady herself as Uncle Harry peeled me off her, complaining, 'Careful, girl. Now give yer old granny a kiss. You can come again soon. Yer poor granny doesn't get many visitors.'

I flung my arms around her neck and plonked a big, wet kiss on her face. 'I love you, Granny.'

For some reason I was overcome, swallowing sobs after hearing Granny's sweet voice sink into a breathless whisper.

'God bless you little Cherry.'

I didn't want to leave her security and peace until I looked at the threepenny bit Uncle Harry pushed into my hand, then I ran all the way home, stopping only to buy a bag of Uncle Joe's Mint Balls and a sherbet dab.

And that was the last time I saw my granny.

6

Patty had arrived to take me to North Wales for a treat. We were going to stay with my big sister Dolly and Alf (her 'queer one') in Rhosgadfan. I was nine and three quarters and had never had a day out of Wallasey or even been on a charabanc-coach.

I was talking nineteen to the dozen. Patty sent me away. 'Yer gettin' on me mam's nerves with yer constant yappin', and I'm warnin' yer, don't get under 'er feet 'cos she may change 'er mind.'

Patty and my mam were getting on better than they ever had before. Mam even let Patty perm her hair with a Pin Up cold perm so she wouldn't have to walk round all day with three spring clamps down each side of her head to make her hair wrinkly. Patty put the big brown hairnet into place to hold Mam's set and stop the straggly bits of hair falling round her lined and worn face.

Bloody hell, I thought, now she starts making a pot of tea. 'Oh come on Patty, hurry up. I can't wait to see Dorothy again.' If she didn't get a move on we would miss the connection near Woodside Ferry where we had to pick up the charabanc-coach to Wales.

'Please. Please. Please. Patty can't we go now?' She took another slurp of tea before slamming the mug on the table.

I thought Patty had gone nuts as she kissed Mam tenderly on the cheek. 'Ta ra well, see yer.'

'What the 'ell 'ave yer got in these bloody cases, our Cherry? I'll 'ave arms on me like Popeye before I'm done.'

Mam came to the front step to wave us off. I stared out of the back window of the taxi as she got smaller and smaller, eventually disappearing from sight.

With only moments to spare we boarded the charabanc-coach. All the passengers were laughing and joking until they clapped eyes on us, then they stopped. Before long they started again in a funny foreign language which Patty said was Welsh. After what seemed like hours of bouncing down lanes past stone cottages we arrived at the end of a long winding pathway which led to our Dolly's cottage. It was just like the one I saw in a Hansel and Gretel book at school. It had titchy little windows with lace curtains and a green-painted door with massive black fancy hinges. The step and window sills were scrubbed clean with a donkey stone. A chimney nearly half the size of the end wall was puffing out white smoke that swirled and then vanished into the blue sky. Funny that, because at home the smoke was grey and hung round the place, making all the clean washing on the line mucky before it had a chance to dry.

Drystone walls marking out the various paddocks surrounded the cottage. Meadows of yellow waving grass stretched for miles. Cows, chickens, sheep and goats all wandered round, seemingly friendly and unafraid. Dolly and Alf had created a fairy-tale home for their little family of girls. The peace and beauty of it all totally overwhelmed me, so different from the life on Merseyside.

Patty and Dolly hugged each other then nattered on non-stop. The wafting smell of fresh bread reminded me that I hadn't eaten since we left home. I was starving hungry and let them know it.

'Geroff to the toilet and wash yer 'ands and I'll get you summat to eat.'

They were too engrossed to notice me still wandering round the house holding myself between the legs, getting more and more frantic by the minute.

'I'm burstin' for a pee our Patty and I can't find the bathroom.'

'Well love, you won't,' laughed Dolly. 'We 'aven't got one. The lavvy is a shed in the back field and there's a tap outside to rinse yer 'ands.'

Hiking across the paddock, keeping my eye on the bull, squatting my little bum on the splintery planks suspended across the oil drum and then washing myself in ice-cold water, added to the thrill and wonder of it all. As I sat on the lavvy with the door wide open I looked across fields waving with bluebells like a fragrant blue carpet, with white butterflies suspended above.

Dorothy and her little sisters were dead lucky. I was jealous of them growing up in a home like that. Although they had experienced many hardships, their house breathed love and contentment. I didn't ever want to go back to Littledale Road.

As I lay in my bed in the room above the kitchen, I overheard Patty and Dolly exchanging stories about their own personal survival tactics before they were married. I began to understand that Dolly had held our family together like a little mother even before I was born. Trying to feed and clothe us had left her with both mental and physical scars. I had never known that before. Even all those years ago, Dolly, being the eldest girl, had taken the brunt of our parents' violence. Her regular punishment for minor offences was to be held by the ears while her head was banged against the wall. She often wore the bruises of drunken fists for 'speaking before she was spoken to'. Sometimes Dolly fainted with the pain, which had left her with recurring headaches. Yes, I could see she really was my sister all right.

69

She was one of us; a curse and a burden just like Patty and me.

I liked Dolly's husband Alf. In fact my family liked him, which was a surprise, him being a 'queer one' and that. A man's man, my dad once said. Alf was full of good-natured banter and teasing. He laughed with me, never at me, and soon had me trusting him even though he was a male like my brothers.

My niece Dorothy taught me a few Welsh words of greeting, which I practised hard until I could say them properly from the back of the throat. Showing off, I recited them on the coach home. Our fellow travellers were stony-faced in their lack of appreciation. Seems I had been cursing and swearing in fluent Welsh.

I had just about given up all hopes on the idea of Joey or Patty adopting me, so I supposed it might be too much to expect that Dolly and Alf would consider it. Then I could live there with Dorothy and the girls and grow up in Wales, instead of Merseyside with the scruffy grey houses and heavily polluted air.

Our Georgie knew someone who could get us a television set for twenty quid, no questions asked. Georgie had seen one at his mate's house and we could have it, with the chance of being the first in our street to own a telly. It would certainly help the Faulkners to come up in the world.

Finally it was time to crack open Mam's money tin. The money tin was a much-prized acquisition from the war. (I heard the grown-ups saying the tin was from a shop with a secret name that people only whispered, 'the Black Market'.) Written on the side of the tin were the words SAXA SALT. The seemingly precious salt had long gone during the war, when it had been swapped for tea, pepper or bits of old tyres for mending shoes. Mam had been saving for ever, it seemed. When asked what she was saving for, the reply was always the same. 'A divorce from the Bloody Reptile.' Funny that, Mam also wanting to escape.

We held our breath as Mam's money tin was ceremoniously lifted from the top of the kitchen cupboard.

Like the Ark of the Covenant it was death to anyone who dared to touch it. Newspaper was spread over the table so that we could all sit round to count the money. We were told to count in ten-bob piles. How exciting! Teddy was betting Georgie that there was more than twenty quid in there. Mam's hands shook trying to work the tin-opener that didn't budge.

'Stop soddin' around. Let me do it,' scoffed my dad.

He lumbered into the backyard with the heavy tin and with his usual refinement, took to it with an axe. We secretly hoped a few odd tanners would roll our way but they didn't. In fact, nothing rolled our way. Nothing rolled at all. Over the years the salt residue in the tin had welded her hoard of coins into a misshapen, oxidized mass.

It looked like we'd missed out on the telly (or the divorce – I'm not sure which).

My dad always yearned for a dog, even though we never managed to keep animals for long. Sometimes, coming back from the pub a bit 'bevvied' as Mam called it, he would haul some poor unfortunate mutt home with his tie wrapped round its neck. The dog would crouch and dig its paws in as Dad dragged it through the alleyway, nearly taking the skin off its arse.

Dad's pathetic story was always the same. 'It just followed me home, lovey.'

But Mam knew full well his drunken obsession with stealing dogs. He would cradle the animal in his arms and nurse it until the drink got the better of him and he fell asleep. The dog was thrown in the wash-house and starved for a couple of days to teach it to be humble and know who its master was. As soon as the wash-house door was opened the dog would always run off.

71

One frightful night next door's cat foolishly howled on our backyard wall. The twins shot at it with the dreaded potato gun to scare it, but the stupid cat returned to its territory. The lads lay in wait, grabbing it and throwing it in the wash-house. Unfortunately for the cat, the latest dog to 'follow' Dad home was a bull mastiff, which had been in the wash-house unfed for three days. I entered the yard horrified by a fearful din of shrieking, crashing, growling and barking. The twins finally flung open the washhouse door. The pulverized cat shot out and straight up the eight-foot backyard wall, before its half-dismembered body dropped dead at my feet.

It was a fatal mistake to let the twins know how my heart ached, but it was impossible to remain indifferent to their incredible cruelty to animals. Most of the time the demonstrations were only staged so that they could delight in my reactions, another victim of their practical jokes, like the trapped animals. I knew with terrible clarity I was hopelessly at the mercy of my brothers.

The twins were unrelenting. They rigged up a skeleton in my wardrobe, daubed with luminous paint to glow in the dark. I didn't lock my bedroom door any more. Locking myself in with God knows what was worse than locking them out. A series of dead mice, cockroaches, plastic shit and vomit was placed in my bed and from time to time I found real sheep's eyes or chicken's feet in my duffel-coat pocket. At one stage my mam came to my rescue after they put an electric charge to the brass knob on my bedroom door.

'That's bloody dangerous. She could 'ave a heart attack! Just leave her alone, there's good lads.' Why didn't she realize that I'd already nearly had many a heart attack without an electric charge? Just simple terror was all it took.

Eventually I learnt not to appear to overreact to their petty dares and the reign of terror slackened off – for the time being.

Life was becoming more tolerable in other ways. After my trip to Wales, with its breathtaking beauty and tranquillity, drawing and painting became my consuming interest – my temporary escape. Having asthma constantly, I'd missed too much schooling and was a dunce. On the day I sat the eleven-plus exam the school was in turmoil after it was announced on the radio that King George VI had died in his sleep. I seized the opportunity and lied to my mam when I went home at lunchtime. I told her we didn't have to go back for the second part of the exam as the school had closed out of respect for our dear King. Just as well really, because I wasn't encouraged to pass – no-one was forking out good money on a bloody school uniform just for a girl.

7

Old Daddy Dawson lived just across the road from us in a bombed house with all the windows blown out and the roof hanging off. We hadn't seen him in weeks.

'Is Daddy Dawson dead?' Georgie asked Teddy.

'I hope so. They've buried him,' he laughed.

How cruel, Daddy Dawson had been good to them. Anyway I'd miss him, the sweet old man who fixed toys for all the street kids. Sometimes he'd give us wheels with tyres on to push up and down the road with a stick. Best of all, he sang Vera Lynn songs with tears in his eyes that only made us giggle.

Before long a family moved into Daddy Dawson's house. The furniture looked too posh for bombed-house tenants, and there'd been someone working on the outside. I noticed that the broken windows were replaced and there was a tarpaulin covering the roof. Watching the progress on Daddy Dawson's house, I saw two girls coming and going. One was about my age and the other a bit younger. They seemed too fancy to be living in the scruffy end of the road. I hung round the streets until the pub threw out, and in months I never saw them playing outside – pity, I could have taught those girls a lot. Having learnt their names were Marion and June Gregory I decided to give them a visit.

'Can't play in the street? How do you manage to get

out of the way when there's a brawl?' I asked them in amazement. Apparently they were treated like film stars. Didn't even do any chores to maintain their warm, inviting home. Theirs seemed a different world to mine: music and dancing lessons, even attending drama groups and amateur operatics. Being in my teens, small and plain, still struggling to survive, I was in awe of these confident, outgoing, pretty girls.

Marion was the elder – born at Easter same year as me, but she wore make-up and stockings and was allowed to go out with boys. 'How do you mean, you've never been kissed?' the girls tittered when we played Truth or Dare.

What else could I mean? How else could I bloody say it?

'I've never been kissed proper-like on the mouth.'

They were puzzled, before confering. 'Maybe we need to do something with her clothes first and then we'll show her how to tart herself up.'

It didn't help that I was undersized for my age with a nose too big for my face. My family taunted me about my nose. 'God knows, what a nose,' Georgie would say. I tried not to care that the louts hanging round the street corners never gave me a second look. No-one ever winked or wolf-whistled when I passed building sites or the gangs outside the pubs.

Being introduced to the girls' pretty world full of glamour, colour and laughter was all-revealing. I became the proud owner of a net underskirt that I could starch and iron wet to make 'sticky-out' dresses. Backcombing my hair was an art I hadn't really mastered yet, but I sprayed it with sugar and water to make it stay in place. (Bloody bees kept landing on my head.) I'd even started to clean my teeth and Patty bought me some Eucryl tooth powder and my own pink toothbrush.

My old school blouse had a transformation since I ironed some transfers of Tommy Steele on the collar and the breast pocket. I decided I must ask my mam for a brassiere. Marion and her sister wore them. I didn't have much to put in a bra, but it would be so grown-up to have one.

The girls took control.

'You need to meet boys,' said Marion. 'If you like I can get you a blind date. I know what we can do; my boyfriend and his mate have both got motorbikes. Can't remember his mate's name, but we could all go out as a foursome. What do you think about trying it?'

I nodded meekly. Marion was so glamorous and wise, I longed to be just like her.

I wasn't so much introduced to Arthur Moon, as pushed in his direction. It was by the ferry building at Seacombe. He showed no pleasure at the encounter; didn't even look at me. Just mumbled while indicating for me to get on the back of his monstrous motorbike.

I was so nervous I thought I was going to be sick. 'But I've got all me good gear on.'

I had my sticky-out skirt, Tommy Steele blouse, and my hair piled up and glued with so much hairspray it was like a bird's nest.

Marion expertly straddled her boyfriend's motorbike and they rode off towards Chester. What a blooming lousy foursome this was turning out to be. There was something odd about this Arthur bloke. I thought he was foreign, as I couldn't understand much he muttered. Arthur was getting impatient and revving the bike; the noise was frightening, doing little to boost my confidence.

'Are you getting on or not?'

Hobson's bloody choice. I'd no bus fare home and I was wearing Cuban-heeled shoes. What the hell? It might be fun.

Didn't know Chester was so far away. What a lousy way to spend your first date. The cheek of this bloke! After arriving in Chester he simply turned the bike around and rode all the way back to Seacombe Ferry without stopping for a drink or speaking. The wind was biting cold, my hair was standing on end like Ken Dodd's and my skirt kept flying over my head. I poked him in the back yelling, demanding to be taken straight home. Arthur for the first time removed his helmet, switched off the engine, and as if remembering why I was there in the first place, decided to comb his hair.

'Who cut yer mouth?' I asked.

He spoke through his nose. 'It ain't cut!'

Pointing to his mouth to press my point, 'Well I know that now, but it's been cut all right, I can still see the scar. See, see, just on the top.'

'It's not soddin' cut I tell yer, I've got a harelip.'

'What's a harelip?'

'I was born with it and no roof to me mouth.'

'No kiddin'? Geroff you daft bugger, I don't believe yer, otherwise yer food would disappear into yer 'ead when you eat.'

Arthur didn't answer, just kicked his motorbike into life and roared off, leaving me standing at Seacombe Ferry and no chance of getting home before my mam and dad's ten thirty nightly Armageddon. I didn't think much of dating. Truth to tell, I'd have rather been swinging round the lamp-post.

'Did he kiss you?' Marion giggled and elbowed me.

I shrugged my shoulders. But Marion wasn't giving up that easily.

'When are you seeing him again?'

'Dunno.'

'What do you mean, you don't know?'

'Well, he didn't hang around long enough to ask.'

'Good grief Cherry, you know what your problem is?'

I wasn't looking forward to what was coming.

'You need to get out and mix more. Even our June gets more blokes than you do and she's two years younger. Hey, fancy trying your luck at the Tower Ballroom on

77

Saturday night? There's lots of hunks there so even you can take your pick.'

Marion's mam enrolled on the 'let's transform Cherry' project. She made me a dirndl skirt with gathered elastic round the waist. Marion offered to lend me her waspie belt when I wore the skirt with my Tommy Steele blouse.

Now I was sure to get a hunk.

Being a teenager wasn't all bad. I was blossoming, filling out, or so Mam said when she noticed my bosoms looking like fried eggs, hidden under my vest. My mam and me were getting on much better.

She whispered, 'Have you noticed any bleedin' anywhere at any time?'

'No,' I was pleased to announce, thrusting my chest out as far as I could, 'in fact they never even hurt, just grew on their own. But ever so slowly, mind you.'

Mam patted me on the back like she was trying to burp me as she quickly changed the subject. She said that she would ask one of the neighbours to give me a Pin Up cold perm to help soften my hard features. Whatever that meant.

When I saw my reflection in the mucky stained mirror over Mrs Higgins's kitchen sink, I panicked. So much of my hair was round my feet.

'Me hair is me best feature,' I told the toothless old girl with the sagging breasts. She sloshed on the lotion and started wrapping clumps of my hair in British Rail toilet paper.

'I want you to do it so I look like Veronica Lake.'

'Who's Veronica Lake when she's at 'ome?' she laughed.

'Only the bestest fillum star I've ever seen.'

After the rollers and the bog roll came the lotion that smelt like pee.

'Am I nearly done?' My eyes were burning and my nose was running.

'If you want to look like a fillum star yer will 'ave to wait a while. Trust me lovey.'

After endless water torture the coloured rods and toilet paper were removed. Then came the curling tongs; I couldn't look, but I certainly felt it when the old hag decided to curl one of my ears. Finally I was done.

'I look like an explosion in a mattress factory,' I yelled to the image in the mirror, rather than confront the old hag. 'Veronica Lake doesn't look like this!'

She slapped me on the back. 'She would do, if I did 'er 'air.'

My brothers didn't think I looked like Veronica Lake either.

'Harpo? Who's this Harpo Teddy said I looked like?' I asked Georgie.

'Oh him, just a fillum star. Thought a woman of the world like you would 'ave heard of Harpo Marx.'

Oh, I preened myself, perhaps I didn't look too bad after all.

'Teddy said I look like Harpo Marx, Dad – what do you think?'

He chided me and chuckled, 'Yes lovey, you do. Now, stop teasin' the baby you boys or you'll get a thick ear.' And with a belly-shaking laugh he headed off to the Brighton.

Even though my confidence was fragile I braved the Tower Ballroom with Marion to hear Ted Heath and his Band. She danced past me with a never-ending supply of partners while I tried to look inconspicuous by shrinking into the corner behind the plastic rainforest between several other stiff dumbstruck wallflowers. My hopes of a dance diminished as the night wore on. I told myself that it was OK, I didn't like dancing much anyway.

The hall was stinking of sweat and stale scent. Longing to escape from the hot smoky place I edged my way to the door to talk to the lady who looked after the coats and kill the time until Marion was ready to go home. Just before I got there, a bloke with a green Fair Isle V-necked jumper and brown shiny trousers nudged me. 'Hey girl, wanna give it a go?'

Luckily for me, it was the last waltz and I knew how to do the slow ones, therefore I gratefully accepted. Now I could tell Marion I had had the last waltz. If I played my cards right he would take me home and ask for a date. That's how it was done, I'd learnt that much.

The stench of vomit hung round him as he staggered drunkenly, resting his head on my shoulder as he started to suck my neck, leaving red marks. He had a comb in his pocket, I thought, as he danced so close something hard was digging into my rude parts.

Grateful when the music stopped I wrenched free and ran out, knowing I couldn't stand the sight, sound or feel of this bloke a minute longer. I grabbed my navy blue school mac and caught the last bus home, alone.

To my surprise Marion was impressed. 'Don't tell me if you don't want to, but I can see by the hickeys on your neck you did OK for yourself.'

Gosh, I had grown in her eyes and no matter how disgusting I found that particular experience I wasn't going to tell her about the slobbering bloke with the shiny trousers, because she now thought I was experienced in the ways of men.

'Can't wait for you to meet Tony who's dead rich. I've been saving him for you. His father has his own business and owns several cars. I'm going out with his friend, so we could go as a foursome.' Marion was at it again.

'Good grief, I 'aven't gotten over the last spotty Herbert who turned up for our lousy foursome,' I said.

She told me that this Tony was different.

'Why? Has he got a proper roof to his mouth?'

'Better than that.'

'Don't tell me – I bet he's got his own teeth as well.'

'Yes. And Tony is handsome. Besides, even though he is very posh, you never know, he could still fancy you.'

I'd never met anyone rich.

'What's the catch? Why would he want to go out with me?' I wondered.

When I met Tony, he was head and shoulders over me. A real dreamboat with blond wavy hair and melting blue eyes that made me go wobbly at the knees. Amazingly, Tony seemed just as stuck on me. That made me feel all warm and happy.

We strolled hand in hand through the local rose gardens on our second date when I experienced that first kiss. Marion had shown me how to part my lips, but he took me by surprise and my teeth awkwardly clashed into his, nearly knocking them down his throat. He showed his irritation as he kept wiping his mouth with a nice white hanky, checking it for blood.

'Sorry,' I whimpered.

'Forget it.'

Fancy me making a mess of that! I'd practised often enough kissing the back of my hand as I shut my eyes and puckered. We walked in uncomfortable silence through the rose gardens, stopping in front of Tony's dad's warehouse, which backed onto a large park of majestic oak trees.

'Would you like to have a peep inside – I've got the keys?' he winked.

Dead right I wanted to look. I had to check out all these cars he said they owned, besides, my new fancy man assured me that the people inside would keep our little secret. Without turning on the light, I could see, true to his word, there were three beautiful black limousines parked behind the shuttered doors. Suddenly I shuddered although it wasn't cold. I was anxious to go now I was satisfied that Tony was the catch Marion said he was. Tony started pulling me by the elbow, past the cars and through a dark echoing passage. I screwed my nose up at the disgusting smell that invaded my nostrils.

Overwhelmed with panic I begged, 'Please Tony, I want to go home now.'

'Soon, when you've met my friends.'

This bloke was starting to give me the creeps.

Slowly my eyes adjusted to the darkness. We were in a huge refrigerated room with several coffins lining the walls and trolleys, unoccupied, thank goodness.

His father was a frigging undertaker! No wonder his business was so close to the quaint church with the rose garden and the park. How many innocents had this weird sod taken in? With blood boiling, 'You go to hell Tony Grafton,' I yelled as he caught the full impact of my swift right hook to his precious pearly whites, drawing enough blood to spoil his posh hanky this time.

Running all the way home without a backward glance, I swore I'd had it with lads. No more, not blooming likely.

I decided to join a nunnery instead.

8

Our front room had to be cleared out. Dolly and Alf and their girls were coming to live with us. Seemed Alf lost his job when the quarry closed down and there was no work in North Wales. I was excited, remembering our trip to Wales and what a good little homemaker Dolly was. Perhaps the burden of housework for me would get easier; besides, she could talk woman talk to Mam and bring smiles back to her face. Now with ten of us under one roof, perhaps Dolly could protect me like Patty once did.

Then I would be safe, cared for or loved maybe.

I lived in dread that I might die soon. My friend Joan Baxter said that if you didn't start your periods before you were fourteen you'd die. I wasn't really sure what a 'period' was but it was something to do with your rude parts: I knew because I'd heard the lads talking.

Just in the nick of time my period did come. I'd had bellyache for ages but my mam insisted it was growing pains. I thought that this meant my bones were all stretching, and if the gripping, nauseating pain made me as tall as other girls my age it was well worthwhile. Almost!

Dolly and Alf stared at me open-mouthed as I

announced to them both, 'Guess what? When I wee it looks like raspberry pop.'

Dolly hauled me upstairs while she unleashed a torrent of disapproval.

'Yer a young woman now so you mustn't talk dirty in front of men. Go on, wipe yerself on yer vest and let's 'ave a look.'

Bewildered, I did as I was ordered. First, I had to have a strip wash and hold a big bandage thing between my legs. Then with the aid of two safety pins it was pinned to my drawers (my vest wasn't long enough) to keep it in place. It made me walk funny – a bit like John Wayne.

'Go and 'ave a lie-down and I'll send you up a nice cuppa and a hot-water bottle. That'll do the trick,' Dolly coaxed. 'The pain will pass soon, it always does.'

'You don't mean this is gonna happen to me again?' I cried.

The days merged into throbbing, distressing nights as I sat on the lavvy with 'growing pains', sometimes drifting into spasmodic, fatigued sleep. At that point my fear of rats in the bathroom was nothing compared to the fear that my insides were falling out.

Every month was the same. Living in terror as waves of pain gripped my stomach, I suffered in ignorance and shame that left me weak and exhausted.

Easter came and with it, again, my birthday. The family discussed and decided that 'the baby' was finally going through puberty. Now I might get a brassiere – lots of girls in my class had brassieres, apparently, as acknowledgement of womanhood. No-one bothered to tell me that it had anything to do with the size of your bosoms. Now Mam seemed to enjoy being able to give presents and could hardly conceal her pleasure as I was handed a bag. There was something delicate inside.

'Yer' growin' up fast now so I thought you should 'ave this.'

Looking in the bag, I saw frills of white broderie anglaise with pink bows.

Finally! 'A brassiere, oh, Mam. Thanks. Wait till I tell Marion.'

Me mam looked confused as I smothered her face in kisses, before running to my bedroom. My hands shook with excitement so much that I couldn't get the damn thing on. It was round my chest and I'd fastened the back, but I couldn't fasten the metal dangly things on top that flopped down.

Finally I gave in. Seeing as I'd got my petticoat on so I was well covered and decent, I went to get help from Dolly and Alf.

'Happy birthday, lovey,' they greeted in unison. 'What the hell do you think yer doin'?'

'See, I've got this brassiere off me mam but me fingers are too small to work the dangly things on the shoulder. What's wrong?'

Stunned silence – they seemed lost for a reply, choking back gales of laughter. What had I said? Alf wiped the tears streaming down his face with the crook of his elbow while I was marched in front of the family for inspection. George finally put me out of my misery. 'It's a bloody suspender belt, yer stupid bitch.'

I was none the wiser. 'So – what's a suspender belt?'

What a birthday – I would take the humiliation with me through the years as the story was embellished every Easter.

The local church youth club was having a dance and a fancy dress party with a prize for the winner. Marion Gregory was going dressed as a gypsy.

'What are you going as?' she asked.

'Not tellin' yer, don't want no-one to pinch me idea. It's a surprise.'

I was determined to come first with my brilliant idea. Nobody would dream of going as an Oxo cube. The

85

empty box I found was perfect with a hole cut out for my head. Naturally, being artistic, I did a good job of painting the box red (and unfortunately, parts of the kitchen floor). After covering my arms and legs with red shoe dye, I was ready to show them all up.

Marion and her dad came to pick me up, but I couldn't get through his car door, as the box was taped and pinned to my knickers and vest, so it wouldn't slip sideways. Down the street I proudly paraded to the church hall as nosy neighbours came to their front steps to catch a glimpse of me. I could see they were impressed as they sniggered behind their hands.

Marion looked OK; I suppose you might say, even pretty, dressed as a gypsy, in a swirly skirt with a white-off-the-shoulder blouse. Her dark hair was curled round her face and big dangly earrings rested on her naked shoulders. But her outfit was not original enough to win a prize – she wasn't smart like me.

As the party got rowdier and hotter I drank lots of pop, I was sticky, uncomfortable, and dying for a pee but it was impossible to get through the lavvy door, let alone sit down. The night was endless, and no bugger asked me to dance. Well they wouldn't – I realized I looked bloody stupid, besides, no-one could get close enough.

I won first prize.

Two bath cubes.

My big brother Joey had had a stroke. His 'queer one' sat in our kitchen crying while Teddy hung round the hospital for news. Boy, him and Joey were two of a kind – in more ways than one. Both brothers had red hair and fiery natures to match; both were witty, but proud with a wilful streak.

One day I came home from school to find a person, who looked like my Joey, sitting in Dad's own chair. He had a vacant stare, couldn't speak properly and slobbered through his crooked mouth.

I was pushed towards him. 'Give our Joey a big love.'

With my eyes focused on the dewdrop hanging from the end of his nose, I stepped back against the big hand my dad held firmly to my back.

'He's got a snotty nose. Someone wipe it first,' I complained.

'Shut up our Cherry, you'll hurt his feelin's, he's not bloody deaf, just paralysed.'

Joey gave a long soulful groan as tears spurted from his lifeless eyes.

His stay with us was short-lived as the district nurse said he was depressed and he needed to be rehabilitated, get back into the real world, get a job, pay the mounting bills and put some cake on the table.

Slowly some feeling returned to his limbs, although his speech and memory were sadly frustrating him. It took over a year for Joey to get some of his speech back although he still stuttered and swore a lot, being so handicapped. And one way and another, he still managed to keep us on hot bricks.

'He's back in the hospital again,' Joey's 'queer one' was telling my mam. 'Don't worry though, he's not in any pain. He was sewin' leather gloves at work and the machine ran over his paralysed hand.'

He couldn't feel a thing. 'Look,' he said to the ambulance attendant, 'I'm in stitches!'

The foreman fainted.

Joey seemed to be coping well – then, for no reason at all, he suddenly became preoccupied with death. He even made jokes of it often. One night he removed his wedding ring and said to the 'queer one', 'Eileen, keep this in a safe place. Don't want the thievin' bloody undertakers gettin' their hands on that. By the way, I must check if they charge for coffins by the inch. If so, mine would cost a soddin' fortune with me bein' so tall. Best get some orange crates from Reid's the greengrocer and I'll build me own.'

He couldn't see he was upsetting everyone when he was morbid like that, but it turned out he had second sight. I came home one day and knew right off that I'd walked into trouble. I could feel it in my bones. Everyone was preoccupied. Even my dad was crying. Patty was visiting and she was crying. And my mam was silent and stiff as usual.

'Go to Mrs Tiplady's till I come for yer,' Patty urged.

'No, I won't. Tell me what's wrong?'

'Do as yer bloody well told for a change. Go on.'

Why was Patty talking to me like that? What had I done? I didn't understand why I was bundled off to the dumpling of a woman from across the road. Mrs Tiplady kept muttering and patting me while feeding me treacle toffee. The neighbours were coming to her front door to have a sneak look at me, whispering behind their hands. With her fat arms folded under her great wobbly breasts she nodded knowingly. I was restrained until seven thirty and then legged it to the pub to talk to my dad. He'd tell me what was going on. He wasn't there – but he must be, it had gone seven thirty!

I ran back to Littledale Road to check things out.

There were a lot of cars outside Joey's house. Of course, our Joey would know. Why didn't I think of that before?

I ran into the house which was full of grim-faced grown-ups. When I saw their faces I was frightened and started to cry, not even knowing why. I soon found out. Joey had had another serious stroke and the ambulance had taken him to hospital.

'Someone take the baby home and see she gets into bed, with a water bottle and a couple of aspirin,' my mam said as she stared into emptiness.

I awoke the next morning having overslept. I hadn't taken my mam her usual morning cup of tea. There would be hell to pay. I rushed to get dressed. As I came down the stairs I could hear all the activity. The family was gathered in the kitchen.

'How's our Joey?' I asked, pressing my cheek to Mam's face.

'He's dead.'

No frills, no dressing-up words, just 'He's dead.' No tone to the voice, no expression on her face, Mam said it again. 'He's dead. Gone.'

Lost for words, I looked at Teddy. 'What does she mean?'

I watched his colour deepen. 'Bugger off and leave me alone.'

Once more I was bundled off to Mrs Tiplady's. After two days I was ushered into our Joey's house to say my goodbyes. The front parlour was crowded with neighbours and family solemnly viewing the body and paying their respects. Slowly and fearfully I approached the coffin to stare at the corpse, cold and waxen.

'Come kiss your brother goodbye,' someone offered.

'What?'

'Kiss your brother goodbye. It's the proper thing to do.'

'No. Dear me no!'

'What's wrong with you, don't you want to say goodbye?'

'Yes, but, dear Jesus, please don't make me kiss him.'

'Don't be selfish, it's nice to remember him this way. Peaceful-like, with no pain.'

That was not my big brother I was looking at. First the stroke, then finally death took him away and left the waxen image. Unable to shrink from the hand that firmly held my head over the coffin, I reluctantly kissed the familiar dead face as my tears dripped onto Joey's neck. Still I couldn't stop staring. My mind found it impossible to accept that after today Joey would be gone for ever. Any hopes of being adopted by him and living safely in his house – shattered.

'You do put the lid on the coffin each night, don't

you?' I asked, looking about the room to all these grown-ups.

'Of course not.'

'You just 'ave to,' I begged, 'otherwise, who will scare away the rats and cockroaches at night if they come near my Joey?'

The firm 'No' made me lose control to hysteria. The sedative that the doctor left for my mam was given to me – what happened after that was dim and vague.

The next day, the day of the funeral, I was rigged out in old ladies' black clothes. Standing at the kitchen door I heard the grown-ups debating whether or not 'the baby' should attend the burial, given her morbid state of mind.

I was sent back to Mrs Tiplady's for treacle toffee.

9

The government letters the twins had been dreading arrived. Georgie and Teddy were called up to do National Service at long last. National Service was all a bit of a lottery, and because of their shared date of birth the twins were both required to do a two-year stint. I was overjoyed. Teddy grudgingly chose the Army. Georgie opted for the Air Force with a vow to be out after six weeks.

Both had a medical. Georgie's medical was not good (for acceptance to the Air Force anyway). Georgie was pleased with himself to be found ailing. Nobody in the family understood why, until he informed us that he had swallowed a cube of chocolate as he was having the chest X-ray and that did the trick, showing a shadow in the area of the lungs. Acting mental in the interviews helped finalize the decision not to take him, but I for one didn't think he needed to put on much of an act. It was all a bitter pill for Teddy, who had to report to the Catterick Army Barracks for training, while Georgie stayed home.

I was panicked at the prospect of Georgie being the one left at home. But he'd got more on his mind these days than finding new ways to torment me. Georgie was working for a local circus and I prayed that the tales he told of cruelty to the animals were untrue. Stories of pigeons being dyed to look like exotic birds. Elephants moved from one place to the next with the aid of a long stick with a nail on the end to prod them along. Bored regal animals in cages with barely enough room to turn around, and small creatures bred and fed live to the larger ones.

I shuddered at the thought of the punishment and cruelty meted out to these poor miserable animals. If my sadistic bully of a brother thought circus life was cruel, God knows what he must have witnessed.

Our Jacky went dancing most weeks with his new fancy piece, June, who lived across the Mersey in Liverpool. He had a proper made-to-measure suit and you could see your face in his shoes that he spent ages spitting on and rubbing circles of polish round and round. He learnt that in the Army.

'If yer a good girl I'll take you to see her next week in the car I've just bought. I've got it outside,' he announced proudly.

Wow! Our very own car.

'How'd you like a spin, Mam? You can bring the baby with you.'

I was dying for a ride in the car, somewhere – anywhere – so the nosy neighbours would look on and see our Jacky had a proper running car, not like the wrecks in the street forever jacked up on bricks.

So there I sat in the back preening myself, nodding and bowing, imitating royalty. Mam sat in the front with her knitting bag of coloured squares and a fag as always dangling from her mouth.

Suddenly Jacky went berserk, shouting at my mam. He was certainly mad about something. 'How could you do that? Of all the stupid . . .'

He stopped the car, leapt out and knocked on the nearest front door.

'Quick Missus fetch me some water. Mam's dropped

her fag end between the window and the door and it's smoulderin' and I can't get to it.'

No harm done, the water did its job.

He continued bellowing at poor Mam, 'Can't you last five minutes without a bloody fag in yer gob?'

The day ruined, we drove home in silence.

The first time I met up with her I couldn't stop staring. Jacky's foreign-looking girlfriend had a lovely dark complexion and almost black eyes. Jacky was so smitten with this June, he said he intended to marry her.

'She's black!' I said, pulling Jacky to one side by the elbow.

'No she bloody isn't!'

'So what country does she come from then?'

'From here. She comes from Liverpool yer daft bitch!'

Mam and Dad were going to have a field day when they saw this dark one with her la-di-da ways.

Georgie acting as father confessor advised Jacky, 'Look kiddo, if you brought the Virgin Mary home Mam and Dad would find fault with her. I don't know what yer worried about, just go for it. Yer've got yer own life to lead.' But somehow his voice lacked conviction.

Any doubts I had about Jacky's fancy piece vanished when she said I could be bridesmaid and have a proper posh frock from a shop in Liverpool. Not bought from the tallyman or the Co-op but from a proper bridal shop.

There were dozens of large shops to choose from in Liverpool. It was a new, exciting experience for me to visit department stores like Tolls, George Henry Lee, and Lewis's. I remembered that one because it had a big statue of a rude man over the front door with his willy hanging out. The statue (or at least its appendage) was constantly the target of abuse, especially by students on capping day who would put a nappy on him.

The city vibrated with noise as hustling street vendors with open suitcases peddled their wares amongst the barrow boys, all yelling to be heard. 'Come along queen,' they called at the shuffling women. 'Genuine pure silk scarves just arrived from Paris France, only two for 'alf a dollar. Give yer ol' man a treat in bed – hide yer curlers!'

Fish and chips and mushy peas from Woolworths were the order of the day before I was measured and fitted for a gold coloured ballet-length dress, with matching head-dress. I looked forward to spending many happy times being spoilt by June's family in Liverpool before the dress was ready for the big day. And I mean 'Big Day' and ever so posh.

The Faulkner clan seemed overwhelmed by the events of the day. The church; the pomp and ceremony; the wedding breakfast, and everything put on as if it were for royalty.

The speeches were not only clean, but left me confused about who the groom was. Didn't sound a bit like the Jacky I knew.

When the band struck up, Jacky and June led the dancing. Like Fred Astaire and Ginger Rogers, they couldn't be faulted with their rendition of the quickstep and foxtrot. Our lot stood lining the walls waiting for the traditional knees-up whilst her lot swanned about on the dance floor. Our Jacky must have been leading a double life – he was showing us a side of him we hadn't seen before.

On the bus home my mam made the comment that them women wore no knickers. Well, what she really said was, 'fur coats and no drawers'.

The *Wallasey News* ran a photo of the happy couple and described the wedding in detail, right down to the going-away outfit of the bride having ivory accessories. I asked Teddy what 'accessories' meant and he said, 'Her soddin' teeth, probably.'

Suffice to say Jacky's queer one was never accepted into the bosom of our family. Lucky cow!

*　　*　　*

I went through school in virtual anonymity. Not by choice – I always dreamed of playing the drums in the orchestra or being a milk monitor. If I could even have had the privilege of cleaning the chalk off the board, maybe passed out the books or refilled inkwells or at least been invited home to tea by someone – anyone would have done, I wasn't fussy.

By the time I reached fifteen I hated school – apart from domestic science and the art classes. I left without exchanging addresses with any of the other pupils or staff. No point anyway. Obviously it would be unwise to invite anyone home, they wouldn't get past the front door or the twins.

The cookery teacher liked me, although she used to throw her hands up in despair. 'Child, your cooking is excellent, but why must you leave the kitchen like a war zone?'

Mrs Coombes, my art teacher, said she wanted to see my parents at school, to discuss my artistic abilities and my job opportunities. She didn't understand. Mam hardly ever left the house except for shopping and the Brighton, and my dad was at work all day.

'Just ask her, that's all. Tell her it's important.'

'I'll try, Mrs Coombes, but you just don't know me mam.'

I was staggered when my mam, without a fight, agreed to visit Mrs Coombes. The contrast between two females, roughly the same age, was overwhelming. The flamboyant Mrs Coombes had bleached hair piled on top of her head, calf-length red fringed skirt with a brightly coloured blouse and huge brass dangly earrings. Mam sat there looking lost. She had on her brown swagger coat and her best cloche hat that she had knitted for the occasion, finishing it only yesterday. I loved both women to death, but my mam was prettier by far.

'As you may be aware, your daughter has won a scholarship which will guarantee her an apprenticeship in somewhere like Weatherall Studios, or even as a trainee window dresser. It's a golden opportunity.' Mrs Coombes waved her red-taloned fingers to dramatize the point.

Mam was polite while calmly listening. 'I'll do me best. I'll talk it over with the baby's father.' Oh no! There it was again: humiliation. She called me 'the baby'. I was in secondary school and she still called me 'the baby'. I was cut to the quick.

According to my dad, 'The world's gone bloody mad. Hairy-arsed, drug-takin' gits, that's what they are. They all need a spell doin' National Service.'

Skiffle, sputniks, nuclear weapons and Bohemian ideas; Little Richard; Elvis; the Beautiful People in the Fifties when my dad was regularly bombarded by 'all these goings-on' headlined in the *Daily Express* and on the radio. Here was the skiffle craze, and the first stirrings of 'Youth Culture'. Seemed like my dad was practising to be an understudy for Moses – with his own commandments. 'Thou shalt not grow up. Thou shalt not have a social life. Thou shalt not flaunt any creative talent.'

The answer to Mrs Coombes's 'golden opportunity' for me to be a design trainee was a definite 'No'.

'No loose, drug-takin' prostitute without no morals will be fillin' her bloody 'ead, or some arty-farty bastard layin' in wait to ravish young girls. I know. No decent father would let his daughter get caught up with that crowd. Anyway, I've already got a good job for her when she leaves school. I've 'ad a word in the right ear. Me mate can get 'er into the Easter egg factory at Cadbury's and she should be grateful for it.'

His last sentence plunged me into despair. Working on the conveyor belt at Cadbury's was almost preordained for women on Merseyside. I refused but it was ages before I touched a drawing pad or showed any further interest in art, until one day when Dad relented a little. I was allowed to go to the School of Art on Saturdays part-time, but not until I had finished the housework and only as an out student.

When I left school to enter the 'Big Wide World of Commerce' I was bereft to leave my art teacher. Mrs Coombes taught me so much about art, but more importantly, she treated me as an equal whose opinion on the subject of art she respected.

About six weeks after I left school, I got an official brown envelope addressed to me from the Education Board. I was afraid they'd discovered a couple of pots of paint were missing. I decided I'd better wait to open it until *they* were at the Brighton. That way I'd have time to think up a good excuse before they read the letter. With trepidation I waited for them all to leave, then I tore open the envelope. I read:

'*Dear Miss Faulkner.*
We are pleased to inform you that you have won the school prize for Geography. The school Speech Day will be held on 20th June when the recipients of awards will be presented with their prizes by His Worship the Mayor, the Right Honourable Harold Tomkins.'

The headmistress signed the letter.

I read the words over and over and over again. It didn't make sense – the geography teacher couldn't stand me. She scared the hell out of me, the rotten faggot, when she singled me out in class for talking too much, then, having placed her dress rings on her bony fingers, used them as a knuckleduster, with my arm as the target. Come to think of it, I didn't even like geography. But the realization that I wasn't the stupid bitch they said I was, made me smile.

As I read the letter again I noticed the footnote.

'*School uniform must be worn by all recipients for prize-giving.*'

97

No child was allowed to start secondary school without a uniform, but the rules were never adhered to after the uniform wore out, except by the privileged few. If I wanted to go to prize-giving, I'd have to buy a new school cardigan. And where was I going to get the money?

I'd originally started Liscard Secondary Modern School with a hand-knitted navy blue skirt and cardigan. My blouses were made from bleached flour bags Mrs Tiplady had put by for curtains during the war.

At that time of the letter I was working at my first job in the Liscard Road Post Office and earning one pound eighteen shillings and sixpence a week. After handing over my wage packet to my mam I was allowed to keep twelve shillings and sixpence. This totally inadequate sum had to pay for clothes, bus fares, make-up and all manner of odds and sods that girls were expected to have.

The biggest loss from my wages was half a crown taken each week by the postmistress as a sinking fund to pay towards any shortages in cash when the books were balanced at the end of each week. Sometimes we got the money returned at the end of the month, but for the most part we would be lucky to see anything. What I wanted to know was why nobody ever questioned what happened to any surplus cash. That certainly didn't come our way.

I shoved in my two penn'orth, constantly complaining at the unfairness. Even though I was the newest and youngest member of staff the other counter clerks happily approved the scheme I came up with.

'OK, this is it,' I explained conspiratorially, 'when the well-dressed or snotty-nosed customers leave their change on the counter, don't draw their attention to it or call after them. Instead we scoop it up with our hot little hands and keep it to one side. At the end of the month we divvy it up.'

For years the ladies had resented the half-crown donations being forcibly taken, so they were quick to agree. It was hard to stop my face from cracking into a grin with anticipation as elegant customers fumbled with bags before retreating from the shop, leaving an assortment of loose change on the counter. Other counter clerks would have eyes fixed on the plunder, not daring to look at each other, but I had no trouble reaching under the wire barrier and scooping it up with relish. (Ta very much!) Our 'bunce' was counted several times a week. Occasionally we got up to five bob each but most of the time it didn't cover the half-crown a week our employer legally thieved.

Funny thing, one of my favourite duties in the post office was last thing at night, melting red sealing wax, and when a big enough dollop landed on Her Majesty's Royal Mailbag, I indented the Government Crown Seal on it for security. This job was not to be taken lightly. I remember when I told my family I was given the trustworthy duty of sealing the registered mailbags, Georgie's reply was swift. 'With your talent for schemes it won't be long before yer in the slammer sewin' them.'

I figured that possibly after nearly a month the bunce tin might give me enough to buy a school cardigan. I could make do with the knitted skirt and even though my blouse was thin enough to spit through, Mrs Tiplady would show me how to turn the collar like I'd seen her do it on Mr Tiplady's shirts. It looked easy enough.

Phew . . . it looked like the problem was solved. I waited for them to come home from the Brighton to wave the official letter in front of their noses. As usual they'd rowed all the way home – you could hear the racket before the backyard door slammed. They wouldn't be receptive to my news so I went to bed, leaving the letter on the kitchen table for them to read if they cared to.

Once the Closed sign was put on the post office door the following night, we examined the contents of the bunce tin.

'We could squander it on cream buns for afternoon tea if you like.' Mazie laughed at the couple of miserable coins huddled in the corners. 'It's been a bad month all round. Sorry kid, you can have my share if it helps.'

I'd deliberately left the headmistress's letter on the kitchen table so my mam and dad could read it but they'd never said a word. So you could have knocked me down with a feather when on the next pay day my mam said, 'You'd better keep all yer wages this week and buy some wool. Nearly five weeks yer've got, that's plenty of time to make a nice school cardigan if you use double knittin' wool which knits up fast. Yer good at knittin'. Remember all the socks you and Patty knitted for the soldiers durin' the war and that was harder, them bein' made on three needles.'

I said that knitting socks was different, a few dropped stitches didn't show with the second-hand wool we got by unravelling old jumpers we were given by the WVS. Pity the poor sods who got the multicoloured socks but we still had a huge selection of buttons left over, enough to supply the rest of the street when they came scrounging. Many was the time the big old Quality Street sweet tin full of buttons was handed to a neighbour for them to hunt through, and sometimes they even managed to get a full set, a rare find just after the war.

Mam said that she wouldn't be a lot of use knitting my cardigan, as knitting navy blue wool would make her 'scabby-eyed' at her age. Besides, she had a lot of work to do finishing her knitted patchwork blanket.

'A blanket?' my dad chipped in. 'I thought you were knittin' a cover for the town hall clock.'

The next pay day I went down to the local drapers.

'You'll be needin' about sixteen ounces,' the lady who sold the wool told me. 'I'll put two ounces by in case you run short, although I can't see you needin' them as yer only a little runt.'

The knitting frenzy began. I knitted before work, knitted at lunchtime, knitted after work and well into the nights. My hands sweated with the wool and the needles became sticky and unworkable. My mam had to keep loosening the wool and picking up dropped stitches for me – I hadn't mastered that yet. A whole week it took me to do the back. Not bad progress I suppose, but I'd have to be quicker as I had two fronts, two sleeves and the front band to make. Should finish it by the skin of my teeth, with luck. Every time I measured the sides with the back, I would give it a little tug to make it longer.

The night before Speech Day I just finished knitting. It was nearly ten o'clock. My eyes were like piss holes in snow, working with navy blue wool at night, but I intended getting up early to finish sewing it up. But, having sewn the sleeve seams, I was struggling to fit the rest together. No matter how hard I tried it wouldn't work; even the pattern didn't give me a clue. Best to ask Mrs Tiplady, she would know what was wrong with the sodding thing. With a smile spreading over her fat wrinkled face, she spread the pieces on the table like a jigsaw puzzle.

'Yer daft bugger, yer've only made two left sides,' she laughed. 'What are yer? A proper gobshite, that's what yer are.'

I didn't think I could cry any more, didn't think I had any tears left, until they came through the door from the Brighton. Blimey! I had forgotten the time – half past ten! I should have known better and been out of the kitchen and up the stairs out of harm's way. This was all I needed.

When he saw my face Dad asked absent-mindedly, 'What's up? What's bloody well 'appened now?' while preoccupied looking through the kitchen cupboards to find what delicious extremity of a dead animal he could demolish for supper.

Angry tears stung my eyes. Furiously I wiped them away and started on my tale of woe, which prompted him to produce two crisp one-pound notes from his wallet.

'Oh, me poor little Topsy. Will that much buy you a cardigan?'

I was flabbergasted. It came so easily. No schemes . . . No effort . . . Two quid . . . just like that.

That was the start of a whole new turnabout for me. Any time I needed a cash injection, instead of making myself scarce at half past ten, I waited up for them coming home and sussed out his mood before making a request.

It turned out Mam had been using the same tactic for years.

'If he's 'ad too much to drink or too little, you will get nowt but a thick ear for your trouble, but if you catch him right, he can be very generous.'

I learnt to be an expert. It became second nature gauging his moods so accurately. Soon I became the family spokesman and got several injections of cash for family members, including my mam whose efforts paled in comparison to my Oscar-winning performances. The downside was having to witness his preoccupation with his beloved suppers, watch him devour unspeakable delicacies such as ox heart, lamb's testicles or sweetbreads that he occasionally offered to share with me, knowing full well the offer turned me green. I would sit and chat like a dutiful daughter while the juices ran out of the corners of his overflowing mouth and down his chin. Then he would finish off by licking his fingers one by one before serenading me with little ditties on his sodding banjo. Nothing my dad ate could shock me. It wasn't that long ago he had pretended to eat Wally, my goldfish (sole survivor from the rag-and-bone man), by slicing carrots longways and wafer thin, and flapping them between his finger and thumb before dropping them down his throat, ignoring my screams and pleadings.

The auspicious Speech Day arrived. My mam and dad naturally declined the invitation from the headmistress, telling me, 'You don't mind do yer lovey? It's really not our bag.'

The thought of going onto the stage and shaking hands with the Mayor made my knees shake and my legs feel like jelly. Couldn't seem to do anything right, me, certain to go arse over tit in front of the whole school.

Suddenly they were clapping as my name was called and I was handed the prize. I forgot my instructions from Mrs Calvey to be, 'articulate, eloquent and coherent' when I said the words of gratitude I'd practised. I was too engrossed in looking at the book prize, and lumbered off the stage. How bloody thick I was, never considering I would get a geography book as a geography prize, thinking they would know I would like a book on art. Instead it was a lousy book on New Zealand, some far-off country in the Colonies.

Mrs Calvey the geography teacher came to congratulate me.

'I never knew I was good at geography, Mrs Calvey. Why didn't someone tell me before now?'

'Oh, my dear child, you weren't. No-one, but no-one can draw detailed maps like you can. Your illustrations are a work of art – well done.'

Sulkily I leafed through pages of glorious coloured photographs entitled 'Spectacular Places of Interest'. Said who? The halfwit photographer I bet.

'Bloody New Zealand, never heard of it!'

Teddy had been posted to the Suez Canal. We had had more communication in the past couple of months than in the previous silent years, when he'd mostly communicated with me by sign language. Mind you, he was writing from the Far East and he wasn't breaking his vow of silence by actually talking to me. It seemed easier for him to express himself in letters and this helped me feel like a sister to him. Almost certainly he faced the possibility that he could get killed in the Suez Canal crisis, as he was in the danger zone. My mam, who never openly showed love to anyone, did admit to sometimes 'God-bothering' for Teddy's safe return.

When I wrote to Teddy he would write back and sometimes he sent photos or postcards. We seemed like old pals, part of a normal family.

Then he wrote to say that he was due home on leave.

Some weeks after his last letter arrived I walked through the door, and my jaw dropped. Teddy had come home on leave. He stood there smiling, so smart in his uniform. Would he actually speak, I wondered.

The short answer was, no.

But I did get a stiff silent hug before he indicated to me to hold out my hand and shut my eyes, which I did. Something wrapped in tissue paper was dropped into the palm of my hand. Remembering my broken trust of years gone by I panicked, instinctively flinging across the room what could likely have been something crawling, or worse, something dead. Teddy's pained expression told me I had misjudged him this time. The new watch he had brought from Egypt was beyond repair. Who was the more upset? Heaven knows – but how could he expect me to trust him?

Mam had a bad attack of the quinsies. For weeks she lay upstairs, burning up, delirious and unable to swallow. The doctor said she would be far better off in hospital but she refused point-blank, insisting she wanted to die in her own bed. Failing to respond to medication, she lay in a dark room rasping, every breath an effort. Medicine had to be forced down her throat as she cried in anguish. She grew weaker by the hour. Her eyes sank into the back of her head. I looked on helplessly while family members took it in turns attempting to coax her back to health. When the doctor shone his torch down her throat I elbowed him out of the way to get a better look for myself at the dark green and white patches that covered her tonsils.

'Well young lady, have you seen enough?' he asked sarcastically, adding that it was the worst case of quinsies he had ever seen.

Mam was sick for over a month. I often sat next to her just holding her hand while she slept. Gradually she became more mellow, even laughed with me sometimes when I did my impressions of Al Jolson singing 'Mammy'. I treasured these times. My mam had been like a friend. Now I knew how Marion felt – her mother had always been like a friend to her.

As Mam became stronger and able to move around, she became (much to our surprise and delight) a regular Fanny Cradock with her cooking and baking experiments. She was a whizz with pickled herrings and tripe and onions. Her spotted dick and plum puddings and bread puddings were wonderful. My favourite was blind stew. She told me that it was a pauper's meal because it had no meat but I didn't care – I loved the bloody big dollops of suet dumplings that floated on the top of the gravy.

'Men need nourishment that sticks to their ribs,' she would say. 'You get chilled to the bones labourin' in this weather, I know.'

Her cooking had always been good, now it was to be envied, but oh I wished she would remember that I was only a girl and I didn't work at a labouring job. My belly couldn't hold them man-sized servings and especially them big 'Desperate Dan cow pies' the men liked so much. Any one of my meals would have been the daily ration for a family of six in the Belgian Congo.

Secretly I was pleased to be grouped as part of the family with no special considerations for being a girl, so if dockers' dinners were part of being included, well so be it.

*   *   *

105

Eric, the bloke the lads called Simmo, began to hang around our house regularly. He called on Fridays when he and Teddy went to the pictures. I was ironing my knickers when he was brought into the kitchen. My face was red with embarrassment as I grabbed them off the ironing board and made a start on the hankies. Simmo looked so smart, standing over six feet tall in his Dick-Barton-style military mac. I'd just clicked who he looked like with his dark wavy hair and gentle features – Michael Denison, that was it. Eric was a dead ringer for Michael Denison who played Boyd QC on the telly. Eric was relaxed and chatty this night, holding my attention as he flashed an occasional beaming smile when his warm hazel eyes connected with mine.

'Did I tell you I'm workin' as a First Class waiter for the Cunard Line, doin' the Atlantic run to America, and sometimes to the Mediterranean for a couple of months on a cruise?'

Gosh, he was really la-di-da now. Smoking coloured cigarettes with gold bands round, and he sometimes discarded them only half smoked. This had not gone unnoticed.

'Can you put the dog-ends in the ashtray, son, instead of throwin' them in the fire?' my mam asked ever so politely.

'Oh, I won't smoke in the 'ouse any more, Mrs Faulkner,' Simmo answered, thinking she objected.

'No, no,' she quickly corrected, 'it's just I collect the dog-ends and roll me own fags with some Rizla paper and your dog-ends are a real treat, them bein' so long.'

Please God let the ground open up and swallow me. From then on, every time Simmo came home from sea, he brought my mam a carton of fags.

'Next time you go to the pictures with Simmo will you take me with you? Please Teddy,' I begged.

'Why would I want to do that?' Awkward sod, he knew full well that I had a crush on Simmo. 'Only if you can get

106

yer blonde girlfriend from up the road to come and make up a foursome.'

We sat in the fleapit in the back row. I never felt his tender touch when Eric finally plucked up enough courage to reach out and take my hand. He asked shyly, 'Do you mind me holdin' yer hand like this?' But I couldn't hear him properly over the movie.

'What?'

He removed his hand. It was then that I realized, with much regret, what the question had been.

It became a regular thing, this foursome, on Eric's shore leave. It worked out great as Teddy was now occasionally talking to me – he had to. He didn't want to look a gobshite, besides, there didn't seem any reason not to, not any more. Eric eventually asked me out alone. When Teddy found out there was hell to pay but I had no problems coping with the return of his broody silence in the months that followed. I was getting emotionally stronger. Eric renewed my confidence in men. He was all right – more than all right.

10

Eric was away at sea on the MV *Britannic*. We'd been sort of going steady for some months, when one day in February a small parcel arrived marked 'Airmail America' and addressed to me. I ripped off the string while my bright-eyed mam looked on. It was from Eric. My first ever Valentine's Day gift. The box was marked 'Nylons – 1 Doz. Pair'. Mam and me excitedly ripped through the packaging between us. We only ever had one pair of stockings at a time. I paid ninepence to have them mended when they got laddered, and they were thick rayon, so you could see where the run had been – like a snail's trail up your leg.

'We can share them Mam.' I knew she would love that – she never had anything nice for herself. Most of her money went on the housekeeping.

I didn't know whether to laugh or cry when I opened the box. We were both flabbergasted – the finest sheer silky nylons – TWELVE PAIRS. But, blimey, they had black seams with a brick pattern in black framing the heels. Just to make matters worse, the legs of the stockings were interlaced with black diamante butterflies.

'If we wear these we'll look like a couple of whores on a Saturday night.'

We laughed together until the tears ran.

Eric was now working on the prestigious *Queen*

Elizabeth as the *Britannic* was in dry dock for repair. He was thrilled to be able to keep his position as a waiter for First Class passengers. In his tuxedo Eric merged with the ostentatious ambience, the silver service and crystal glasses.

Eric wrote often, saying that his cabin mates received delicately perfumed love letters, which they kept under their pillows so that the smell helped them to recapture the sexy memories of their girlfriends. I never had any perfume, but not to be outdone, the next time I wrote I filled the envelope with talcum powder before I sealed it.

I got a short, polite reply to my last letter asking me to picture him in his tuxedo and cummerbund, covered in white powder and looking and smelling like a baby's bum in front of his mates and with hungry irate passengers waiting to be served.

After that I went to Woolies and invested one and ninepence in a bottle of Ashes of Roses scent, but Eric was worth every penny. Next time, I wrote a loving letter and before sealing it poured several drops of Ashes of Roses into the envelope.

Eric showed me the letter when he came home on leave. 'Not that I don't appreciate yer efforts love, but the letter was all smudged and I couldn't read it. The perfume must 'ave been so strong it took the colour out of the ink.'

Actually, if you've ever smelled Ashes of Roses it was a wonder it didn't burn a hole through the paper.

Eric's letters came regularly. Bless him. Some days I got four or five all at once if he'd been at sea and couldn't post them until the ship reached a port. Occasionally he'd written a poem. Mostly they were about what he loved about me. I was choked that he could see me like . . . like he did. No-one else could and I'm buggered if even I could. I was afraid. Something wonderful, something precious had plunged light-heartedly into my drab existence and I couldn't bear to think I could ever lose him, or this new love.

Eric's shore leave was only one week out of every four or five, which suited me fine. I didn't have enough nice clothes to see him more often without him knowing what a shabby individual I really was.

Working at the post office wasn't fun any more, in fact downright boring . . . all those stamps and postal orders to count night after night. Then I saw in the *Liverpool Echo* an advertisement for an office trainee at Frankenstein's Air Sea Rescue, the manufacturers of life-saving equipment. Anything had to be better than glorified shop work, I thought. I phoned to arrange an interview. Then I told my bosses I needed time off for my uncle's funeral.

With her face like a smacked bum she snapped, 'You must hold the world record for uncles with an untimely demise.'

Smarmy cow.

The sign on the door said Boardroom. Sitting at one end of a polished table (the sort I had only ever seen in pictures of the Last Supper) an old gentleman with white wavy hair interviewed me. He kept telling me not to yell, as well as reminding me, 'Hold your tongue young lady, it is I doing the interviewing.' I thought he hated me until he grinned. 'The pay is forty-seven shillings and sixpence a week. When would you like to start?'

My mouth hung open like a stunned mullet.

Then he added, 'Oh by the way, please refrain from calling me Mr Frankenstein. My name is Mr Evans to you. I'm the General Manager here. Mr Frankenstein, our founder, died many years ago.'

My first day, like the following days in my new job, was a total and utter disaster. Not that it was my fault – well really. I was installed in front of a fearsome contraption like the engine room of a submarine with wires crisscrossing every which way.

'It's only a switchboard, it won't bite,' said Peggy the other junior, trying to coax me into using it.

I was surprised to learn that Peggy lived in Birkenhead and she wasn't even common. She had really flash clothes, including a different cardigan each day, and she even had a 'pure gold' watch. Funny that, because Peggy said she had never had a dad, only uncles. Mind you, her mam was lucky, had lots of visitors and sailors who called at night and brought presents.

So on that first morning I watched Peggy push rods in and out of sockets every time she heard a nasty buzzing noise. Little metal shutters above the sockets clicked open and shut like Big Brother's eyelids.

'I'm not touchin' that friggin' thing.' I wailed. (I remembered my sister's recent ordeal when she had an electric perm at the hairdressers and they'd used a contraption with dangly wires.) 'I could get burnt, even worse, electrocuted.'

My concern fell on deaf ears.

'Now for the tannoy system. You will have to learn this so that you can inform personnel in the building of incoming calls or visitors at reception.' She picked up what looked like a metal ice cream cone, pressed the On button and spoke, plum in the gob like. 'Calling Mr Daley. Calling Mr Daley. Will you please call at reception? Thank you.' I could hear her voice echoing round the factory.

'It's all too hard. I'm too nervous to do that,' I told her.

'Don't be daft, you will soon get used to it,' she laughed, sitting me in front of the giant switchboard once more and continuing to pull and push plugs in and out when the buzzing devil with the winking eyes demanded attention.

It only took a matter of days for me to make my mark at Frankenstein's. Having cut off overseas calls, put angry callers through to the various wrong offices and caused chaos in both factory and office alike, everyone knew

111

who I was. At the end of the first week I had to endure the pointing and sniggering as I handed the factory workers their little brown wage envelopes on Friday night.

After that first week I was demoted to a job in the Gestetner duplicating room – my next great cock-up. Reams and reams of black smudged paper and sticky black printer's ink spewed from this contraption and ended up decorating the bottom half of two walls. At the end of most days I looked like a tar baby, but worst of all was my ability to ruin the original master type, which had sometimes taken hours to produce.

I was finally condemned to the post room where they said I could do no real damage. My penance was sorting incoming mail as well as shoving things into envelopes and tearing long strips of stamps and sticking them to a pile of letters with a grudging thump of my wrist. Licking and sticking relentless stamps was to me like torture. I might just as well have been back at the flaming post office.

One fateful day I was handed a message to relay through the tannoy system. The message said 'Please call Mr Bishopsprick to the main office.' Not realizing I had my finger on the On button, I announced for all and sundry to hear. 'You must be soddin' jokin'. Bishopsprick? He'll need to change his bleedin' name if he expects me to call that out loud!'

Well, I hadn't been there long enough to get holiday pay but they kindly gave me a week in lieu of notice.

As if I cared. I hadn't felt any benefit of my increased wages at Frankenstein's, as I was docked pay nearly every day for being late to work. I had to travel over the Penny Bridge or Duke Street Bridge, which were often raised during rush hours to let the Mersey tugs and small boats through. Endless days of leaving home in the morning before light and arriving back in the evening in the dark.

I was only out of work for one week when I got a

smashing job in a garage in Bidston. Sole charge position: Receptionist/Accounts Clerk. This meant catching three buses with an hour and a half travelling each way. No matter, I was in my element. Bidston was nice and clean. None of the shop windows were boarded up to stop vandals kicking them in. No packs of dogs ran riot fouling up beneath the mighty trees, leafy and magnificent, that lined the pavements. I vowed that one day when I was older I would marry some rich bloke and live in Bidston.

Like a duck to water, I took to working at the garage and loved everything that the job entailed, learning quickly to recognize all the makes of cars, their engine capacity and horsepower. I loved all the new cars but my favourite was the Wolseley 1500. Dead classy. It had leather seats and interior, with a walnut dashboard. Sometimes I liked to sit in the cars just to get a whiff of the newness.

I worked long and hard at the garage but to the frustration of the owner, Mr Davies Snr, I spent more time in the workshop amongst the muck and grease, knowing that I was as handy as any of the lads were. Watching how to do a grease and spray, an oil change, tune-ups, how to grind valves and decoke cars. Surrounded by engine parts, oil and grease, I felt blessed out of my socks.

'You're supposed to be in the office, young lady, but somehow you manage to slither into the workshop every time my back is turned. This practice must cease,' Mr Davies Snr raged as I slyly wiped my greasy hands on a mutton cloth for the umpteenth time that day.

Try as I might I couldn't stay away from the workshop, the cars, or the muck. I agonized over what excuses I could give if he caught me, as I didn't want the sack, but I hated being abandoned in the front office.

Being part of the BMC group, the garage had to take all new models of car into stock to tie up with the nationwide publicity campaigns. The revolutionary Mini

113

Minor had just come on the market and the company was forced to take three of them into stock (much to the disgust of the owners, sales staff and mechanics, who didn't think the radical new car was much cop). Everyone said it was a dud. 'No-one will buy that piece of junk.' 'Just like a Dinky car.' 'Too gimmicky.' 'They'll never catch on.' 'Doesn't even look safe.' On and on the criticisms went.

They couldn't have been more wrong. The public took to these new cars like donkeys to strawberries. The success of the Mini was such that stocks had to be rationed by the manufacturers, and only the most valued customers on the waiting list took priority for delivery.

Business boomed because of interest in the now top-selling Mini, doing nearly sixty miles to the gallon and priced to enable the so-called working class to own a new vehicle for the first time ever. With the higher turnover and profits, the garage was given a facelift and new faster benzene pumps were installed to put 'tigers in tanks' more efficiently. Extra funds were made available for advertising. My boss even had his own calendars printed: chose the pictures and had his name printed below. I didn't know the bloody calendars would be my final downfall at the garage.

Mr Davies Snr told me to send the calendars to all the valued clients, and enclose a complimentary card with an invitation to a viewing of the 'all new' Mini Minor.

I did as I was told, no problem – apart from adding my family and friends to the valued client list. Nobody I knew could afford to buy a new car, but some would be chuffed to get a calendar and I could write my own personal message on the complimentary card, things like,

The calendar comes for nowt, but if you want the car it will cost you an arm and a leg. Let's hope you win the pools
Love Cherry. XXXXXX

I would never have been caught but for the nosy old tart in the post office. I had sent the last batch out to the customers with insufficient postage. The ones addressed to Auntie Nellie, Uncle Harry, Mrs Tiplady, and my friends. The tart at the post office handed them back over the counter to my boss. Mr Davies Snr said that was thieving. But it wasn't proper thieving – not in my book anyhow – not like the priest when he took away the money tin that I was saving money in to buy a black baby.

I was heartbroken to leave the garage. Aside from the workshop I would miss young Mr Davies Jnr, who had befriended me and taken on the task of my sex education. I learnt that the term 'queer' didn't mean funny man or clown (or in-law). I sat with my mouth open in disbelief as he described in intricate detail a homosexual's love preference. He told me about lesbians and massage parlours and prostitutes. He used words like 'penis' and 'testicles'. (When I heard him use words like those for the first time, I was so embarrassed I just giggled and giggled.) As I tried to hide the blushing behind my fingers when I felt the heat creep up to the roots of my hair he took great delight in embellishing his knowledge, telling me about erogenous zones, ejaculation and lots more rude words. So explicit! Surely he was having me on. I needed to check it out with someone, as I was not sure he wasn't just trying to shock me. In the end I asked Georgie. Georgie then took great pleasure in not only confirming but also embellishing even further all I had been told.

To top it all, I learnt for the first time in my life that I didn't have to swallow Tampax, should I decide to use one. That revelation was as much a relief as an enlightenment.

My next job was closer to home. Another garage, this time in New Brighton. I couldn't do shorthand proper like, but as I explained at the interview, I could write fast.

What I didn't say was that I couldn't always read what I'd written, mind. Anyway I got the job. Mr Fitzgerald, my new boss, said it was because I was so bloody hard-faced that he found me amusing.

Didn't think much cop of Mr Fitzgerald, but he wasn't around much. Just as well, because I soon discovered he had a rare sleeping illness, which meant he couldn't drive. Odd for a garage owner, I thought, not having a car.

Sleep could come over him suddenly when he was shaving, talking or even eating. Only lasted minutes, mind you, and most of the time he was unaware of what had taken place and continued on as if nothing had happened.

The first time I witnessed his illness was when he fell asleep mid-sentence. One fateful day, halfway through dictation his head dropped. He was sleeping like a baby, which I found most unnerving. Even though it tickled my fancy I'd never cracked on, until another staff member entered the office to bring morning tea.

I joked, 'Don't bother Noddy, he's away with the fairies again. Wonder what his wife thinks when he drops off on the job?'

How we both giggled. Me, because I thought I was dead funny, her, because she knew the rotten sod often faked it just to catch you out. As he did then.

Didn't like the job much anyway so it was no loss to me; but I'd have a lot of explaining to do when I got home.

11

I had been out of work for nearly three weeks so I supposed I deserved the silent treatment along with the sighing and door-banging. Just as I was looking forward to my Sunday dinner Mam handed me a plate. I stared in disbelief. 'Where's me meat?'

'No meat for you. It's only for the workers.'

Bloody hell. Now *I* banged the door.

Fancy being out of work and almost broke with Christmas coming up. I couldn't have timed it worse. Hadn't done any Christmas shopping and I needed some warm boots that didn't leak.

The next day the walk to Birkenhead market seemed to take forever over Duke Street Bridge. Luckily I managed to pick up a second-hand pair of boots for ten bob and got my Auntie Nellie a proper bread bin – red and white plastic. She should be able to see that OK even with her failing eyes.

I began the long walk home. With my luck the bridges could be up and my mam would curse me for being late. I'd done some messages for her and got my dad smoked kippers for his tea.

Walking through Hamilton Square always got my imagination going; a feeling of timelessness filled the quadrangle of office blocks surrounding a miniature park. The paths were laced with tiny neatly clipped privet hedges leading to green velvet lawns. I sat down to get my breath back, feeling dwarfed amongst an expanse of majestic trees. My dad once told me some of the trees were planted hundreds of years ago when Hamilton Square was full of residences for the gentry, bought with money from owning sweatshops, slave trading and exploiting the wretched mine workers. If I shut my eyes my imagination conjured up decades of fashionable folk coming and going. Starchy uniformed nannies sitting in the park with their precious charges in big prams like the one Prince Charles and Princess Anne had.

I always looked in awe at the regal old sandstone office buildings, with tall fluted columns seemingly reaching to the sky, supporting porticoes topped on each corner with a gargoyle. Black-painted wrought-iron railings were interlaced with brass scrolls to match the brass plates at the sides of the buildings. I stood at the base of the magnificent marble entrance to one building to squint at the notice pinned on the colossal carved door:

<u>VACANCY</u>

BOOKKEEPING MACHINE
OPERATOR REQUIRED

Please apply within to J.J. Stansfield & Sons

That could be the job for me. I reread the notice. Yep, I decided to give it a go even though I didn't have my good gear on. I'd had enough interviews now to know how I should present myself. I felt very self-conscious, clutching my Marks & Spencer's bag, my Auntie Nellie's bread bin, Mam's kippers and my boots, all getting in the way of the revolving doors. Unfortunately, I also knew that I couldn't afford the bus fare to come back tomorrow. Besides, I'd chicken out. With nothing to lose I entered the foyer.

'I've come about the job.'

The doorman in the black get-up and the bowler hat appeared not to hear.

'I've come about the job,' I yelled to his retreating back. By the look on his face when he turned you would have thought I had trod in something.

'You will be requiring the second floor, the office of J.J. Stansfield and Sons,' he said, pointing to the stairs.

'Ta.'

The second set of revolving doors located at the top of the stairs proved to be more of a challenge . . . I got well and truly stuck. I couldn't get in or out. I heaved and pushed free myself and landed on my knees in front of a large polished mahogany desk.

'I've come about the job,' I said, looking up, concerned in case I'd cracked my Auntie Nellie's bread bin. Now I was flustered. The heat was seeping up through my body, finally turning my face red.

It was a Mr Walmsley who interviewed me. Such a nice bloke. Dressed in a dark grey suit, white wing-collar shirt, and his spectacles hanging from his neck by a chain, he appeared to me to be dressed in keeping with the surroundings. Couldn't help feeling I had gone back in time – it all reminded me of the Charles Dickens era we read about at school. I must have been nervous because my brain couldn't keep up with my gob as I gave him all my work-history details – well, not quite all the details.

'Hey, you look just like Eamonn Andrews, you know, on telly. You do, you do. Yes, you look more like him than he does,' I laughed.

He didn't reply, just cleared his throat and smiled. 'Hmm, just so.'

I thought I was probably doing better than I had first

expected to. Then I started feeling cocky as I rabbited on inconsequentially.

'He does *What's My Line?* Do you watch it? Me dad loves it.'

'Miss Faulkner, let me remind you this is not a social gathering, I'm attempting to conduct an interview,' he said, still with a glint in his eye. I could tell he liked me.

'Sorry, I was enjoyin' it so much I almost forgot why I was here.'

After that I was ushered into the inner sanctum to meet a Mr John and a Mr Henry Stansfield. They nodded for me to sit down in a deep, buttoned wing chair covered in brass studs. I did as I was told. In spite of the leather being stiff and cold I remained seated in the huge chair, my arse colder than a penguin's chuff. There was no way to ease the discomfort, as my miniskirt couldn't be pulled down over the bare bits. Couldn't even sit on my hands as I was still clutching my parcels.

After some thirty minutes' interrogation I was informed the advertised position was 'Accounts Payable'. I would have me own office and two pounds five shillings a week.

'Oh!' My face dropped.

The Eamonn Andrews lookalike quickly interjected, 'Plus luncheon vouchers to the value of twelve shillings and sixpence per week of course.'

I chattered on happily now. 'I've never 'ad luncheon vouchers or worked in a place like this with a canteen before.'

I'd be on a pig's back; I could feel it in my bones.

'Oh, but we don't have a canteen,' said Mr John, looking uncomfortable.

'But I can smell cheese and onion.'

It was Mr Walmsley's 'Oh, my word!' that got my attention.

He cleared his throat before lowering his voice. 'Perhaps I should have mentioned . . . urm, you see we appear to . . . urm have a slight problem, in that Mr John's secretary has . . . a . . . small failing . . . so to speak . . . urm inasmuch as she is somewhat remiss in . . .'

There was an uncomfortable pause while he scratched his head. I waited, wondering what the hell was coming.

'. . . Urm somewhat remiss in attending to her bodily hygiene and ablutions.'

There it was – out like a bad tooth.

He went on then full steam. 'Unfortunately, combined with the intermittently faulty central heating it sometimes makes the work situation uncomfortable, not to say very delicate. Very delicate indeed.'

I got the gist. With mixed emotions. I mean, who was I to talk, having had similar problems in the past because of the garlic and onion chest rub. But I was grown-up now and we could afford Lifebuoy toilet soap in our house.

'So can't yer just tell 'er she stinks?' I asked without malice. I seemed to have developed this amazing talent for rocking the boat.

'Well I'm afraid not. The situation is rather sensitive. She's a family friend and has been with the company for many years. It's not insurmountable and you will soon get accustomed to occasional odorous overtures.'

Of course I never did. Birthdays, Christmases, I always bought Miss Jackson some bath salts, scented soap or smellies of some description, as did other members of the staff. When Miss Jackson came into my office I would fling open the windows in an exaggerated manner and make sarcastic jokes. Sometimes I sprayed air freshner round the office when she entered the room. My attitude gave the three other office workers a new-found courage to address the problem, and Miss Jackson eventually left in tears. Being young, I never for a moment considered her feelings. It was many years later, when I recalled the incident, that I realized tact and a kind word would have been more merciful. But tact and kind words were few and far between in my young life.

These were hard but happy times for me at work. I was well thought of at J.J. Stansfield and Sons. The fact that they made hammer crushers to sell to the mining companies was of no interest to me. In all the years I worked there I never learnt (or cared) what a hammer crusher was. All I knew was that I was better off than most of my friends who worked at Littlewoods or Vernons pools marking off football coupons. I actually looked forward to going to work.

Each week my mam handed me a meagre fifteen bob out of my wage packet, but she didn't know that I had nearly that much again in luncheon vouchers. I soon had another scheme under way. This time I struck a deal with the owner of the general store on the corner of Hamilton Square. We traded luncheon vouchers for nylons, fags, magazines, fireworks, Easter eggs, make-up, etc. (anything but lunch). Needless to say I was always hungry. Sometimes, for special occasions, I would trade a month's luncheon vouchers in advance, so I couldn't afford ever to be off sick: unused vouchers were supposed to go back to the pay clerk. What a slice of luck – I *was* the pay clerk.

Part of my regular duties was to take Mr Henry his elevenses. Up two flights of granite stairs I crawled each day, balancing a cup of tea with two arrowroot biscuits in the saucer. By the time I placed the tea on his desk, the soggy remains of the biscuits floated in the saucer. Mr Henry's patience wore thin. This was a constant source of irritation to him.

'Child, you will have to hold your back straight and learn to balance the cup so the contents don't spill over the side,' he implored.

Try as I might I failed. Sometimes I even got as far as his door and just as I knocked the tea would slop over.

Gosh, our Georgie was smart. He said one day just out of the blue, 'Hey stupid, why don't you balance the saucer with the biscuits on the top of the cup till yer in the door.'

I wanted to please Mr Henry, and dry biscuits put me back in his good books again. He reminded me of the Duke of Edinburgh and didn't pick his nose and flick the bogeys like his brother Mr John did.

Mam was caught in never-ending 'menopause madness'. She started having blackouts in the street. Many was the time she had to be brought home by a neighbour. But it took more than a few blackouts to keep her down. The day after one she ventured out again. It was only a matter of minutes before one of our neighbours was yelling through the letter-box slot in the front door, 'Yer mam's on her way 'ome. Someone's bringin' 'er.'

'Oh no. She'll 'ave to see a doctor. This can't go on,' my dad groaned.

Mam's eyes were swimming with tears as she staggered through the door. She seemed to be in pain – not the usual blackout this time.

'Me 'ead's on fire!' she yelled, sticking her head under the cold water tap, cursing. 'Who left the flamin' *Fiery Jack* on the mantelpiece? I thought it was me brilliantine, without me glasses on I couldn't read the tube.'

Please God don't let her see me laugh or she'll kill me.

Her head became scabby and inflamed and she couldn't comb her hair for nearly a week.

Life went on in Littledale Road without further incident, until my mam's luck changed – she had a big win on the nags.

Teddy was in the kitchen counting out the money with Mam.

'There must be over a hundred and fifty quid on the kitchen table.' Teddy yelled the news to Georgie who was glued to the lavvy after gorging a whole jar of pickles for a bet.

'What's she goin' to spend it on?' Georgie yelled back through the closed door.

'Dunno.'

123

'If you must know, I'm goin' to open a shop,' she boasted. You could have heard a pin drop. 'You heard me, I want a shop of me own. I've always fancied a little business venture.'

Me dad didn't know what had got into her. 'What sort of bloody business venture?' Now he was obviously getting annoyed.

'I dunno, just a shop. Maybe fancy goods or some such. Why don't you lot get it into yer nappers, I'm not the thick'ead you all take me for. I don't say nowt but I keep me eyes open and me ears an' all.'

My mam was the oddest person, I thought, with parts of her character you only glimpsed now and then. What was it with shops and the family? Jacky had opened a shop when he got out of the Army. Soon got tired of being a shopkeeper. According to June he aspired to be the executive type if you please. Someone suggested that Mam take over our Jacky's old shop lease. The shop was still empty and boarded up. What could be better? It even had the name FAULKNERS painted over the door already. It was easily the most interesting shop in the street with a pub or a betting shop or chip shop on every other corner.

The writing on the windows stated 'Fancy Goods'. That wasn't even the half of it because Mam didn't want to miss out on any potential sales. She stocked everything: paraffin, coal bricks, soap powders, pet and garden supplies and pets (well . . . goldfish, budgies, gerbils and white mice).

In no time at all Mam had made Faulkner's a thriving little business and our house was the first to benefit from the profits. First on the list was a brand new 'shop-bought' telly. Then followed a fridge, log-effect electric fire, feather pillows, warm winceyette sheets and lots of home comforts that our less fortunate neighbours didn't have.

*   *   *

124

As our house was rented, it had never been painted since before the war.

'That's next on me list,' said my mam. And true to her word, after another record month, the paint was got. Unfortunately, Georgie knew this bloke who knew a bloke who made an offer Georgie couldn't refuse. The house was duly painted battleship grey with the paint left over from the war.

'Looks like the bloody *Ark Royal* troopship,' the neighbours laughed. Of course they were jealous, because it was the only house in the scruffy end of the street with a new coat of paint.

Me dad helped Mam out at the shop on his time off work just to give her a break, although Mam never had a holiday, ever. The routine at the shop was always the same. Every morning, she wrote all the bargains of the day on the window in whitewash. Then she hung all the brushes, mops, plastic buckets, plant pots and garden tools outside, over the door and round the windows. Eventually the police and the Council threatened to close Mam's shop down for trespassing, because her stock was blocking the public footpath.

'Daft buggers, I've got to hang them out, there's no bloody room for customers inside the shop if I don't.' She continued to do as she pleased. Good for Mam! She was queen of her domain, besides being acknowledged and respected in the community, so much so that I was invited to the prestigious junior Mayor's Ball.

My School of Art training came in very handy when I became the official window dresser. Not an easy task, although my dad wasn't a hard act to follow. Usually his display looked like a jumble sale, given the con- glomeration of assorted wares.

One night I was sitting on the front wall at home when a passing neighbour said, 'Yer winder must look good me girl, there's a crowd lookin' in.'

Of course, I couldn't resist. I had to see for myself and

125

hear the flattering comments. It was true – there were eight or nine locals crowded round the window – but they were pointing and laughing. I pushed my way through to see what held their interest.

Rats, that's what was holding their interest. Bloody rats running in and out of the displays, round the dinner sets, pots and pans, and one was dangling from the swing inside the most expensive parrot cage.

I scurried away.

Never losing heart, I changed the window display on the first of every month. Some of the office staff from the local town hall came over regularly to watch my latest creation taking shape. They stood in the front of the shop window staring, as they ate their hot chips.

Feeling smug about my latest display, I boasted at the tea table, 'It must be good you know, Dad, 'cos they wouldn't come to look, if it wasn't. They can't even wait till it's finished.'

'Like hell. It's only the bloody lads from the town hall and they come to look up yer miniskirt. When you prance round they can see yer drawers. I've seen more cloth on a bandaged toe.'

126

12

'Honestly Cherry, what do you think? Do you like it?'

How could I not like anything with diamonds? Marion, the lucky beggar, was engaged to a hunk called Mike. I'd only seen him a couple of times and found him very charming not to mention gorgeous, tall with vivid blue eyes and blond hair you would die for. Like James Dean, he wore a leather flying jacket with a fur collar. They made a handsome couple, especially now that Marion had enrolled in modelling school.

'Why don't you come with me to modelling school? It's only five quid for six lessons – excellent value. You learn to do your make-up properly instead of the way you use Panstik, like slapping putty in the cracks. They teach you to walk straight and wear proper hats gracefully. And guess what? You even learn how to play the lady and how to set the table; which knives and forks to use when you're being posh.'

'Lord knows I need all the help I can get,' I replied. 'If me dad's in the right mood and will hand out the dosh I'll give it a go. Best I tackle him when he comes home from the pub.'

Must have picked the wrong time. Maybe he'd just not reached his generosity level at the pub or else he'd cottoned on to my scheme.

'I'll give yer the five quid but yer workin' now so you

can pay me back at five bob a week. How does that suit yer, Topsy?'

'Ta, Dad.' I smiled falsely. I must be losing my touch.

Now, full of hope, I would show the lads I was ready to break free from the chrysalis, and emerge as a delicate beautiful butterfly, not a bleeding moth.

Teddy started on me first. 'You a model? What are yer goin' to model for, toby jugs or gargoyles?'

Georgie next. 'You 'ave to be kiddin'. They're just after yer money. Probably they'll take anyone who'd pay. Mind, they're scrapin' the bottom of the barrel takin' you. Yer've got a gob on yer like a billposter's bucket. Come to think of it, they could just be lookin' for some short-arse like you to model doll's clothes.'

Rotten sods – I'd bloody show them.

On the first day of the modelling course we paid over our five quid, then were put into groups according to our attributes. Miss Forsythe-Brown, the principal at the modelling school, decided after some consideration that my best features were my hands and that I should work on them, softening them with Vaseline and trying to make them look delicate. I looked down at my hard-working hands with their broken nails and chafed skin. (If these were my best features what the hell did she think of the rest of me?) She must have been joking. It's impossible to improve anything that's regularly immersed in soapy water, bleach and Jeyes fluid. However I was eager to get started, so I invested all my savings in a pair of rubber gloves and a jar of Vaseline, a nail file and cherry red nail varnish.

On my next visit to the modelling school I ran up the steps two at a time, anxious to show off my 'smoother than a baby's bum' hands. The door was locked. The sign in the window said 'Offices to Let'.

I could have done better wasting the five quid on some decent clobber.

*   *   *

128

Eric had transferred back to the *Britannic* now, the last of the White Star Line doing a three-month Mediterranean run, and was due home in a week. Most of the time we were apart I drifted, feeling empty without him. When I was with Eric I thought of ways to look nice for him, since my physical rebuilding at the modelling school had proved to be a dead loss.

He'd phoned me from the docks to say he would wait for me outside Stansfields' office in Hamilton Square the following Tuesday. When the big day arrived I was too dithery to work. I kept looking out the window.

'Hey, is that your fella? The one across the road in the military mac who looks like Michael Denison?' one of the girls yelled.

Just as I looked out, Eric saw me and waved.

Proudly, I swanked. 'Girls, notice he wears leather gloves and a silk scarf, not knitted ones like your blokes?' My heart went out to Eric, standing round now with four gawking females weighing him up.

Before going home we sat in the bus terminal café at Woodside. I was happy listening to Buddy Holly and the Everly Brothers on the jukebox and hearing Eric's stories of the glamorous 'rich bloods', a name given to First Class passengers. We sat drinking expresso coffee and me stuffing my face with sticky buns.

'Where do you put it all? I've never seen anyone as small as you eat so much.' Eric couldn't know that I'd spent a month's luncheon vouchers on necessities like hair lacquer, stockings and make-up, which left me with an empty belly.

I told him about my dismal efforts at the modelling class.

'Why would you want to change? You're perfect the way you are.' He planted a butterfly kiss on the tip of my big nose before putting two bob into the jukebox to serenade me three times with the record 'Five Feet of Heaven in a Ponytail', and I blushed because at the time I had a ponytail.

I told him that I wished I could be tall and pretty with a page-boy hairstyle – like Veronica Lake.

'Who's Veronica Lake?'

'Veronica Lake, the fillum star.'

'Never 'eard of her. But to be honest me favourite's Jean Simmons, she's lovely.'

Jean Simmons? She had *black* hair! I decided Eric must prefer women with black hair. Unfortunately mine was blonde. Needless to say, my next month's supply of luncheon vouchers was spent on Radiant Hair Dye – Black Henna.

Saturday night when Eric and I were alone, I announced, 'I'm goin' to dye me hair, will you give us a hand?'

Eric seemed keen so I sat on the floor between his knees and read the instructions, while he dabbed the lotion to the left-hand side of my head.

'Where's the other bottle?' said Eric.

'What other bottle?'

'Well I've only done one side and I've run out.'

With black dye running down my face and neck and splattered all over my mam's good towels, I looked in the mirror. Jet bloody black down one side was bad enough, but even worse, the shops were closed until Monday. I'd have to live with the harlequin clown image all weekend.

Teddy and George called me 'The Blackhead'. All hell broke loose when my dad clapped eyes on me. He refused to have anything to do with me, telling my mam, 'All that little madam needs is a tambourine and a caravan. And wasn't I right? Always said we'd spawned a soddin' gypsy.'

I kept out of my dad's way until I could afford the hairdresser at the end of the road to complete the transformation.

Nobody liked it, least of all me, but if it meant I looked like Jean Simmons I'd stick with it until Eric went back to sea. I was upset that he was leaving me again but anxious to put my hair right. After we said our goodbyes at the Seacombe Ferry building it was back to the shop for me, this time choosing to be Ash Blonde.

At least that was the intention. I stared, at a loss for words, at my reflection. My hair had turned a mouldy green with the texture of Mam's pan scrub. The humiliation was almost too much to bear as I stood in the hairdressers. It didn't need a Brain of Britain to tell why I was there.

'Blimey Charlie, who the hell did that? Don't tell me. I don't need to ask,' prattled the tarty-looking proprietor. Did she have to add to the humiliation.

'Well, we'll do our best to fix yer. Won't we, Gloria?' she said, turning to her assistant, as she ran her practised fingers through my wiry green hair.

'Gloria will see to you. Take a seat.' I was duly passed on to Gloria who was busy spitting on the mirror and wiping off the soap marks with a corner of a towel, which she then wrapped round my neck.

Gloria grinned in a conspiratorial way and whispered, 'Don't you worry yer 'ead, queen, I'll make yer look the gear.'

When she had finally finished she stepped back. 'That's the best I can do, chuck. Warm Brown. Suits you, and anyhow it won't take too long to grow back to normal – whatever that may be.'

I'd been promoted to Accounts Manager at Stansfields, and they'd advertised for a new office junior. No-one could have foreseen the mayhem this junior was about to cause in the quaint old family business. Suzanne (Sue for short) had long red hair and freckles; was supremely confident, with an incredible sense of mischief. My word, how she brought joy into my life. We had so much fun at work that the old Dickensian office turned into the London Palladium.

Poor Mr Walmsley bore the brunt of our jokes. Each

night when the post was weighed and stamped, Sue placed the heavy brass weights off the scales in his brief-case. This he took to his home and back to work the next day without being aware of the excess weight he carried to and fro, on and off the train each night and morning for nearly a week. The longer the prank went unnoticed the funnier it seemed.

We wished that we could have been flies on the wall when he tried to open his *Financial Times* to read on the train. It became our habit to staple the pages together, or draw glasses and moustaches on the photos. Poor sod, he never uttered a word of reproach, even when the stapling extended to the pockets and sleeves of his overcoat. The three old gentlemen bosses seemed to be continually shell-shocked after we took advantage of their meek, introvert natures.

Mr Henry Stansfield simply looked devastated when again faced by a morning cuppa, this time the cold tea deliberately slopped over his biscuit in the saucer. And we were afraid to even look at Sue when Mr John Stansfield was giving her dictation, as she sat facing him with a finger stuck up her nose, mimicking him. The meaning was totally lost on the poor bewildered sod.

I knew Sue had gone too far one day when Mr John and Mr Henry called me into their inner sanctum. They were clearing their throats nervously, ummin' and ahin' between them. This could mean real serious busi-ness.

'Now please take note Miss Faulkner,' Mr John said, clearing his throat yet again. 'Miss Clarke is sitting at the reception desk with holes in the knees of her black stockings. This simply is not acceptable. Neither is her uncontrolled hair.'

Mr Henry butted in with his two penn'orth. 'And urm . . . and urm . . . yes, yes, I think it is worth mentioning that she, Miss Clarke that is, appears to be wearing gold slippers.'

'Really?' interjected a blushing Mr John. 'Is that so? My word.'

After a short exchange of glances between the two, Mr Henry continued, 'Please Miss Faulkner, relay our distaste and disfavour of her wayward appearance to Miss Clarke.'

The realization of what they had said dawned on me. Before I could protest, Mr John blushed again and he and Mr Henry legged it out the room to take refuge behind their respective office doors.

As I expected, Sue didn't take it too well.

The following morning saw her sitting at the reception desk with wire threaded through two plaits, bent to make them stick out from each side of her head, with extra brown freckles dotted round her nose. Pippi Longstocking rebelliously greeted all comers at her reception desk.

None of the bosses ever dared to attempt further comments on her increasingly bizarre appearance.

Probably it was because I was from the scruffy end of the street that Eric's family didn't warm to me. His mother never made me feel welcome. She always hoped he would meet a nice young lady on board ship or somewhere exotic. (From what Eric told me, there weren't too many nice young ladies on board them ships.)

But Eric and my mam were getting on famously. He could always make her laugh as they shared their knowledge of the horses and enthusiasm for the jockeys, Lester Piggott or Gordon Richards. Mam bet on them regardless of their mounts, whereas Eric studied the form more seriously and managed a few big wins.

Eric shared his fags and his hot racing tips with Mam and even on the days she was giving me the silent treatment she always made him feel very welcome. So much so, that each Saturday night after the ritual of cooking the joint for Sunday's dinner, Eric was honoured with a hot meat butty with pickles. He was unaware that he was eating my Sunday dinner portion, because I didn't get any meat on my plate on the Sundays he was on shore leave. After hearing that, he politely declined Mam's future offers.

On Pancake Tuesday it snowed. Eric and I were finishing off the first batch of pancakes my mam had made with fresh snow instead of milk. While my mam was busy with the next batch I whispered to Eric, 'She only ever makes pancakes on Pancake Tuesday if it snows – she's convinced it's a sign of lasting good luck.'

'Oh good, so do you feel like gettin' engaged?' he asked.

'What?'

'Thought I'd try out some of me good luck, do you feel like gettin' engaged?'

I did hear right, then. 'But yer mam doesn't like me.'

'Me mam's not askin' to marry yer, I am.'

'You like me that much?'

'No . . . I love yer that much.'

Mam said she didn't care one way or the other whether we got engaged or not. She had great difficulty demonstrating her love for anyone, there was never a cuddle, never a caress or words of love. Probably it wasn't that she didn't care; she put an enormous amount of effort into the intricate Fair Isle sweaters and endless nourishing meals she made for all of us.

I longed for the day she could say that she loved me, seemed like she never would. But if I asked her outright, 'Do you love me?' the reply was always the same. 'I curse the day I ever 'ad you. I should 'ave put you in a home when I 'ad the chance.' She reasoned I could do a lot worse than Eric for a husband and stated matter-of-factly, 'Listen, just take my word for it. All men are bastards, it just takes some longer than others to show it.'

But there was no doubt Eric loved me. He said I was sweet. (Sweet? Me?)

'Cherry, I think it's time I 'ad a talk with yer dad.'

'What for?'

'To see if he will agree to us gettin' married, me love, what else?'

'I wouldn't bother. They'd give their blessin's to Jack the Ripper if it meant he would take me off their hands.'

To my utter amazement my dad said, 'No.'

He went on, adding insult to injury, 'Sorry son. Yer only a lad and you 'aven't even got an apprenticeship or the backin' of a good union for the hard times. I'm not keen, not keen at all, besides she's not yet eighteen. Still a baby and far too young to be engaged.'

Mam told me later that during the Depression Dad had walked the streets, sometimes as far as Manchester and back, looking for work to put food on the table. He'd slept in doss-houses and hanging over ropes suspended across empty rooms because there was nowhere for him to lie down.

Years of hunger, poverty and frustration had knocked out most of the romance there might have been in my dad; he was a grim realist. He was haunted by the deaths of his first two babies, Elizabeth and Patrick, both through circumstances of poverty and ignorance.

'He wants better for you. He wants you to 'ave a secure future,' my mam insisted.

They amazed me, absolutely bloody amazed me.

Secure, when had *I* ever felt secure?

The best he'd ever done for my future was to jack up a job for me in an Easter egg factory. But all the lads in our family had had apprenticeships. Joey, and Jacky, the eldest, were once apprenticed asphalters like Dad, Georgie was always destined to be an apprentice electrician. Teddy became an apprentice bricklayer, his over-developed brain taking a well-earned rest after all his hard work at college, suffering pain and humiliation at the hands of the Jesuit priests.

It was years before I understood that the Faulkners'

highly acclaimed tradesman tradition wasted the talents of these highly intelligent men. As for intelligent women, well they didn't have a cat's show in hell.

To be fair, my dad had always thought he'd done his best for me, even if he thought the best way to protect me and especially my virginity was to keep me childlike and ignorant.

Despite Dad's resistance, Eric and I agreed on a secret engagement. A ring would follow when Dad came to his senses and Eric had completed another three-month Mediterranean run on the *Britannic*. The tips he received now that he was First Class waiter would give us the start we needed.

Patty and Dolly were nicely settled with their families in houses of their own. They were in the same neighbourhood in Poulton and met regularly for a cuppa and a chat.

Patty's youngest son was a bit of a problem. At nearly four years old he was still being breastfed. The boy was thriving, unlike Patty who was haggard and drawn, with tits like spaniel's ears. She had been advised to stop breastfeeding, but the child continued to help himself to the breast whenever he pleased. Mam told her if she didn't wean him off soon, she'd have to shove her tits through the school railings at playtime for him.

Everyone had his or her own ideas about how to encourage him off the breast. Someone suggested she put mustard or bitter aloes on her nipples. After many failures Patty's own idea worked best – she painted a face on her breast with soot to scare him off.

Soon Patty perked up enough to take on a home job – packing pipe-cleaners. Ten pipe-cleaners to a band, twelve bands to a packet, one hundred and forty-four packets to a carton, ten cartons to a container. She soon became an expert, learning to count, pack and talk at the same time. In her sleep, she said, she counted them. 'No more erotic dreams for me, I just dream of countin' soddin' pipe-cleaners all day and every day, week in and week out.'

Their little two up and two down home had been taken over by pipe-cleaners. White fluff covered the furniture, the cat, and even settled on Patty's eyebrows and hair. On her busy days her house looked like a snowstorm.

'Can't stop now lovey,' she would say when anyone called in. 'Put the kettle on, I need to wet me whistle. The bloody fluff sticks at the back of yer throat.'

Years later my beautiful brave Patty died prematurely, her lungs choked up. She had fought a constant battle for breath, laboured and painful, even with the aid of an oxygen machine.

The death certificate stated she had died from emphysema.

But had she really? Some believed that the real cause was the fluff from all those pipe-cleaners.

13

By the end of 1961 I was turned twenty and my horizons were beginning to broaden. I could go to Liverpool with Marion any time that I saw fit. Or at least any time I could afford to catch the bus to the ferry to travel across the River Mersey and catch another bus to Matthew Street. On top of that we had to pay a shilling to get into the Cavern Club. Just to be part of the queues winding round the brick bomb sites and derelict warehouses hoping for a chance to get in was like wrestling for positions in the January sales.

Marion and I ranked amongst the other 'Cavern dwellers' who sat like pigs in muck on the hard-backed chairs in the sweaty, dank and dingy basement. I was armed with a bottle of Fanta (laced with vodka of course); Marion was armed with jelly beans to throw at George Harrison. George was partial to sweets and was Marion's favourite member of the Fab Four. Now if I was ever asked to marry one of the group I would have picked Paul – he had the longest eyelashes and the tightest arse. That was a dead turn-on, as was the kinky leather gear they all wore.

When the parade of local talent walked on stage we all went berserk.

'Shurup, shurup,' I would yell. 'I didn't pay a shillin' to listen to you rowdy lot.'

Us Merseysiders were known for our witty charm –

born in us, so they say. But them lot, at the Cavern, they were the real side-splitters. I don't know who was the more undisciplined – them on stage or the audience. The pong of sweaty gyrating bodies in the haze of choking cigarette smoke and who knew what else had me gasping for air, so we always left before chucking-out time. Anyway we had no need to hang around to pull a bloke; we were both spoken for. We would run to catch the *Royal Iris* ferry boat, hoping it wouldn't be too late for us to connect with our last bus home.

It was a time of great changes, excitement and activity, internationally. Yuri Gagarin completed the first successful space flight. This was seen by some as good news and bad news, because the fearsome Russian Empire was debated by all and sundry. It was thought that with its mighty power and strength it was planning to take over the world, and not before too much longer. After all, anyone could see how easy the Berlin Wall went up, so what chance would we have if it started on a little country like ours? Films about the end of time and nuclear holocaust were fashionable. Our generation was too young to remember much about the Second World War, but had become expert on predicting the Third World War and the rise of Communism. The media was rampant with news of the nuclear power stations and missile silos being built around Great Britain and Europe. We talked big and matter-of-factly about a probability of a hopeless doomed future and the possibility of annihilation.

Our generation had also found a voice, so we marched for change; we marched for peace; or we simply marched. At long last I was coming into my own, being privileged to be part of the radically changing Sixties, although sexual liberation seemed almost too late for me. The Beatles with the unique Liverpool sound had started to play a major hand in shaping the international music industry. They were in the papers and on the telly. Dirty old Liverpool was on the map. It was OK now to speak

139

with a thick, nasal, gutteral voice. It was better than OK, it was desirable – cool, man.

Peace reigned in our house for a time. The coloured fags kept coming and Mam's blackouts, rages and depression subsided. Occasionally I would catch her eyes shining with half-hidden tears, although she cried less and less these days for her dead babies and Joey. None of *my* bottom-drawer items ever got thrown out of the bedroom window like Patty's had. In fact, my mam helped me out with my collection, buying odds and sods such as tea towels, tablecloths, pillowcases and bits of bedding and hardware, but always handing them to me without comment. No mush, no sentiment, other than occasionally saying 'I thought this would come in handy,' or 'you may need this some time.' If I made a fuss or showed appreciation with a hug she would get all embarrassed and push me away. However, she always watched my face, smiling to herself at the degree of pleasure she brought.

Now what had I done? I thought things were going to well, for too long, and now the silent treatment again. Well, two could play at that game. I tried not to force the conversation before I left for work, slamming the door behind me and quickening my pace as the vision of her coming after me with the poker suddenly leapt into mind.

When I got home the atmosphere was still thick. Mam's eyes met mine, brimming with tears.

'What's up Mam? Can't yer talk about it? Can't yer tell me?'

She grabbed a piece of paper from behind the mantle clock. Silently, she thrust the note across the table, her eyes fixed on me as I read.

> *Won't be back for tea –*
> *gone to get married.*   Georgie x

Oh no! Poor Georgie. Poor Mam.

Teddy also had a fiancée. Her name was Liz. She was pleasant and easy-going. We got on famously. We were the same age with the same hobbies and interests – rock'n'roll and shopping. Comparing our bottom-drawer collection, we shared ideas on our future nest-building and housekeeping.

One day I casually mentioned to Liz, 'Our Teddy is not nearly as moody since he took up with you.'

'Moody? Surely not? I've never thought of him as moody. Teddy's very kind and loving. He makes me feel special and Dad and me mum think the world of him. He's very clever, done a lot of renovation work on our house and we have a cottage in Wales, which he's helping to rebrick and decorate. My folks think of him as the son they never had.'

I gave her firm warning not to mention Teddy's building prowess to our mam; that news would go down like the *Titanic*. My brothers were all skilled in working with their hands – our house in Littledale Road saw little evidence of this.

On the other hand my dad's do-it-yourself exploits were legendary. Like the time the vestibule door stuck shut – rain blowing under the front door had made the layers of lino underneath swell, so the door didn't fit properly. Dad took control of the problem. Stubborn paint on the hinges finally submitted with the help of the chisel and then the axe. He took the big carved oak door and laid it across Mam's best dining-room chairs in the good front parlour.

Not to be defeated simply because he lacked the right tools, my dad finally finished the task with the usual swearing and cursing. In an effort to remove the bottom bit of the offending door, after hours of blood, sweat and tears (Mam's), my dad gave up on the blunted saw and resorted to finishing the job with the axe.

Like apostles round the Communion table we all stood

looking at the battered door that was still suspended across the now chipped and scratched dining chairs, unable to see why Mam was giving him the evil eye. After all, she had longed for my dad to take an interest in the house. Finally, with the twins' help the heavy door was up-ended to be rehung on the now twisted, battered hinges. We looked on at the mad axeman's revenge, the door more crooked than a parson's smile.

With the axe in his fist my dad's mood quickly changed from willingness to belligerence. 'I'm given' yer fair warnin', don't no-one say a bloody word.'

Like me, mam wasn't going to let an opportunity like this slip away.

'Paddy, yer soft git, yer've only sawn the top off the soddin' door instead of the bottom.'

In a fit of temper my mam took to the offending lino with the bread knife. By the look on his face my dad, for a minute, feared she was taking it to him. No real harm done, apart from the gale that regularly whistled over the top of the door and down the hall.

And now Dad was going on about a fish tank he'd found. Since he retired at the end of last year he had threatened to get more involved with Mam's shop. Even bought an old fish aquarium from the rag-and-bone man.

'It's only got two sides and the bottom is missing, but I can soon fix it up,' he proudly announced.

Mam's eyes looked to the ceiling.

'It'll cost next to nowt, Lil, and we can stock tropical fish. Very fashionable now is tropical fish.' She was not convinced and offered no words of encouragement.

He didn't need or expect them – he was determined to have his own way whatever the cost.

After the usual threats and blaspheming he managed to replace the glass in the fish tank. The tank then took pride of place on the kitchen table and the garden hose was attached to the cold water tap.

'It'll take quarter of an hour at least to fill at this rate. I'm just goin' to the lavvy.'

The deluge of water went everywhere: over the table and into the table drawers. The rag clippie rugs Patty made were floating out the door to meet him on his return. The only thing not full of water was the fish tank.

Mam yelled, 'Paddy, I wish you would bloody well listen to me and leave well alone, yer daft bugger. Yer've still only got three sides of glass fitted.'

As usual the door was violently slammed in the customary Faulkner show of temper. One thing could be said for my dad, he didn't give up easily; Mam's vengeful words only stirred him to try even harder. Many tantrums and trials later, all the glass was fitted. The tank was tighter than a duck's arse. Dad was a happy man although Mam had lost interest altogether in having anything to do with fish. But not Dad, he was still keen as mustard, happily putting coloured chips in the base of the tank, then carefully placing little bridges and plastic plants for the fish to swim round without getting bored. For the finishing touch he collected a choice rock from the beach, which had to be soaked and boiled to get the salt out.

Now, highly chuffed with himself, he boasted, 'If a job is worth doin' it's worth doin' well,' and with that, he picked up the heavy tank with one hand and swung it off the table.

The rock, so carefully soaked and boiled, smashed through the side of the tank. The air turned blue as I legged it out of the back door followed by a lunatic Dad in hot pursuit. The remains of the tank were flung over the yard wall into the back alleyway for the rag man.

Eric had been away on a cruise for three agonizing months. God, how I missed him, although he wrote every day telling me how much he loved me. In his last letter he gave the time that his ship would tie up at Canada Dock, Liverpool, saying he wanted me to meet him at his house

143

after work as he was bursting with news of some kind. Mr Walmsley said I might as well go home early, as I was hopeless in that excited state.

After a long embrace Eric covered my eyes and led me through his mam's front door into their best parlour, with his family hot on our heels. I opened my eyes to an Aladdin's cave of furniture and presents. Amongst them a table and chairs, the likes I'd never seen. Not your usual old-fashioned walnut, but chrome with pale blue plastic cushions. A set of bathroom scales with a fur cover to stop your feet getting cold; a hundred-piece cutlery set; a dinner service; chunky soft blankets bound with satin, and much more.

Bewildered, I looked at Eric's grinning face.

'Hope you like them lovey. Most of the stuff I got in America but the beddin' came from Venice. Only the best for you.'

This gem of a man loved me as much as I loved him. Silent tears poured from my eyes, tears of happiness. Never was that good with words – bit like Mam, I suppose.

When the time came to talk to my dad again about our engagement, as usual I put my boot right down my gob.

'Dad?'

'What?'

'Eric's outside. He wants to come and see you because now we've just got to get married.'

He threw his newspaper onto his vacated chair and paced the kitchen while my mam hid behind a veil of cigarette smoke. Eric was not even through the door proper before Dad pounced. 'The baby tells me you 'ave to get married – how's that? Well, what's the bloody idea?' He roared like a tiger with a hangover.

'Well urm . . . you see Mr Faulkner,' Eric stammered, 'it's just that me mam's 'ouse is bulgin' at the seams with all the stuff I just brought home from me big trip and no-one has room for it.'

We squeezed hands with a new-found boldness, I spouted, 'And we're gettin' married anyway so why not sooner rather than later?'

Speechless for once, my dad dropped into his chair.

So finally we got 'officially' engaged with a diamond ring to prove it.

Soon after that Eric announced to his family that he was looking for a shore job, because we didn't like being apart for so many weeks at a time. Now I was certainly not in their best books, spoiling his Merchant Navy career not to mention the weekly allowance he had been sending home to his mother for years.

'Two quid a week – are you sure Mam?'

'Yes. The woman was in the shop yesterday buying her dog food. Such a dirty old witch she is – insists on me opening the tin and her tasting the dog food before she gives it to her precious mutt, but I don't mind humourin' her – she's a cash customer.'

'Only two quid a week, you know that for sure, Mam? That's not bad to buy a house in Bell Road.'

'Yes. The full price is only six hundred pounds. Why don't you nip round after yer dinner and talk to the woman?'

'You think so?'

'Won't hurt to talk will it?'

Eric and me stood outside Number 35 Bell Road trying to imagine us possessing our own love nest. Before we got a chance to knock the yapping dogs from inside drowned our voices out. The front door creaked open, releasing a stench of neglect and damp.

'Hello girl, you must be little Cherry. Come in girl, yer mam said to expect yer. Not many like her. Such a lovely obligin' woman, broke the mould when they made her.'

Eight or nine of the ugliest mutts I'd ever seen, all yapping and having trouble with their breathing, immediately surrounded us. I was struggling to find something constructive to say as Eric backed away.

'Hey Eric, how about his place? Isn't it lovely?'

No comment came from him, just a shudder.

'What unusual dogs. I 'aven't seen any like them before, not with flat faces,' I said as I bent down and stroked one on its mangy head.

'Pekinese. Surely yer must 'ave seen a Pekinese before. One's in pup now, see? It's the pretty one over there. Park yer arses and I'll make us a brew.'

Our firm 'No thanks' came in unison. I was trying to take shallow breaths so as not to fill my lungs with the stench of dog's muck.

'This 'ouse is just the ticket for a young couple startin' out. Just say the word and it's yours to buy for only two quid a week and a hundred quid down. I'm movin' out before the end of January,' she rambled.

'A hundred quid down?' Eric said in shock.

'That's the deal – cheap at half the price.'

The house was the usual terraced two-up-and-two-down, with an outside lavvy. Filthy windows hid an equally neglected yard that was surrounded by crumbling brick walls with tufts of grass and weeds growing through the cracks. Mind, the house did have an old iron bath complete with pedestal basin inside, so it was better than some two-up-and-two-down houses. Eric, bless his heart, had won thirty-four pounds on the horses, plus we had seventy pounds saved. We had our first fiscal meeting in the doorway of the local betting shop. The proposal was passed unanimously and the money was paid to the woman's solicitor that week.

Once the witch moved out we got a closer look at our monumental investment. It was far worse than we imagined. She was a real dirty bitch for sure. We ended up working most nights and weekends. Like navvies we started to try and make the house habitable – for normal people. Eric started scaping the stinking, rotting lino

146

from the floors, whilst I burnt what the 'vendor' had laughingly called 'curtains'.

But the stench lingered.

The good news was that there was no obvious sign of rats. Slugs and snails left their shiny trails up and down the damp walls, as armies of spiders scurried into dark corners. Seething black masses of cockroaches carpeted each room; some were crunched underfoot and the rest scattered in every direction once the light was switched on.

But the stench lingered.

I opened up the kitchen cupboards – nothing but dirt and mice droppings. Then at the back of the kitchen drawers I found it – or them. I screamed, slamming the drawer shut. Eric raced to my rescue and discovered for himself the remains of dead, stiff and decomposing puppy dogs wrapped in tissue paper, whose last resting place had been at the back of these drawers.

Eric was now working all the overtime he could as a conductor on the Wallasey buses, and when he was on split shifts I went to work on the Bell Road house at night on my own, stripping the wallpaper, sanding the walls and woodwork. Next day after only a couple of hours' sleep, Eric came to carry on with the work on the house. He would find upside-down jam jars, buckets and plant pots scattered around the room, imprisoning some obscene vermin or creature that I couldn't bring myself to deal with. After years of witnessing the twins' vendetta against the animal kingdom, I was, without doubt, extremely squeamish.

I collected pictures of elegant houses from *Home & Garden* magazines. One of the pictures showing a serving hatch between kitchen and the dining room took my eye.

'Eric, could you put one of these in – between the kitchen and the back kitchen?'

'Yep – probably. Could even put slidin' glass doors in to keep the draught off the back of yer neck.'

He started well enough. He bought a heavy great lump

147

hammer and knocked a bloody big hole in the kitchen wall. Naturally I was impressed. He'd been at sea since he was fifteen so it never occurred to me that he might not know about fixing things.

He certainly didn't.

'Let's make a feature of it and make it bigger,' he said when he saw how clever he was.

We had to call the Gas Board in to fix the fractured pipe that had, until then, been safely buried in the wall. Apart from that, I loved the serving hatch, even though we couldn't slide the glass doors because it wasn't square for some reason. We managed by pushing the small dishes and things through the top of the V-shaped gaping hole left at one side.

A while later we asked Teddy, who was still bricklaying, to give us his advice on how to fix our sloping floor in the bedroom over the kitchen.

'What's the problem – how come you think yer've got a slopin' floor?'

'Put it this way,' I said, 'the tallboy with the castors keeps slidin' across the room to the middle wall.'

'Well take the bloody castors off – problem solved. Look, if I get a chance I'll call round tomorrer night after work.'

When he came to examine the floor Teddy spotted the serving hatch. Bet he didn't think we were capable of doing that on our own! In fact, he said as much.

'You know what you've bloody well done, don't yer? You've only knocked a soddin' great hole in the supportin' wall.'

'What's the supportin' wall?'

'Spare me! It's only the soddin' wall that holds up the bedroom floor that holds up the bedroom walls that holds up the roof! It's a wonder the lot didn't come down on yer heads. Just see where it dips, you'll never be able to close the door on yer servin' hatch, not without puttin' a beam over the top.'

We decided it was all too complicated and too hard to fix. We could live with the sloping floor so we left well alone, covering the serving hatch with a picture. A lot of fuss about nothing – so we thought.

Our heart's desire was a proper white wedding. But the deposit on our house took all our savings, so we had to improvise, suggesting family and friends save the plastic carnations the makers of Omo soap powder were giving away free with every packet. Sprayed with a bit of scent, no-one would know the difference, in the photos anyway. Teddy jokingly suggested that I should tackle Mam and get her to knit me a wedding dress – that's if I didn't mind it being square-shaped.

When it came to making the cake we knew that old Mrs Tiplady would oblige, although she was prone to use egg powder and gravy browning instead of wasting the good brandy that she insisted her customers supply. We were also warned that the icing on the cake turned brown and mouldy after a couple of weeks, therefore it would be no good putting the top layer away for christenings, as was the custom. No matter, neither of us liked fruit cake anyway, and Mrs Tiplady was easily coaxed with the prospect of acquiring a drop of 'the good stuff'.

Eric had nearly paid off his suit at Burton's the tailors. The wedding service itself was turning out to be problem to arrange – no clergy would agree to marry us. My dad said it was because I was a 'left-footer'. Even though I was brought up Church of England, I was still christened a Catholic, and Eric was a Protestant. I even tried slipping the clergy the odd couple of quid by way of a sweetener, but it didn't work. There was only Mam's High Church in Liscard left to ask. Normally we wouldn't have dared approach them, but it was that or a registry office wedding. When we met the vicar he introduced himself as the Reverend Pope. I nearly cracked up – imagine us pulling this one off and being able to say the blooming Pope had married us. To our surprise and relief he agreed, bless him.

The date was fixed for March 31st so that we could get the full year's tax rebate.

We didn't want to start a family too soon because we needed all our money to fix the house up to make it habitable. Knowing very little about sex, birth control, babies or such, I tried asking my mam. But Georgie always turned up to eavesdrop and make disparaging remarks, such as, 'How would Mam know about babies? When you were born she threw the baby away and kept the afterbirth.' It probably should have hurt my feelings but didn't – I had no idea what afterbirth was at that time.

I gave up trying to ask Mam and eventually made an appointment with the family doctor to get his advice, and he in turn referred me to a family planning clinic. Eric, thank goodness, came to the clinic with me. Boy, the things they talked about would make your hair curl.

'This is a diaphragm, more commonly known as the Dutch cap. Safer than a sheath and there is still a lot to learn about the new birth pill. I suggest you go for the Dutch cap,' said the counsellor.

I tried to concentrate on what she was saying, but my mind kept wandering to what this frail old bird, with the mauve candyfloss hair and varicose veins criss-crossing her legs which looked like a map of the London Underground, could possibly remember about sex and birth control. I tried not to be put off when she talked of the withdrawal system, or the temperature and ovulation-period check. Wanting the best value for our ten quid investment for the sex and birth control session, we decided to go for the Dutch cap; at least you left the building with more than a red face for yer trouble.

I was given a tube of goo and the Dutch cap, to take home and practise inserting and testing for comfort and fit. They put all the paraphernalia in a discreet dinky little blue purse for me to take home. Feeling very grown-up, I announced at the tea table, 'I got a Dutch cap from the family plannin' clinic today.'

That grabbed their attention.

Teddy, as usual, took the mickey. 'Oh, Liz got one of them but it hurt her ears.'

I didn't think he was so bloody funny. Ignoring him I produced the Dutch cap for everyone's inspection.

'So why 'ave you got it so soon?' Mam snapped. She seemed upset, as though I had delivered a mortal wound.

'Oh, it's only so I can practise with it.'

I should have said, 'So I can practise insertin' it.'

'By the time you've finished practisin' you'll probably need one as big as a bin lid.'

I could always bank on Teddy for support.

Mam pushed her dinner away. The door banged. Now I had to face the usual Faulkner silent treatment at a time when I really wanted my mam to talk to me about woman's stuff. There was so much I still needed to know.

Instantly, Teddy's mood turned to concern. I thought he must have understood my anxiety. He whispered, 'Have you considered condoms?'

I was grateful for someone being prepared to discuss such matters, considering Mam's obvious lack of support, which Teddy put down to her lack of knowledge.

'Well to tell the truth,' I said, 'we did. But do yer know they're 3/9d a packet and we can't really afford them.'

'What about the washable ones? Works out a lot cheaper.'

'What a good idea. Never heard of them.'

'Oh yes, I always used to use them, until recently.'

'Recently? You mean they're no good.'

'Bloody marvellous, but I had to stop usin' them.'

'How come?'

'Liz's mum put a stop to it, said it upset the neighbours when I pegged them out on her washin' line.'

I fell for it again, heaven help me. When would I learn to stop taking his bait?

14

March 31st 1962, our BIG day. After today we'd be living in our own little house, with our precious few sticks of furniture including the treasures Eric had brought from abroad.

The wedding was at three o'clock. I didn't know how I was going to get through the day. I seemed to be the only one working, cleaning the Littledale Road house from top to bottom, scrubbing the step, donkey-stoning the window sills and polishing brass. The resentment I felt started to melt as I remembered that after today I wouldn't have to do this any more. But I still needed to spend some time alone with Mam.

I found her, as usual, lapsed into a preoccupied silence. I took her hand and looked into her tired face. 'I do love you, Mam. Tell me truly, you will miss me, won't you?'

'Don't ask daft questions.' She muttered some sort of embarrassed apology. After removing her trembling hand from mine Mam bristled back to life, then quickly got changed and left in one of the earlier cars.

Alone in my room I got dolled up in my wedding dress. A pearl crown for my head and a pair of satin winkle-picker shoes completed the ensemble. Proudly, I carried a white Bible with a spray of real flowers, all paid for in full by selling my sewing machine.

My father's hands, warm and strong, covered mine. We

were alone, the last to leave. 'Oh, Topsy darlin', it does me heart good to see you standin' there, lookin' just like a princess. No, no, girl, you look like Veronica Lake.'

The familiar tightening in my throat when faced with kindness threatened to overwhelm me. I laughed through the tears. After all these years, he'd remembered my childhood fantasy of looking like Veronica Lake.

'Thanks Dad for helpin' pay for the reception, and, you know, for everythin'.' My eyes burned, as I forced back further tears that threatened to spoil my make-up.

'Don't talk bloody daft. Anyway I don't suppose I've been much of a dad. I wish I could have afforded a better send-off, especially since you're the last one to bugger off, if you know what I mean?' He gave me a hug and wiped his eyes, tried to blow his nose on his hanky, but forgot it was only three fabric points glued onto cardboard, sticking out of his top pocket to look real.

'Let's see a smile from me special baby.'

As was the custom, all the neighbours were gathered round the front door calling out, waiting for a glimpse of the blushing bride.

Dad braced himself. 'Let's knock 'em dead, Topsy.'

March 31st also happened to be Grand National day. To make matters more complicated, the wedding ceremony was due to start at the same time as the big race. Dad and me arrived late at the church, having decided at the last minute to watch it on telly. By the time I was ready to walk down the aisle Eric was distraught, fearing my earlier emotional state.

I gazed into his loving face, squeezed his hand and whispered, 'Kilmore won.' He winked.

It was a good omen – he won thirty quid.

Wedding ceremonies were supposed to be serious formal occasions, and this one was, until I heard sniggers and laughs coming from the congregation. I couldn't believe the lads would mock this day, of all days, for me. I kept turning round to check what was going on, but the

154

Reverend Pope insisted I pay attention. Afterwards, at the reception, I learnt that the reason for the laughter was when I knelt at the altar I still had the price of 39/11d chalked on the bottom of the shoes that I had bought from the Birkenhead market.

After the service, which lacked spontaneity and singing, was over, the immediate family went into the vestry to watch the signing of the register. Amongst the animated talk around me I heard a groan – a piteous little sound coming from somewhere behind us. Then I caught sight of Mam, standing in the distance alone, her eyes drowning in tears. I ran over and embraced her. She lifted her arms in a clockwork gesture to pat me before returning them limply to her sides. I suppose she just didn't know how to embrace me after all this time, although I knew in my heart that she must have wanted to.

Another precious moment lost in the sin of silence.

After the photos, it was back to the Melody Inn in Wallasey village for the reception. Everyone charged their glasses of Babycham and cheered when Dad proposed a toast to his precious baby daughter and her new husband, who was almost everything a father would want in a son-in-law – although he was still lacking a trade. He hoped Eric would always love me as much as he loved my mam. He was choking with emotion as he bent and kissed her smack on the mouth.

The guests all said it was a lovely spread. Like me, they didn't know that after the meal Dad would take up a collection to help pay for the waitresses. Funnily enough they obliged, thinking that this was a giggle and part of his Irish humour, and not to make up for the loss of profits because my parents had to close the shop for the afternoon. (The only other time the shop was closed on a Saturday afternoon was when Liverpool played Everton and some disgruntled fans kicked the windows in.)

We planned a weekend in London for the honeymoon. But stopping on the way for our first night in a Whitchurch pub, about thirty miles from home, we realized that we wouldn't get far with the seven pounds we had left after paying for the wedding and the night's rest. We decided to sneak back home, where I cooked our very first meal of egg, chips and beans in our own pans on our own stove in our very own house. After our feast we washed the dishes in our very own washing-up bowl and took off to the pictures.

We sat and giggled in the back row of the Wallasey Gaumont British Cinema. At half-time when the lights went up for ice creams and Butterkist popcorn, we discovered we were sitting next to Teddy and Liz. I don't know who was more surprised. It was a wonderful film. We snogged all the way through Anthony Newley singing 'If I Say I Love You, Do You Mind?' It became OUR song.

Who could ask for a better honeymoon?

The family always believed that I was youthful and unworldly; they discouraged any interest in 'grown-up business' such as news and world affairs. This left me with a hunger for documentaries and talk shows on the television. Such programmes gradually increased my general knowledge and confidence to join in conversations with some family members. The news stories and personalities of the day come back to me as vividly as my own memories.

Eric and I were amongst the first generation of television addicts. *Six Five Special, Juke Box Jury* and *Top of the Pops* kept me riveted to the telly the nights when Eric was on late shift. Richard Chamberlain as Dr Kildare and David Janssen as Richard Kimble, The Fugitive, forever searching for the One-Armed Man, were not to be missed.

The summer of 1963 was wet, windy and stormy; by

heck, stormy in more ways than one. *Mrs Dale's Diary* and *The Archers* paled in comparison to the real-life drama being enacted before the eyes and ears of the world.

Like the rest of the country, we were following the exploits of Mandy Rice Davies and Christine Keeler in the sex scandal involving John Profumo, the Secretary of State for War. The ongoing revelations shocked the country. We watched the news and read the papers, only interested in the grisly bits, still not wordly enough to understand the possible threat to the nation as a whole and the dilemma of the Government. Thirteen years of Tory rule came to an end and my dad was overjoyed, like it was all down to him that Harold (bloody) Wilson won the election.

November 22nd 1963. The news flash announced President John F. Kennedy had been assassinated. Why was it I was so devastated, not just shocked? He was very much a man of his time, and the Kennedy clan were constantly in the news. We were all familiar with details of the wedding, the children, the Inauguration. I felt involved because I was now a mature adult at twenty-two and quite able to think for myself. The event also became more personal to me as Jacqueline Kennedy was some-one I admired – an icon, attractive, intelligent, strong-willed and a trendsetter to boot. The tears of genuine grief I wept were tinged with guilt at having been so involved in the past in my own misery, never considering the tragedies that touched others. I learnt that Cherry Simmonds did not have a monopoly on suffering; but in a perverse way it was strangely comforting to know that the rich and famous could also be victims of circum-stance.

Neither Eric nor I could manage money; me because I'd never had enough to manage (only what my mam gave me back out of my pay packet every week), and Eric, being at sea since he left school, wasted most of his on gambling. Though he did unfailingly send home a weekly allotment to his mam.

So thank the Lord for the corner shop, which introduced us to the world of revolving credit. Every day we booked food items – bread, milk, Spam, fish fingers and jam. The bill at the end of the week usually amounted to around the sum we had over on pay day after seeing to the mortgage, tallyman, gas and electricity. There was never enough to stock up on groceries for the next week. So, as I said, thank the Lord for the corner shop, where the whole process started again. Some days I didn't have enough bus fare to get to work, so we would scrounge around the rubbish bins in the park and sometimes behind the chip shop, looking for empty pop bottles to return for threepenny refund.

Marriage was a challenge, no doubt about it. Not quite like the glossy magazines led you to believe.

Eric was a saint with his never-ending cuddles and caresses. Now I slowly began shaking off some of the years of garbage and self-doubt, although my self-esteem didn't suddenly develop overnight. No, that would take a long time, but I found a quiet confidence and freedom. Freedom even to watch what I wanted on the telly – all the wonderful long-haired gits and throwbacks my family disparaged: the Beatles, Herman's Hermits, Adam Faith, The Yardbirds, Sonny and Cher, Emile Ford and the Checkmates and Cilla Black (whom I liked best of all).

Now I could go openly to the Cavern to enjoy the Sixties performers full flood on stage. Up and coming singers and groups that sent me into a frenzy included Gerry and the Pacemakers, Wayne Fontana and the Mindbenders, and the genteel melodies of Peter and Gordon left me mesmerized. The surroundings of the Cavern were now heavily autographed and the fake dungeon walls were covered in graffiti.

I also had freedom to choose my own wardrobe. I

wore poppit bead necklaces, crocheted mini dresses, maxi plastic macs, chisel-toed and winkle-picker shoes. All these became part of my cool wardrobe and no-one to say, 'Yer goin' ta ruin yer bloody feet.' The Gossard Wonder Bra was all the rage – made mountains out of molehills – a must for any young girl trying to attract a mate. (Not cheap, I paid nearly two quid for one out of our Patty's mail-order catalogue.)

Eric looked smashing with his hair quiffed like Elvis and his long sideburns growing to the bottom of his ears, rigged out in his drainpipe trousers and shoelace tie, his outfit complete with luminous socks and crêpe-soled shoes.

Fashion victims? No chance – we loved it.

Both Eric and I were in for a rude awakening.

Until I got married, I thought I had an excellent grounding in housework. I couldn't have been more wrong because all I could really do was scrub and clean. I couldn't cook, not proper meals like the ones featured on the pages of the 'How To' books or like my mam made. Eric never complained that my culinary delights of egg and chips, sausage and mash or beans on toast were the best that I could conjure up in those first months. And coming from a family of manual labourers, our meals were MEALS, so huge that they spilled off the dinner plate onto the table. 'The only way to a man's heart.' Mam lied.

What a culture shock for Eric, having served six years as First Class waiter on the Cunard liners.

Marion, my old friend from Littledale Road, invited us for dinner with her new husband Mike. We had posh food. Mince with vegetables on a bed of rice, followed by apples stuffed with raisins. Gosh, she never failed to impress me – always doing everything perfectly. Eric enjoyed his meal so much that he expressed his gratitude. In fact, he expressed his gratitude more than once, to the point I was good and mad.

'Hey Mam, how d'you cook mince?'

'Dead easy. A quarter-pound of mince will do you two. When it's boiled add a handful of rice in to swell it up, it could last you two days.'

'What else? What about vegetables?'

'Handiest and cheapest is a tin of mixed veg. Best to pour it in when the meat's nearly cooked.'

Well, I'd followed her instructions but I wasn't doing too well. I looked in the pan at the snotty mess, slime and grease floating on the top. Each time I stirred it in, it floated back on top. Not wanting to waste really good food, I dished it up anyway. It was times like this we needed a dog!

'Don't know what I did wrong,' I told my mam the next time I saw her. 'I put the tin of vegetable salad in last just like you said.'

'Vegetable salad? Yer soft bitch, that's vegetables in bloody mayonnaise. No wonder you 'ad problems.'

Eventually my cooking skills started to improve (by trial and disaster) at least to the point where I could peel a potato without alerting the casualty department at Victoria Hospital.

Unfortunately, my first efforts at the laundry were even more disastrous. I bought three bottles of bleach for half a crown, a dolly blue and a packet of starch. Didn't need soap powder. After the wedding we had enough to last a lifetime. (Teddy still teased me, 'Guess what kid? Buy the plastic carnation and get all this Omo soap powder FREE.')

Determined to have my whites 'whiter than white' on my first washday, I carefully put Eric's work shirts and his best wedding shirt, along with the string vests his mum knitted for him, all in a bucket to soak.

What did Mam do next? I remembered: she soaked the whites in bleach overnight. I figured one bottle of bleach for two nights would probably get them whiter. Perhaps two bottles for good measure.

160

In the end I left them soaking until the following Saturday when I had a bit more time to do the job properly. When I tipped the contents into the stone sink in the wash-house and started to wring out the shirts like I'd seen my mam do, I ended up with two halves to everything. One half in each hand, apart from the vests, which simply disintegrated.

Undaunted, I was determined to try harder next washday. I'd been given a wooden mangle that we kept in the backyard, as it was too big to fit in the wash-house. In a washing frenzy I washed anything and everything including the eiderdown, even though it was nearly new. Being full of feathers, the bloody thing wouldn't go through the mangle as the feathers had all gone to one side in a lump. Up to this point the washing had gone very well, except that the clothes were coming out of the mangle just as wet as when they went in. It was then that I noticed the rollers were bandier than a jockey's legs, so no wonder. I stood on tiptoe and heaved, forcing the handle with all my weight. Pain shot through my back.

I fainted.

The doctor came and ordered me to lie on a hard surface in bed for a week. Getting me to sit still for five minutes was a problem, getting me to lie still for a week drove us both nuts. Eric unscrewed the back lavvy door and placed it under the mattress to make my half of the marital bed into a hard surface; he was so good to me, then and always. Never a curse or a banging door in our house. (Well, not from him anyway!)

The laundry problem was solved. We bought an agitator washing boiler from the gas showroom on the never-never, at only half a crown a week. We were both working; we could afford a few luxuries. And just as well, because the alternative was to give Eric's mum our washing so that she could take it on her weekly pilgrimage to the local wash-house. I could just see Hetty, her pram full

161

of washing and her head full of gossip about her new daughter-in-law's carryings-on.

Mam said my 'growing pains' would stop when I got married. Mam was wrong. Month after month, the gut-wrenching pain and nausea left me in a weakened state for days. It was worse in the winter, with only a small brick lavvy in the backyard where I would sit shivering for hours with a blanket wrapped round me in an effort to keep warm. Icicles hung from the cistern and icy water ran down the mossy walls, giving them a green glass-like surface. Eric would bring the occasional cup of steaming tea to fortify me.

He was at a loss to help, until one day he announced, 'Try this Indian brandy. Me mate Barry says his wife was bad every month, but finds this works a treat. She swears by it.'

'OK. How much do I need?'

'A cupful.'

I was willing to try anything. It tasted putrid. It burned my gullet.

'Bloody hell! I can't drink this!'

'Just try,' he yelled.

'No, no. I 'ave tried!' I yelled back.

'Look, if you really wanted to get better, you'd drink it all right. Just hold yer nose and down it in one go. Don't be such a baby – just try it.'

I struggled, managing to down about a third of a cup before being violently sick. My mouth felt like dragon's breath. Choking tears joined my runny nose and streamed down my face. I sent Dr Crippen packing with the immortal words, 'Just you bugger off and leave me alone to die.'

Eric told his mate the next day how uncooperative I was and how I'd failed to respond to a cup of Indian brandy in one go.

'A cup of what?'

'Indian brandy.'

'Well no wonder she was bloody sick – I told you it's a *teaspoon* of Indian brandy *in a cup* of hot water.'

The 'growing pains' continued.

Eric was promoted from bus conductor to full-time bus driver. Not front-page news, but we welcomed the increase in wages. Bus conductors were paid a pittance, although we did get the occasional bonus in the form of perishable goods left on buses; if these weren't claimed by the end of the shift, Eric brought them home. Many was the time we were grateful for a bag of bananas or a packet of bacon. One time we had nothing much in the house for a square meal but Oxo cubes. I had planned to make soup using up the stale bread for dunking, when Eric turned up at the end of his shift with a fresh loaf of bread and a packet of kippers. Ravenously we scoffed the lot – talk about a variation of a theme on the loaves and fishes miracle.

We had joked about sending Ronald Biggs and his mates a begging letter; after all they were worth two and a half million quid. The Great Train Robbers were seen as modern-day Robin Hoods by a lot of working-class folk. We tended to forget that the thieves had seriously injured the engine driver. The newscasters, with tongue in cheek, reported nightly of the efforts of the police to capture the country's so-called heroes.

Never did keep up with what happened to the Great Train Robbers because the second-hand nine-inch telly that Georgie 'procured' and gave us for a wedding present conked out. We started going for walks in the evening instead.

One particular evening we pressed our noses to the window of the local funiture shop. It was then we spotted and fell in love with a multi-patterned green plastic couch and two armchairs. Much nicer than the big overstuffed chairs we were used to. The notice said they were a bargain at only four shillings a week.

'Four bob a week, what do yer reckon?' Eric nudged me. 'Go on, what do yer reckon?'

He was as bad as me. 'You know what me dad said, we shouldn't get in over our 'eads.'

'I can always clean windows for extra cash.'

We daydreamed and argued outside the shop for nearly an hour.

'We really need a headboard first,' I said. 'Yer Brylcreem's markin' the wallpaper over the bed, and what about some curtains for the front parlour? I hate the whitewashed windows.'

On and on we talked ourselves in and out of the idea.

To hell with it!

We had the suite delivered the next day. It took pride of place in front of the fireplace in the kitchen.

Modernization was a craze and we were caught up in it. (And the style police still have a warrant out for our arrest.) The ugly old carved oak doors got a bright new coat of paint on their new flush hardboard panels. Out went all the elaborately carved mahogany banisters and handrails that looked old-fashioned, they were sawn off and replaced with the elegant clean lines of orange-painted hardboard. Leaded-light windows were a bugger to clean so they were the next to go. Picture rails were discarded in favour of starting the wallpaper three feet or so down from the ceiling, edged with a patterned wallpaper border. We couldn't afford to replace the kitchen cupboards at this stage, so we gave the heavy brass handles and knobs to the rag-and-bone man (declining his lousy goldfish). Now we had nice new orange plastic handles to match the plastic light shades. My dad was furious at our fashionable colour scheme – called Eric a 'bloody protestant soft git'.

The most expensive and frustrating work to date was done by a psycho plumber who spent two weeks mucking up the plumbing system and flooding the kitchen. The entire works were put right in a weekend by a couple of unlikely butch women whom our Georgie knew. They worked day and night to provide us with the luxury of running water.

Mind you we still couldn't get our Saturday night bath, since Eric had painted the bath the previous month and the paint still wasn't dry.

Our little palace was finally taking shape.

Eat yer heart out, Mary Quant!

15

We were still in love after almost two years in our own home. We both had jobs, and my asthma attacks were less and less frequent.

February was extremely cold, 'brass-monkey weather' my dad said. One evening, blindly unaware of the impending tribulation, Eric and I arrived home at the same time. With icy fingers he opened the front door, using the solitary key hanging on a string behind the slit we had for a letter box in the middle of the front door.

We gazed, open-mouthed, at a dirty river of shoes, brushes, soiled laundry and even potatoes floating down the hallway to greet us.

The unopened bags of cement stacked in the hallway were solid lumps and our new lime green wallpaper had shrivelled up and hung limply from the wall like wilting lettuce. The new electric fire was already turning rusty. The musty smell and damage was indescribable. It didn't take long to figure out the disaster's source. We had never foreseen the possibility of burst pipes, although we had experienced them most winters as we were growing up. The main pipe above the ceiling in the kitchen had burst and judging by the bulge in the ceiling there was a lot more water still to come down.

We gazed broken-hearted at nearly two years' hard work and savings literally down the drain. Couldn't even warm ourselves, it wasn't safe to leave the power on, with water everywhere. We closed the door on the deluge and retreated to Eric's mum's to get warmed before deciding what to do next.

'I know it's a tragedy. We all face them at one time or another, you can't expect to live in England without the prospect of burst pipes. Now tomorrer you soldier on and get the insurance company round to 'ave a look.'

Eric stared at his mother. 'What insurance company? We don't know nothin' about any insurance. Nobody told us anythin' about insurance.'

After staying at Eric's mum's for the night, we took time off work the following day and laboured all through the night to salvage what was left of our bedraggled love nest, although hardly anything was worth saving. The smell of dampness and the cold was a major concern, with no obvious solution in sight.

Reluctantly I conceded I had to ask my family of tradesmen for their expert advice. None of them took any interest except for our Jacky.

'Never mind,' he said. 'I bet yer got rid of yer vermin. Only thing to get rid of now is the crabs.' Trust our Jacky, the know-all, to see a funny side.

We just couldn't laugh.

Our debts were mounting. We'd spent nearly every penny we had on repairing the first winter's flood damage. Now we were over three months behind with the mortgage payments, with no hope of catching up. I remembered what my dad had said when we told him we'd bought the house. 'You know what happens to capitalists who bite off more than they can chew? They bloody well choke.'

We continued to ignore the little brown envelopes, some still unopened, jammed behind the clock on the mantelpiece – that was until the gas was cut off.

After reading an article in the *Liverpool Echo* about a company offering up to a thousand pounds for terraced houses, I rang on the off chance to see if they were interested in Bell Road. Two men arrived the next day to check it out.

'You have a bit of subsidence in the kitchen and the bedroom above has a sloping floor,' said the bloke with a red spotted tie and a face to match. He took me outside to show me how the roof had sunk in the middle. Subsidence was apparently very common due to the damage from World War II (obviously they had never seen subsidence caused by a serving hatch – especially one hidden behind a picture of the Queen).

I gave them my best Doris Day saintly look. That did it. They thought they had me by offering only seven hundred pounds.

'Take it or leave it!' he said as he rubbed his hand over the flaky surface of his face.

'We'll take it,' I snapped. Even Mam said some houses were unlucky, and this one certainly was heading that way.

'By the way darlin', what happened to the bath?' the other bloke asked smarmy like, 'the bottom half is pink and the top half is white. Don't tell me a lovely girl like you gets her looks by bathing in pink champagne.'

I smiled coyly as I lied through my teeth. 'I dunno. It was like that when we moved in.' The real truth was we'd been invited to a swank dinner dance and I didn't have a posh frock, so Eric and I tried dyeing my wedding dress pink in the bath. The wedding dress was a dismal failure – the net part went crimson and the rest the colour of a dirty elephant. But the bottom half of the bath came up a perfectly lovely shade of pink.

'End of the month, OK girl?'

'What?'

'The end of the month. We want you out at the end of the month . . . comprendo? Sign this, here,' he said, indicating exactly where while stuffing a pen in my hand.

It was like something out of the *I Love Lucy* show. For

two days I kept meaning to talk to Eric about it, but the timing never seemed quite right. Then at teatime on the third day the same two spectacular blokes walked in without even knocking, sticking the document that I had already signed under Eric's nose.

'Just here, pal,' the smarmy one said, pointing.

'What?'

'Sign this will you pal and make sure you're out by the end of the month?'

'Why? What's goin' on? Where am I goin'?'

'Well the company's purchased this property and since the end of the month suits this sweet young thing,' he said with his arm hooked over my neck, 'that OK with you?'

A lesser man would have committed homicide at this point. Eric just nodded, dumbfounded.

We heard of a house for sale at 23 The Summit, Liscard. Had a nice ring to the name, so we went to have a look. The sign outside was from one of the local estate agents, Boughey's. Eric's sister Dotty worked for Boughey's, so that was a plus. We knocked at the door to ask for details, and the obliging owners invited us in. We were suprised how big the house was. Eight spacious rooms and all smelling of new paint. The bathroom not only had a toilet, but also a bath and a shower. We were relieved to see gas fires, as we couldn't face another winter like the one we'd just had in the damp, cold cave in Bell Road.

'Well if that doesn't beat all, look at this lovey.' Eric had found a cupboard with an ironing board that folded out from the wall. The amazing gadget was all it took to make our decision. We sat in the estate agent's office and Mr Boughey explained the Halifax Building Society's criteria on loans, having made a few scribbles on a pad.

'Sorry to disappoint you, son, but you don't earn enough to cover the payments. It's close but . . . well, all I can do is to try to get you an appointment to see their loans manager. But don't hold your breath.' Our appointment was arranged for the end of the week.

It was proving all too much for me, this buying and selling houses lark. I woke in the mornings sick as a dog with the worry, scheming on how we could make up the shortfall on Eric's earnings. I must have wanted the house pretty badly, as I was making myself ill, with my head down the toilet most days. Friday came round quickly, and the interview with the building society manager was going well until it came to income.

Sensing his reluctance, 'Eric cleans windows on his days off and gets half a crown a pop,' I lied. 'And, apart from that, there's me own wages and . . .' He didn't let me finish.

'Unfortunately we never include women's wages in our calculations of income.' It didn't seem right that this little upstart was playing judge and jury, having some control over our future.

'But I get over three pounds a week,' I stammered.

'And what if you have a baby?' he said exasperatedly, clasping his hands behind his head as he tilted his chair backwards.

'What? Oh! I see now what yer gettin' at. But I won't 'cos we need the house furnished first and we both want to wait until we're in our thirties. Besides, I've got a Dutch cap.'

His face coloured as he half-rose from his chair. 'Well, thank you for coming in. I'll be in touch,' he answered stiffly, then busied himself by thumbing through papers on his desk.

We were dismissed, but I continued to argue.

'You see, it's like this . . .'

'Yes, yes,' he put in hastily, while his eyes caressed the ceiling. 'Yes, I understand.' But he wasn't listening. 'Good day Mr Simmonds.' He shook Eric's hand after opening the door.

'Jumped-up arrogant sod never gave us a fightin'

chance.' I was choking back the tears. 'I've a good mind to punch his bloody lights out.'

Eric, as usual, was kind and said, 'He's only doin' his job, love. Anyway, what will be will be.'

'Please God, just this once – give us a fightin' chance.'

The stress of the interview made me even sicker, if that was possible, apart from being so overtired with not sleeping. The worry of where we were going to live was getting to me. I couldn't even eat, and tea and coffee tasted putrid. Now I could see what my mam meant when she said I was highly strung. I felt I had not been throwing up in vain when Eric's Dotty rang me the following Wednesday.

'Congratulations, yer've got yer house. Our Mr Boughey 'ad a word in a few of the right ears for you.'

I couldn't believe it. 'Hey, kiddo.' I said to Dotty, 'did I tell you we 'ave a dinky ironin' board that folds out from the wall?'

'Yes you did, every bloody day, in fact. I'm waitin' to see it printed in the *Liverpool Echo*.'

Once the loan was officially approved I grew impatient.

'Eric, why can't we move now?' I pestered.

'Dunno. We'll go and see if we can catch the owners tonight, I've got a split shift.'

We waited on the step of 23 The Summit, and when no-one came to the door, we peered through the windows. 'Great, looks like they've moved out already. We could move in tomorrer if we can borrer our Jacky's truck for the big stuff, the rest we can fit into the old Ford Thames van. That old bomb just might make it round the block.'

'Don't you knock my limousine – it was a good investment.'

'Liar!' I shouted. 'You said you won it in a card game.'

Even moving out had its problems. We understood when you left a house you took everything. We would make sure of that, as Dad said he thought that we were

171

dealing with Rachman, a notorious property dealer. The last few things were loaded in the car, including the washing line, the light bulbs and the dustbin.

'Oh, I've just remembered, we've forgotten the immersion heater. You go and switch the power off, and I'll unscrew it out of the cylinder,' Eric said.

I went down to the meter board and flicked all the switches. 'All done,' I shouted.

Seconds later, there was an explosion. Eric was thrown across the room. He lay semi-conscious with the melted screwdriver in his hand.

'What happened? Oh please, please talk to me. What happened?' I pleaded. His eyes bulged like Marty Feldman's as he took some time to find the words.

'You silly bitch, you just turned all the power ON. Someone must 'ave turned it off, already.'

I was overdue for a big cry, and so I cried. I cried because I could have killed my husband; I cried because I was unsure of our future; I cried because I was covered in bruises from struggling to help Eric to drag the heavy furniture down the stairs. And on top of everything else my nervous stomach was still playing havoc. I even cried about Jasper, my tortoise and my first very own pet. Being winter, Jasper had been allowed to hibernate in the kitchen in the potato rack, to keep warm. When we were packing, Eric said, 'Shall we throw this bloody thing out? I think it's dead.'

'Don't you dare! Don't you know anythin' about tortoises? It's hibernatin', stupid.'

He picked it up and peered through the shell. 'Don't think so, its head's rotted off and it stinks.' To think I'd been mopping round Jasper for months in case I disturbed him.

Didn't have much luck with animals.

We duly arrived at The Summit the next day but hadn't thought of getting any keys with all the drama and excitement.

'Don't worry, I'll go round the back and see if I can get in, if not I'll break a little window in the toilet.'

Eventually Eric opened the front door from the inside and in his poshest voice announced, 'Welcome to yer new home Mrs Simmonds,' and with that, he picked me up and carried me over the threshold, collapsing on his knees just inside the door.

'Bloody hell girl, yer a lot heavier than you look.' Like a couple of kids we rolled round the floor laughing and tickling.

Soon we realized that our few sticks of furniture looked comical, lost in such a huge house. There was just enough to furnish the kitchen and one bedroom. No matter, we had a lifetime to furnish it the way we wanted.

After a week in our new place I still couldn't hold food down and even Eric was looking piqued. He continued to do all the overtime God sent in order to pay off solicitor's fees *and* the insurance premiums. With a weekend off together, we were sitting at the kitchen table, Eric eating a fry-up of bacon and eggs I'd unenthusiastically cooked for him. Both of us were in our dressing gowns when we heard our front door bang shut. There stood an irate old geezer clutching a bunch of keys and glowering at us.

'What the bloody 'ell are you doin' 'ere?' he demanded.

'That's priceless, mate! What are *we* doin' 'ere?' Eric challenged.

'We've just bought this 'ouse. We own it,' I said, equally belligerent.

'Not bloody yet yer don't. It's still my son's 'ouse, so you two can just bugger off. The deeds and title are not sorted. It's not settled yet, not by a long chalk.'

Seemingly our occupation of the house was really trespassing, quite aside from the matter of breaking and entering before we got the full deeds to the property. The solicitors for both parties decided that the transfer could be hurried along if we paid eight pounds to the previous owners as back rent. Not knowing how we could come up with an extra eight pounds, for the sake of peace we just agreed.

I couldn't ask my dad to lend us the money, as owning houses was still a sore point with him. He was dead against owning property of any description. Only bloody Tories needed to own houses and property, according to him.

We'd worked so hard to keep our little van and now we decided it had to go to pay the bills.

'How will you get to work?' I asked Eric.

'Actually chick I was goin' to tell you, I've got me eyes on a job with the Ambulance Service where I won't need the car because the ambulance station is just round the corner in Liscard. I've got an interview this Monday, so keep yer fingers crossed.'

Eric was a dark horse. I was gradually discovering things about him and beginning to understand my mam's description of his black-and-white character. There were no grey areas; any decisions he made were clean-cut.

We painted our little van blue and I made a leather steering-wheel cover to hide the cracked one we couldn't afford to replace. With shoe polish on the tyres and freshly sewn seat covers, we had no trouble in selling our pride and joy.

'Fifty pounds, not bad seein' as we got it for nowt in the first place and it's done us well.' Eric was laughing, flinging the pound notes in the air like confetti. 'Look lovey we must put money away for the rest of the solicitor's fees and clean up the other bills, but tonight we shall dine out. What about an Indian curry? How does madam fancy a vindaloo? And if yer a good girl I may even shout yer a bottle of bubbly.'

After conjuring up a vision of an Indian curry I couldn't answer. I was back up the stairs, on my knees with my head down the lavvy.

*　　*　　*

174

Mam always made me welcome when I visited. Though she never said as much, I could tell she looked forward to my visits and hearing gossip from the office, with little stories about Sue's latest pranks. Now Eric was working on the ambulances, she was captivated by his stories, sometimes sad, sometimes funny.

The latest story I had to tell was from Eric's last tour of duty, when he had called at the home of a bedridden old codger to take him to hospital for chest X-rays. When Eric arrived, the old man was naked and helpless in bed. Eric lifted him gently from the bed and sat him carefully in a slat chair while he hunted for some pyjamas. The sparrow-like patient squawked and screeched incoherently. With an authoritative tone and firm hand, Eric told him to sit still, coaxing him gently back down. Again the old man whimpered and again Eric asserted his authority, having firmly pressed him back into the chair, until he noticed the old man had tears in his pleading eyes. Clasping the old man's hand between his hands, Eric patiently went to great pains to explain why he must take him to hospital, and why he needed to be adequately dressed. The impotent old man now had tears freely sprouting but, too weak to get off the chair, was pointing between his legs. Eric gently lifted him and still cradling him in his arms inspected the chair for sharp edges. No sharp edges, just a kitten that had been reaching up and clawing playfully at the poor old man's limp testicles as they hung tantalizingly below the slats.

Mam also had tears in her eyes, laughing at the story, before she wiped them away with the corner of her apron.

As usual she was ready with a cup of tea, cake and biscuits, which I normally devoured with great gusto as our meagre budget didn't run to such luxuries.

'Don't want none, Mam.' I pushed the plate out of sight.

'What do you mean you don't want none? There's custard squares, fresh today, yer favourite.'

'Sorry Mam, I'm really not hungry,' I mumbled.

'Yer always bloody hungry. You were born hungry, even more so lately. I can see you shootin' up like rhubarb under a shitty bucket.'

She stirred her tea with slow turns of the spoon and peered unseeingly into the cup, before she spoke again. 'How are yer growin' pains?' she asked.

'Haven't 'ad any for months. Seems like I've come right.'

Me mam stopped making swirling motions with the spoon. 'Yer not pregnant are you?'

'What do you mean?'

'I can't say it much different,' she said as she carried her cup of tea across to her armchair next to the fireplace. She plonked herself down. 'Does green go with red – I'm buggered if I know – what do you think?' she said, reaching for her knitting.

'What?' My mind was in turmoil.

She fumbled amongst the mound of knitted squares. Like Tommy Cooper attempting to conjure a rabbit out of a hat she proudly brandished a lone green square. 'Would you say I've too many of these green ones?'

'Sod yer bloody squares Mam. What do yer mean, me pregnant?'

'Well are you in the club? Because if yer not pregnant I reckon you should pay a visit to Dr Arthur. It's not right bein' poorly like that.'

How could I be? I still had six and a half years to go before I was thirty, and like I told the man at the building society, 'That's when we plan to 'ave children.'

16

Why was I crying? Why so fearful of what Eric would say? Blimey, I couldn't think straight. I read somewhere that fear is a sign of intelligence – in that case I must have grown up dead smart.

What was it Dr Arthur said? 'Three months pregnant, date of forthcoming birth around mid-January.' Glad I didn't know beforehand what the examination was about. Would have lost my nerve; besides, I wondered what the doctor's wife thought about him feeling around pregnant women's rude parts. There must be a better way to examine them, surely.

Over and over I rehearsed how I was going to break the news to Eric. Hadn't I seen it done on the telly, waiting for the right moment? Candlelit dinner maybe, or perhaps sitting in front of the fire listening to Johnny Mathis. I planned every minute detail.

He was hardly through the door, hadn't even got his coat off.

'I'm pregnant.' There it was, out of my mouth like a bad tooth. Eric looked at me blankly. Ha – poor sod didn't know what had hit him.

'What?'

'I'm pregnant.'

There was a terrible shocked silence followed by, 'How do you know? Are you sure? Who told you?' He hoisted me up and swung me round as if I was a child. 'Oh, lovey, aren't you a clever girl? Hang on, I'll put the kettle on and then you can tell me all about it.'

Eric's mum took the news badly.

'For goodness sake it's early days. Yer've only been married five minutes. My Eric's just bought you that lovely house,' she added, looking at me. 'You couldn't 'ave timed it worse.'

I fought the urge to apologize. 'Me mam is thrilled,' I lied. 'So are we.'

We left without another word.

Eric's new job on the ambulances didn't help me with an unsettled stomach, what with all the stories of blood and gore. Worse by far were the tales of the strange occurrence of fearfully deformed babies, some with no hands or hands growing out of their shoulders, and the extreme cases of babies with no limbs at all. It was all too close to home for my liking.

At six months pregnant I was still being sick. I found it difficult coping at work with the never-ending tiredness and nausea. My friend Sue with her usual sense of mischief regularly suggested bacon and fried-egg sandwiches or fish and greasy chips for lunch, knowing full well my vivid imagination made me throw up. Even the pills the doctor gave me to prevent morning sickness didn't help, other than to put me to sleep. I was good for nothing so reluctantly I said goodbye to all the friends that I'd made at J.J. Stansfields.

Eric's mum eventually came to terms with the prospect of another grandchild in the family, so much so that she began knitting. She started with small things like booties, hats and mittens.

'Have you decided on a name?' she asked Eric, without even looking at me.

'Anastasia,' was the reply. 'I've always liked that name. Possibly Darren for a boy.' Over my dead body, I thought. Darren's OK for a boy but I hadn't met anyone from Merseyside with a handle like Anastasia.

For some time I had been making jumpers on Mam's old knitting machine and selling them for a quid each. The leftover wool came in handy to make baby clothes. The problem was, navy blue, shocking pink and bottle green were not the best colours to dress a newborn baby in. Trouble started when my belly got bigger, I couldn't get close enough to the machine without getting back-ache.

True to my prediction Eric started cleaning windows part-time at half a crown a house. It took him ages as he was so soft-hearted with the cadging old buggers in the street who had him doing the high windows and inside for no extra charge. When he was on early shift at the ambulance station he also drove taxis at night and some-times at the weekend.

The stories he told made my hair curl; he even had an encounter with one of the all-time-great 'urban legends'. I didn't believe it at the time, but nowadays everyone has heard a version of this story. But Eric still believes that it's true.

'It happened about one o'clock this mornin',' Eric told me. 'I got back to the taxi yard and found me mate leanin' over the back of his taxi. Said he was waitin' for the police. The boss thought it best to call them.'

'Go on. Go on, get on with it, what happened next?'

Eric hesitated as if he was regretting starting the story.

'Bloody hell, will you get on with it.'

'Well, my mate Barry, you remember Barry? Seems he 'ad this call to pick up a fare by Duke Street Bridge. Couldn't find anyone hangin' around but when he was drivin' back along the Dock Road, four or five louts ran out of the dark yellin' for him to stop. Well you don't stop for no-one around there, so he puts his foot down. When he looked through the rear window he saw them tearin' after the car swingin' chains and throwin' bottles. He heard somethin' hit his car, but didn't stop to find out what it was till he got back to the yard, and then he saw it.'

'Saw what? What did he bloody see?'

'He said that over the boot handle was hangin' a big chain and caught up in it was four dismembered fingers. Must 'ave been wrenched out of some bloke's hand when Barry hit the gas. He's very upset.'

Blimey, there's one born every minute!

One thing we had learnt in buying a big house was that you never have enough money to heat it. With high ceilings and lots of rooms, the heating went through the roof in both senses. When you talked in our house your voice echoed round the room, and in the winter you could see your breath before you. Worst of all, when you opened the kitchen door a cold blast from the hall blew straight through.

The weather had turned bitterly cold and the Power Company was threatening to cut off our electricity. I was convinced that the bill had been paid until I challenged Eric.

He was sheepish – the horses again.

'What do you mean it was a sure thing?' I shouted. 'How could you put our money on horses?'

'I was given a hot tip on a horse. It would 'ave won too if it 'adn't fallen on the last hurdle.'

Always the same story. All we seemed to fight over recently was Eric's losses on a 'sure thing'.

'It's the only interest I 'ave, chuck, the nags and an occasional game of bowls.'

The bastards from the Power Board eventually turned the power off when Eric was on nights. I was terrified in the dark, scared of bogeymen and ghosts, but most of all I feared there could be rats lurking just waiting to get me.

Eight o'clock in the morning Eric was on his way home.

I could hear him whistling halfway down the street as I waited to hear the key in the lock. I was angry, cold and stiff from spending the night in the chair, too afraid to go to bed. I remembered all the warnings from my mam about men. Could it be she was right after all? I blew my stack.

Finally, after I finished yelling, threatening and eventually sobbing, Eric managed to calm me down.

'It was just a hobby and a chance to make a couple of bob, but if me betting upsets you I won't 'ave any more bets, honest. It's just an interest at work to 'ave a bet and follow the races on the telly. When we don't 'ave any call-outs it helps to beat the boredom.'

'How do you think I feel each time one of the neighbours says they've seen the ambulance outside the bettin' shop and asks if you're on duty. It's a wonder you 'aven't 'ad the sack before now.'

'Well, it's only when we are takin' outpatients, never when we 'ave a life and death case in the back.' He smirked.

'I wouldn't bloody put that past yer,' I muttered.

True to his word he didn't continue to back horses, but unbeknown to me Eric was now the In-house Bookie, taking bets off the other fire and ambulance workers, and worse still, holding onto them without placing them with the betting shops. Up until now he was just about financially even, but hoping for the big break and business to pick up once the news got round to the crews on the other shifts at the ambulance station.

Most Saturday afternoons when Eric wasn't on duty we shopped at Birkenhead market for crabs' legs, which I craved; visited both mams and spent the rest of the afternoon watching telly and gorging on sweets and bottles of pop. This particular Saturday was full of tension. Eric was watching steeplechasing in *Racing at Doncaster* when he started screaming and yelling.

'Fall yer bastard, fall!'

'Have yer been lyin' all this time? Eric? You promised not to back horses any more?' I grizzled.

'Shurup woman!' he shouted, pushing me out of his line of vision to the telly. He kept yelling obscenities at the box. This was an unfamiliar side to Eric, a side that I had only glimpsed on rare occasions. His emotion spent, he slumped in the chair, grabbed me where my waist used to be, and buried his head between my breasts.

'Sorry, so sorry. I didn't mean to shout and upset yer.'

'What the hell's got into yer?' I said, pushing him from me. 'Yer frightened me.'

Eric went on to explain that he had taken on a ten-bob treble from his mate at work, and (in Eric's opinion) the bet was on three donkeys with 'no chance', so he held onto the bet as we needed just ten bob to pay off the overdue rates.

The first horse surprisingly won, at 18/1, which meant nine pounds, ten shillings went on to the next horse, which also won, at 16/1. The accumulated figure of one hundred and sixty-one pounds went on to the last horse, King of Thurls, at 33/1. The horse was supposedly another no-hoper. So why was Eric turning white? The hurdle race started. King of Thurls ran next to last all the way. The favourite was ten lengths ahead. It was an eleven-horse race, and coming to the last few hurdles, six horses had fallen. King of Thurls caught up to the favourite. The favourite fell at the next-to-last fence and King of Thurls was well ahead. The sweat ran down Eric's face.

King of Thurls clipped the final fence and down he went. So did Eric. Collapsed into the chair, sweat now mingled with tears, he stammered out the inconceivable consequences.

'You realize what a hundred and sixty-one pounds at 33/1 equates to?'

Eric promised never to play bookie again.

*   *   *

It looked like we might get a white Christmas after all, judging by the snow sticking to the pavements.

Eric's mum invited us to Christmas dinner along with the rest of the Simmonds family. After our few years of marriage she appeared to finally be warming to me and accepting the marriage, although it was Hobson's bloody choice. Gratefully, I accepted. Being over eight months pregnant and broke meant that there wasn't an awful lot we could do to celebrate Christmas. Anyway, it was a lot warmer in his parents' house as they had a backyard full of coal. Eric's mum was being especially kind. Even asked me to stay the night before.

'With Eric on duty we don't want you on yer own on Christmas Eve do we?'

Everything was prepared for the festivities; we'd made the apple sauce and mince pies, we'd even wrapped the shiny sixpences in greaseproof paper and put them in the Christmas pudding.

Eric told me he had won the raffle at work for a piece of pork. We were so chuffed we could put something towards the Christmas dinner, also it was a chance to please Eric's mum. Pork was a favourite of Eric's and we could never have normally afforded a joint of meat, let alone pork. I told Eric's mum that he would bring the pork in the ambulance at lunchtime because he couldn't carry it on his bike.

Eric arrived empty-handed. 'Where's the pork?' we asked in unison.

'I didn't bring it. I didn't think you would want it.'

'Why the hell wouldn't anyone want a piece of pork?'

'Because it turned out I'd won a pig's head. I sold it to one of the blokes who said he can make brawn with it.' As an afterthought, 'Got half a crown.' He grinned.

'Great, just enough to pay for the soddin' raffle ticket,' I snorted. It was hard to see the funny side of it at the time. I wanted desperately to please his mum and family and now I felt I'd let them down.

'Don't worry,' his mum said. 'I can open the tin of ham Eric brought off the ship. Had it for a couple of years. I was saving it for a rainy day, like today.' By my reckoning the 'rainy day' was a long time coming – about eight years. So the tin of ham saved the day and in spite of the pig's head it turned out to be a great Christmas. We wandered down to the Five Bars pub at Seacombe Ferry with the family and had a singalong round the piano, started off in true Simmonds tradition by Eric's grandma. In fact it was more than tradition, she threatened to kill anyone who dared break out in song before she did.

Only person missing was George, Eric's older brother. He was a postman and doing his final Christmas delivery, which was the second delivery of the day at lunchtime. He had been doing the same round for years, therefore he got lots of tips. Problem was, not everyone paid him in cash; some paid with Christmas cheer. George wasn't a drinker. In fact George was the most sober person I ever met, very starchy and proper.

Come two o'clock, throwing-out time at the pub and George still hadn't turned up. On wobbly legs we staggered in the direction of home en masse. Everyone offered in turn to take my hand just in case I went arse over tit on the icy pavement, but I reckon they needed me for ballast. I was the only one sober, me being pregnant and all.

'Look what I found in the front garden,' Eric shouted. 'A funny-looking gnome with a red nose, dressed in postman's get-up,' he laughed, while attempting to heave legless George to his feet. George couldn't stop laughing. I could see why, when they tried to undress him and put him to bed, George had his Christmas tips money stashed everywhere: in his pockets, down his shirt, in his bag, in his hat and seemingly every spare orifice – well nearly.

A bumper Christmas all round.

*   *   *

After I left J.J. Stansfield & Sons Sue and I remained close friends. She had married Jeff, who, like Eric, was also in the emergency services, but he was a fireman. We got to know their friends, most of them from Hoylake. One couple had just returned from New Zealand. I felt I had something in common as I still had my school-prize book on New Zealand. Couldn't for the life of me figure what they were doing back on Merseyside if they or the book were to be believed. Nearly all of our other friends lived locally. Few of them could afford a car, but mostly we kept in touch through the Fire and Ambulance Service. One couple we spent a lot of time with was Yvonne and Dick Pink. (His parents had a sense of humour.)

Yvonne taught me more about practical housekeeping and budgeting in the few months I had known her than I had learnt in the past twenty-odd years. For instance, I could get broken biscuits late on a Saturday afternoon from Woolies, for half-price. I could put water in butter and whip it up to make it go further. I learnt how to cadge vegetables from the local shop for a non-existent rabbit, and bones from the butcher for non-existent dogs, all to make nourishing soup.

She told me, instead of hair conditioner, I could get my hair to shine if I rinsed it in vinegar. It worked until our Jacky put me off, saying I stank like a bloody chip shop. So I switched to beer, which my family failed to detect.

For most of my pregnancy the stomach aches persisted; I continually vomited. My worry increased daily about the baby growing inside me, since Eric's main duty at work was taking crippled babies and children to specialist hospitals round the country. Regularly I heard about babies with no limbs and how they coped with just their fingers growing out of their shoulders; and how courageous mothers coped with their delightful, bright but deformed children. It turned out that many of these

185

mothers had been given a new morning sickness drug called Thalidomide.

So what about me? I'd been swallowing a variety of pills like they were Smarties. I'd take almost anything to stop the awful nausea.

Trying to glean information from Dr Arthur about what I had been taking for the morning sickness made the last few months a living hell.

Some good news. The budget announced that tax refunds would be given for each additional family member born before 31st January 1965. According to the doctor our baby was due before then. I worked the refund out to be thirty-two pounds, which would pay for a new pram, a baby bouncer – a must for a child born in the Swinging Sixties – and an extra dozen cotton nappies.

With only ten days to go I felt better than I had in ages, until all the superstitious local old crows gave their opinions on the confinement.

'You 'aven't dropped yet, must be a girl.'

'Should take castor oil, helps the baby slide out smoother.'

'Don't nurse a cat when yer pregnant or the baby will 'ave ugly birthmarks.'

The only thing they agreed on was that I wasn't done yet, and would be at least two weeks over my time. Couldn't they understand that was unthinkable – we needed a pram. If the baby didn't come before the 31st January it would have to walk everywhere!

17

Eric was working nights on 14th January when the endless stomach ache worsened, leaving me distressed and exhausted. Unaware that I was in slow labour, I remembered the old crow's advice about the castor oil. I spent the rest of the night going both ends, not able to lie down, stand or sit. I was alone and terrified. I dragged myself to the neighbours, who let me use the phone.

My knuckles white from gripping the table, I pleaded with Eric. 'I've got unbearable growing pains. Can you bring some painkillers from work? Please hurry!'

'But I can't get away just yet, we're short-handed. I'll bring something as soon as I can. It could be when I get off duty in the morning. Sorry lovey.'

We were still talking, and with eyes screwed tight to fight off the searing pains now ripping through my back, I begged. 'It's all going wrong, I want me mam. I hurt all over. Quick, get me mam.'

'Hang on love, I'll be there in a minute.'

Eric arrived at the front door with the ambulance, and he and his mate Trevor Morgan tried to load me in the back between my contractions. I learnt too late that the castor oil had been shitty advice. I was not only frightened but very embarrassed.

After being prepped for the birth by a tart of a nurse I was put in a labour ward at Highfield Maternity Hospital.

The ward held ten or so other women in different stages of labour. The various pitches of the screams and groans sounded like the Vienna Boys Choir with sore throats. Naturally I joined in.

The tart came back, slapped me on the arse and said, 'If you carry on much longer young lady you'll be removed from the ward. It's nearly visiting time and I don't want you upsetting the visitors with your cursing and bad language.'

'Piss off.'

True to her word, I was shunted into a large tiled store cupboard along with all the linen. I continued to swear and cry in vain for my mam.

Eventually, the nurse came back with an oxygen mask, saying the oxygen in it would relax me but it didn't help. Bloody thing must have been empty.

Eric knocked off work early to be with me. With eyes like saucers he sat holding my hand until after visiting time.

'They say I 'ave to go now, but don't be afraid love, it's nowt to be frightened of.' He bent to kiss me.

'Well you can bugger off then.'

'Is there anything else you want?'

'Yes, I told you I want me mam.'

Thirty-six hours later, although in a much weakened state, I was still stroppy. The nurse was back, approaching me with a tray set with scissors and instruments. 'Keep yer hands off me. Yer not cuttin' me open. I want a proper doctor.'

Now she was all sweetness and light. 'Don't worry chuck, I'm only going to break your waters. It won't hurt, then things will be much quicker after that.'

Well I knew she was dead right – it wouldn't hurt her! But was she telling the truth or was she about to cut my belly open without an anaesthetic?

Suddenly everything happened at once. I was soaked, stripped off and changed then soaked again. I was wheeled into the delivery room without being changed for the second time. I was half aware of Eric lurking in the background. The doctor was there, telling me to push. Daft bastard – if he'd had a baby, he would know you couldn't help but bloody well push.

It was forty-two hours of heavy labour before I held our son in my arms. I was crying, Eric was crying and our son was crying the loudest.

Some far-off voice said, 'We will 'ave to pop a few stitches in where you're ripped.'

I didn't care. I was happy, lethargic and a mum. Now they could do what they wanted with me. We had a beautiful son, Darren. After dropping into oblivion I slept the sleep of the righteous. It was some hours later I woke up, having slept really heavily.

'Hey nurse, I'm hungry, where's me tea?' I called.

She held her finger to her lips to shush me. 'Sorry sweet, it's 2 a.m. nothing now until breakfast. I'm part of the night shift, only a couple of us on duty.'

I started to get upset. 'It's days since I 'ad anythin' to eat.'

'Well maybe I could make you some toast. How do yer fancy that?'

'Smashin'. Ta!'

I feasted ravenously before slipping back into a drug-induced stupor. I woke in a green-walled dormitory with twenty or so green-blanketed beds, all occupied. Instinctively, I felt my stomach. With the realization that it was empty, I yelled for my baby, not knowing the rule that apart from feeding times, babies were kept in the hospital nursery. I wasn't having that! I yelled again. In no time I was nursing him. With a flurry of activity the rest of the complaining new mothers were also handed their babies by way of a 'special treat' – today the local dignitaries were going to tour the hospital. Obviously the staff wanted to avoid any possibility of renewed outbursts of complaints from us new mums.

'Someone special to see you, Mrs Simmonds,' said the bosomy sister.

Whoever the dignitary was he spoke with measured charm. 'What have you called this young man, may I ask?'

'Darren. Yes, Darren,' I said proudly of our son, who had arrived with a thick black ready-made crew cut. He looked like a little bruiser.

'Not much like a Darren.' He laughed, looking for acknowledgement from the entourage for his half-baked wit. He continued to laugh at his own observations and proceeded to the next bed.

Cheeky bugger, but he had me thinking. 'Hey Sister, come 'ere a mo, do you think my baby looks like a Darren?'

'Yep, reckon that name would suit him down to the ground. That or Rasputin.'

Salt of the earth, Merseysiders.

Twice a week the Registrar of Births, Deaths and Marriages called at the hospital to issue birth certificates. Three shillings and ninepence for a simple certificate or twelve shillings and sixpence for a gold-edged one, inscribed in Old English writing. For me there was no debate, since I vowed my baby would always get the very best.

'What is the name of the child, madam?' the registrar asked.

I had a sudden rush of blood to the head.

'Richard. No. Richard *Eric*.' My reply surprised me; we had never considered the name Richard. After completing the rest of the details, I paid the twelve shillings and sixpence and went back to the ward.

Visiting time.

'How's me little Darren then?' Eric cooed into the cradle.

'His name's *Richard. Richard Eric*.'

'What do you mean his name's Richard Eric? I thought we decided on Darren.'

190

'Well, I was thinkin', he doesn't look much like a Darren, you 'ave to admit.'

Eric laughed, 'Well he doesn't bloody look like Dr Kildare. He and that fugitive fellow 'ave a lot to answer for. Next time you get pregnant I'm getting rid of the telly.'

'Next time? Next time? There won't be another bloody next time. I'm so sore. Do you know what it's like? Since they've sewn up my rude parts I feel like I'm sittin' on broken glass, and squattin' on this rubber ring hasn't helped.'

Eric admitted that he hadn't thought of the name Richard but he actually liked it better than Darren, although he was concerned in case the name Richard got shortened to Dick. Good job he wasn't a Faulkner or it would have been Dicky.

My stay in hospital lasted for ten days, during which time I didn't get a visit or flowers from either family. Not even a lousy card. I cried buckets all day, which was to be expected. Post-natal depression the nurse called it. Seems everyone feels the same after they give birth. Maybe so, but everyone didn't have indifferent families like ours.

After spending ten days in the hospital I couldn't help wondering how some women faced going back again. When I was leaving a hard-faced nurse said, 'See yer next year.'

'Not bloody likely you won't.'

Eric had been outside the bathroom door for nearly half an hour trying to comfort me. I couldn't be comforted, lying in the warm bath not wanting to get out.

'Please Cherry, open the door. I can hear you cryin'. Can't you tell me what's wrong? Surely things can't be all that bad. Let me in.'

Eventually I opened the door and broke into sobs telling him. 'After I 'ad the baby, you remember what they did?' Without waiting for the answer I sobbed on.

191

'Well the cow of a nurse sewed up the hole in my bum for some reason. She said that the stitches would melt. Well they 'aven't and it hurts, so how do they expect me to go to the toilet? I 'aven't been properly since Richard was born.'

'Believe me my love, they wouldn't sew the hole up in yer bum,' Eric laughed.

That did it. 'How the hell do you know? You don't know everythin'.'

Still craving the comfort of the warm water, I climbed back into the bath and sulked. Later Eric took my temperature, then called the district nurse. When she arrived she gave me an enema and a pep talk. She explained that the hole in my bum had not been sewn up like I thought; it was just a case of severe constipation resulting from the iron pills the hospital pumped into me. Apart from that, she surmised I subconsciously held back, fearing ripping my vaginal stitches.

Boy! She wasn't wrong there.

Life started getting easier. Because baby Richard came on time, the pram, the baby bouncer and two dozen nappies were all paid for by the Labour government's tax-rebate scheme.

Richard got to be the most well-known baby in the district. His pram was frequently sighted outside all the local betting shops when Eric took him for walks. He was a good baby who didn't cry much and slept well. Most days he slept in his pram outside the back kitchen door where there was at least a pretence of fresh air. I couldn't leave him on the front doorstep as the soot from the chimneys floated down into the pram. Besides, he was also a sitting target for the local pigeons. Dirty buggers.

It was nearly six o'clock one evening and everywhere was quiet – we'd had fish and chips for tea and Eric was getting ready for work. Richard still hadn't woken for a feed.

'I think you should bring him in now, Cherry before it gets too damp outside, and I want to give him a cuddle before I go on duty.'

I stood at the back door in a cold sweat, words strangled in my throat.

'Someone's taken me baby. Oh God please, please, no,' I cried out.

Eric was beside me in a split second, shaking me by the shoulders.

'When did you last check him?' he shouted into my face.

My mind went blank. I couldn't think. 'Dunno, before tea,' I shouted back hysterically.

'Calm down Cherry, you must concentrate. What was Richard dressed in?'

I was in a frenzy, wondering why he wanted to know what he was dressed in. Suddenly I realized Eric was going to contact the police. It was all too much, too terrifying to take in. Numb with shock I just stood silently and unseeingly shaking my head. Heaven help us.

'Calm down, Cherry. I'll take you to yer mam's, and then I'll go on to the police station. Did you hear what I said? Better we run down the back streets, quicker than waitin' for a bus. Are you sure yer up to it?'

He didn't wait for an answer before he threaded my limp arms through my coat. Hand in hand we ran through the dark streets, turning left into Mill Lane and running to the end of the block of shops before turning right. One shop, with a sprinkling of customers, still had its lights on.

It was the chip shop. And outside the chip shop we spotted Richard's pram with Richard safely inside, gurgling away. I was speechless – understandably, Eric was more than upset with me.

'How could you do it? How the hell could you leave our baby in a pram outside the chip shop and come home without him? Sometimes, Cherry, words bloody fail me.'

'I'm sorry, so sorry,' I cried. 'Please, I'm so sorry. It's

hard to remember wheeling the pram to the shops. I was so concerned with wanting to get home before the chips got cold, I must 'ave forgotten him.'

I was still trembling as I reached for my baby. Eric's anger soon turned to relief and grateful laugher.

'Sod work. I'll ring in sick so we can 'ave a quiet night together, just the three of us. Please Cherry, stop cryin'. Everythin's OK now.'

The lovely bedroom-cum-nursery we'd done up for Richard looked delightful with the Rupert the Bear transfers on the white-painted furniture. Only problem was we couldn't afford to heat the room during the extreme winter. The paraffin heater in the hall proved next to useless as ice formed on the inside of the windows. We survived the bitter weather by going to bed after tea where we all snuggled together in sleeping bags for extra warmth, falling asleep listening to Radio Luxembourg.

'This just can't go on,' Eric complained. 'It's the coldest winter on record, with all me wages going on heating and trying to keep the baby warm. Besides we'll never be able to afford to furnish this place, not now anyway. How about we keep our eyes open for a smaller house?'

The following autumn Eric was on duty picking up a patient from Wallasey village when he noticed the house next door to his patient pick-up had a For Sale sign outside. Like most post-war houses it was a compact pebble-dashed semi-detached, with bay windows. Eric was impressed with the unobstructed view over to Bidston Windmill and the absence of nosy neighbours to look into the backyard.

Once again, we tried the direct approach by knocking on the front door. Immediately, Eric recognized the owner from his schooldays, so we were invited in and shown through their home except for the middle bed-room where their son, whom they didn't want disturbed, was still sleeping. Such an extraordinarily warm, cosy house, but we were more worldly now and would seek a second opinion, someone to give it the once-over. On our next visit we turned up with our Teddy in tow. Again, we weren't allowed to disturb their sleeping child in the middle bedroom. The house passed inspection, so everyone shook hands on our agreement to purchase, pending the sale of our house in The Summit.

We were so excited, although we didn't know what we were going to do about selling our own house. Eric took the initiative and stuck a For Sale sign in the front garden. The paint on the sign barely had a chance to dry before a young couple fronted up. Hard to believe – like us, they were so taken with the ironing board that folded out from the wall they didn't give a thought to heating the place. We didn't tell them that the bloody ironing board was positioned too high on the wall, so unless you were seven feet tall or stood on a box to iron, it was as much use as a chocolate teapot.

Caveat emptor!

After getting the nod from our solicitor that our house sale was definitely going to go ahead, we settled the contract and cautiously moved into the little semi-detached in Mosslands Drive. While we were busy unpacking boxes and putting bits away, one of our helpers, who had just completed a tour of inspection of the house, said, 'Hey, do you know what's wrong with the ceiling in the middle bedroom?'

'No, you whistle it and I'll sing it,' I joked.

'I'm serious, girl. I'm asking you, what's wrong with the ceiling in the middle bedroom?'

'Why? What do you think's wrong with it?'

'Absolutely nothing – there isn't one.'

We eventually learnt that the water-holding tank had come through the ceiling (along with all the plumbing) during the same winter we had the flood in Bell Road.

The previous owners had conjured up a sleeping child to avoid repairing the ceiling, after they had replaced the holding tank and fixed the plumbing. We sure learnt the hard way.

Caveat emptor!

For the most part, the house was modern and cosy. We met our immediate neighbour Joyce, a lovely lady. She told us that her husband Ken was a detective inspector, with the Wallasey police, which I thought could be a bit of a problem once he found out my maiden name was Faulkner. I was right – it didn't take him long. We saw him eyeing our visitors with suspicion. Obviously he knew all about the Faulkner boys.

After we settled in we had trouble with the electricity supply. We had a word with our Georgie.

'It's obvious,' he scoffed, 'yer another MANWEB [Merseyside and North West Electricity Board] benevolent society.'

'Say that in English will yer?'

'Charlie, a bloke from the King's Arms pub, rigged some of the local electricity meters so that they didn't register all the units that were used.'

Small wonder the house was warm and cosy. Our meter was so obliging that, if we didn't have enough appliances plugged in, the meter wheel actually went backwards. We thought that the electric-meter reader would soon get suspicious about the few units registering on the meter so we eventually bought a gas fire for display purposes only, the pipes disappearing through the floor to nowhere.

One cold, bleak, snowy winter's day there was a knock at the door. I opened it to find our neighbour, the detective inspector. I kept my foot behind the door in case he caught the blast of warm air wafting through the house.

'I've just driven down the road opposite your house, and being on a hill, it gives an overview of all the roofs below. What amazes me is that your roof is the only one

196

in the street with no snow sticking to it. Snow lands, melts, and runs off. What do you make of that?'

I thought I would choke. Not very convincingly I stammered, 'Dunno nothin' about roofs, you will 'ave to talk to Eric when he comes home.'

Now fixing me with a hard stare, Ken quizzed, 'By the way, what are those brothers of yours up to?'

I told him I neither knew nor cared what they were up to. Without waiting for further comment I slammed the door and leant back against it. With a long sigh I vowed to find this Charlie bloke who had rigged the meter, and get him to make it right. But Charlie's meter-fiddling days were over – we learnt he fiddled one meter too many and blew his arm off. He wasn't having much luck. His previous venture was to empty the coins from his gas meter into the electric and vice versa, depending on which inspector was due to call. One fateful day his son spotted the meter reader coming up the street.

'Dad, it's the gas man.'

The electricity meter was quickly emptied to replace the money he had taken from the gas meter. Charlie had time in gaol to reflect on his son's ignorance in mistaking the gas inspector's uniform for the electricity inspector's.

The day after Detective Ken's visit I fronted up to the Power Board, tongue firmly in cheek, telling them we were having problems with the meter, which was making a funny buzzing noise. The following week a nice man, somewhat perplexed, obligingly changed it for a new one.

We were back to being cold and hard up, but we could at least sleep at night.

18

It was a long walk to my mam's house, but I called twice a week when she had time off from the shop. She sat surrounded by knitted cushions, puffing on her Woodbines and knitting squares by the dozen with wool unravelled from old sweaters. Over the years she had sewn hundreds of squares together to make patchwork blankets. She still never said she was glad to see me, but now I was a mother I had a little more insight and understanding of her total demoralization. Every time I left to go home it was always the same.

'Take that packet of bacon with you before it goes off, yer dad won't eat it.' Or she would say, 'Take the rest of the cake home. We don't like it. Chuck it in the bin if you don't want it.' She was trying to make it easier for me to accept her thoughtful little luxuries, but I never had any problems saying 'Yes'.

Occasionally she would slip me a quid. 'Get the baby something.' For years she subsidized our meagre groceries.

She found it so easy to give and so hard to receive.

When would the screaming stop? I gazed desperately into the cot, not knowing what to do next. Oh why was Eric always on duty when I needed him? Richard's screaming turned to gasping and choking. He was violently sick, his eyes rolling. All my efforts to comfort him were fruitless. Before I knew it he went into a fit.

'Please come home. Hurry.' I begged Eric, over the phone. 'I don't know what to do. I can't hear the baby breathing.'

Within minutes a black limousine screeched to a halt outside the front door. Eric had arrived. All the ambulances were out on emergency calls so he'd taken the boss's car. After one look at Richard, Eric bundled him up and we sped off towards St Catherine's Children's Hospital in Birkenhead.

'Not this time please God,' I prayed. 'Please don't let the bridges be raised.'

God must have heard my prayer. Only Duke Street Bridge was raised.

Our child was turning blue and having difficulty breathing, as was I. My heart pounded as Eric took a diversion to the Penny Bridge, stopping only to check Richard's oxygen before he radioed ahead to the hospital. The nurse at the door took Richard from my arms and ordered us to wait in the lobby. Nursing staff, shrouded with masks and gowns, rushed around; nobody talked to us.

After a long silent wait we discovered that Richard had been sent to intensive care isolation.

Nobody explained why. I reprimanded myself for the rotten mother I was, for not knowing enough about children.

'He's not going to die is he?' My piteous appeal remained unanswered.

'Hang on, love. Whatever happens Richard is in the best hands and we've done all we can,' Eric said, his own eyes swimming with tears.

After several hours sitting alone in a white and stainless steel ancillary room, we were collected and taken down endless corridors to a sterile ward. A doctor wearing a mask and gown told us that we must dress in protective clothing if we wanted to have five minutes with our son.

My knees gave way as I looked at our child attached to tubes and flashing gadgets to monitor his vital signs. At least he *had* vital signs.

The doctor put his hand on Eric's shoulder. 'We will ring you if we need to get in touch during the night. The paediatrician will see him in the morning.' There was nothing else anyone could do and he insisted we go home and get some sleep. Without adding another word the night nurse patted Eric comfortingly on the back before she abandoned us. We just stood there, at a loss as to what to do next.

'Where now,' Eric asked.

'I want me mam. I want to see me mam.'

Eric checked his watch and said he didn't think that it was a good idea, but with my voice getting higher with hysteria, he reluctantly agreed.

Mam and Dad had just got back from the Brighton. Dad was sitting at the table tackling his plate of tripe, while Mam gazed into space, smoking. The fact that it was after eleven o'clock and no-one ever visited them at that time of night didn't seem to register as odd with either of them. Mam seemed to be in a receptive mood and welcomed us with her glazed smile. They both had a skinful, that much was obvious.

'Fancy a cuppa?' Dad asked hospitably.

It all came out in a rush. 'Our baby is sick. He could die. He's in St Cath's. I don't know what to do because they won't let me stay with him and won't even tell us what's wrong. I can't bear it – what should we do?'

My mam calmly stubbed out her cigarette and attacked a fresh packet.

'Poor little mite,' she said blearily. 'Well love, babies are born and babies are taken away from you. That's yer lot in life.' Then she shrugged. 'And yer just 'ave to make the best of it. Anyhow, yer've still got Eric.

That's a lot to be thankful for, 'cos good men are rare these days.'

Her calm acceptance of the situation made me sick. I looked to Eric. 'Please take me home. I should 'ave known better than to try talkin' to *them* at this time of night.'

Eric dropped me back at home, returned the limousine to the ambulance station and arranged for a substitute man to take over his duty for the night.

We never really found out why Richard was in intensive care and isolation, but it was to be the first of many asthma attacks that plagued him. After over twenty long, hard years of my own asthma, I had failed to recognize the first threatening signs in my own child thrashing about fighting for breath. Richard survived many more severe asthma attacks. At least as time went by we were able to recognize the warning signs.

There was a note in our letter box. Ken, the detective inspector from next door, wanted to interview Eric urgently. He left his contact phone number, which put me in a flat spin. What had he heard? What had we done wrong?

'Don't worry Cherry, it'll be about work. When he comes at six o'clock tonight I'll take him into the front parlour.'

'What do you mean about work? Why, what happened?'

'Don't worry, I'll tell you later.'

'Later won't do. I want to know now.'

I prised the story from him. It seemed Eric was witness in a murder case. He took his ambulance to an emergency call at the brickworks in Moreton. The caller said he had found his friend beaten and strangled.

When Eric arrived it was apparent to him that the patient was well and truly dead. After calling the police on his radio he tried to comfort the distressed friend as he treated him for shock.

201

During the grilling in our front parlour, Ken told Eric that the man who called the ambulance was in the holding cells, their only murder suspect at that stage.

'Wouldn't like Ken interrogating me as a murder suspect. I was only a witness and he put me through the bloody mangle. Scared me shitless he did with his questions.'

Eric was convinced that the police were barking up the wrong tree. 'If there's one thing I do know, it's people. And this bloke was so nice, and so concerned about his friend. The police are grasping at straws.'

Later that night Ken called to thank Eric for his help, informing him they had in fact arrested their suspect, the man who called for the ambulance. He had even confessed that he had killed his friend after a heated argument.

So much for my husband the detective.

Marriage and motherhood agreed with me. We were coming up to our seventh wedding anniversary. Eric and I were not only lovers; he was the first male I learnt to trust. Fancy having a man in my life that could accept my ways, and me, without me being cursed, violated or belittled.

Having heard about the seven-year itch and being superstitious, I was afraid something might spoil our happiness, a happiness that deep down I felt I didn't deserve. With this in mind I was reluctant to rock the boat by broaching any subject that might upset him, for instance, my going back to work. Goodness knows we needed the money, but more than that, I craved the stimulation and companionship of other adults. After growing as a solitary being, I still lacked confidence, although outwardly I was cocky or 'a class act', as my dad would say. Anyway I had a hunch that three-year-old Richard would not only enjoy, but also benefit from playing with children of his own age.

I met Brenda, a friend of mine from school, in the knickers department of Marks & Spencer's. She told me she worked for her dad who owned a big plant business in Cleveland Street, Birkenhead and who was looking for someone, only part-time mind, to work in the office doing accounts. Ten o'clock until three; good money, and she said the job was mine if I wanted it.

'Great! Ta.'

'Start on Monday if you can. Just turn up.'

At first Eric was adamant. But the money was too good to resist.

'I hope you told her no, that yer 'ave a kid not at school yet.'

'Eight pounds a week, can you believe it? Eight pounds a week. Only three pounds less than you get for all them hours and you shovellin' bodies off the street an' all.' I finally convinced Eric to let me try for just a week.

Ann, the lady down the road, said that she would love to look after Richard, as it would be company for her two infants. She used to be a nurse and adored children; and Richard got on famously with her kids.

I was looking forward to working at a plant nursery. We'd never had a proper garden. For some reason I'd always had jobs involving machinery, workshops, grease and oil. On my first day I got off the bus at Cleveland Street, Birkenhead and started looking for a large building with flowers and trees outside. After walking up and down for ages my feet were killing me, but all I could see were workshops, factories and big yards with huge machines painted the colour of egg yolk.

I finally noticed that one of the buildings had a sign, 'Stevenson Plant Limited'. The nursery must be tucked in behind there, I thought, so I entered. After I rang the bell for attention a young lady at reception opened a little glass sliding panel.

'Yes? Can I help yer?'

'I'm lookin' for a flower shop,' I said politely. 'I've

walked one end of the street to the other and I can't find it, and me soddin' feet are killin' me.'

'Don't know no flower shops, girl. 'Ave yer got a street number?' I handed her the card with the address on. She burst out laughing as she read 'Stevenson Plant Ltd, Cleveland Street, Birkenhead'.

'Oh girl, that's us. We're Stevenson Plant.'

'So where's the bloomin' flowers?'

'We ain't got none. We're a plant hire company, yer know, PLANT hire? Machines for buildin' roads, puttin' in drains and liftin' things. PLANT! 'Aven't yer heard of them big yellow buggers being called plant and equipment?'

'Oh hell. I knew it was too good to be true. I thought it was plants hire,' I muttered. 'Trust me to read the card wrong.'

I'm still waiting to get a job in a flower or plant nursery. But in spite of my original disappointment, I enjoyed the job with Stevenson's where I was given a lot of responsibility. Mr Stevenson my boss liked me; what was more, he liked Eric. He took a real shine to him. In fact he gave him a job repainting the big yellow machines for five bob an hour, when he wasn't on duty at the ambulance station. This took some of the pressure off and Eric stopped taxi driving and cleaning windows, so we could have more time together.

Everything was coming up roses.

Richard had another crippling asthma attack, brought on by playing with next door's cat. I took him back to St Catherine's Children's Hospital where he was immediately admitted. He was the first child to be privileged to use an expensive new piece of hospital equipment. It was a scary-looking tent-like contraption that covered Richard and the whole top half of his bed. A small machine pumped steam into the tent through tubes. Richard was terrified, all the while struggling to breathe.

204

The sister tried to calm him down as the tent filled with vapour.

'Don't be afraid, sweetheart. It's only a steam machine; we call it Puffing Billy.'

When they got him settled we were finally allowed back in to see Richard breathing easier and sitting up. With enormous eyes he stared at us walking down the large ward towards him. Unblinking he yelled at us, 'Hey Dad, look at me, I've got a new machine,' gasp, gasp.

'It's called Fuckin' Billy.'

I swear he didn't get that kind of language from *me*.

19

Dad seemed to have aged; become frail, even missed a few nights at the Brighton, said he couldn't make it down the back alleyway. Somehow he didn't have the same zest. He'd completely lost interest in playing his beloved banjo, although he was only allowed to play it indoors at weekends now anyway, since he had been murdering the ukulele as well as the banjo, driving everyone round the bend with his rotten imitations of George Formby.

Because I was worried I dropped in at Littledale Road as often as I could.

Mam said, 'He's OK, just under the weather, but you should know we 'ave 'ad the shop up for sale for some time. We simply can't carry on any longer. It's gettin' too much for us. Problem is, no bugger has any money. Yer dad wants to run the stock down and close the doors. Such a bloody shame. Sad end to a good little business.' She was whispering even though we were alone.

The following Saturday I stood looking round the shabby run-down shop. Dad crouched behind the counter, a shadowy pathetic figure, almost willing the customers to stay away. After making Dad a cup of tea, I stayed to keep him company. As there was sod-all stock to worry about, we had time for a heart-to-heart. I was surprised when he started to confide in me about the imminent state of collapse.

'Yours or the shop's Dad?' I tried to joke.

'Both.'

'What's the shop worth, do yer think?'

'Dunno. Dunno anythin' any more,' he mumbled in a dejected tone.

'We did hope for six hundred pounds,' chipped in my mam, who had just been out to buy a 'nice piece of fish' to tickle the old sod's appetite. She went through the back and hung up her coat. 'Now where was I? Oh yes, like I said, good little business. We don't make a hell of a lot of money you understand, but it's done us OK, helped us get a few comforts around us. Would suit you and Eric down to the ground, wouldn't it Paddy?'

Dad just nodded.

'And Richard could stay with you durin' the day till he starts school.'

Not that she was twisting my arm or anything.

That night I lay awake until after three o'clock, my mind doing overtime, wanting to buy the shop and trying to work out how we could afford it. But who would lend us six hundred quid? The fact was . . . no-one.

As the weeks ticked by, I discovered my dad was now regularly attending Central Hospital in Liscard. Said it was for his chesty cough but Mam thought it was probably his heart. Patty was sure it was his piles. We were all guessing, as Mam wouldn't go with him to find out. Her morbid insistence was due to her idea that once they get you inside those places, the only way you come out is in a wooden box.

'I've got some good news,' I announced almost before I was through the door. 'Eric and I would like yer shop.'

Mam, who had up to that moment been memorizing the racing page (her favourite jockey was no longer Lester Piggott, but Gordon Richards), put down her paper and looked at me over the top of her glasses. Dad sat motionless.

For once I had their undivided attention.

They looked hopeful. 'But, hang on,' I said, 'there's a catch. Eric and I talked it over and we decided that the only way we could take over the shop is if you would let us pay it off on the never-never. We'd give you five or ten quid out of the takin's every week till it was paid for – and you could 'ave yer paraffin and cat food for nowt.'

I never really expected them to go for it, but they were more worn out than I realized. 'Yes,' they snapped in unison, fired with relief and hope. Dad's spirits lifted visibly and his enthusiasm was infectious.

'I'm sure you won't be disappointed, chuck. The hours are long for small profit, but quick return. Yer mam can show yer the ropes.' Then, as though it was his own original thought, 'And Eric can give yer a hand on his days off duty.'

The deal was sealed with hugs all round.

We took over the shop on the first Monday in January 1968. Unfortunately Eric was on ambulance duty, much to his disappointment. Dad sat behind the counter ordering me around and telling all the old cronies who came in for their regular natter, 'This is our baby, the youngest of nine. She and her husband own the business now. Yer will 'ave to speak nicely to 'er if yer want to keep gettin' yer bits on tick.'

Good old Dad never changed, long on sympathy – short on cash.

An ambulance stopped outside the shop. As usual, a small crowd of ghoulish, goggling women and push-chaired toddlers clamoured very quickly around the shop door to get a look. They probably hoped to find out if some unfortunate had met a tragic end or was being whisked off to hospital – or better still the morgue.

'Sorry to disappoint yer, ladies,' Eric said, pushing past them laughing, before calling to me as he came through the door. 'How much 'ave yer taken?'

'Nearly thirty bob,' I laughed, 'and it's only ten o'clock.'

Lunchtime – same procedure. Without getting out of the ambulance parked at the kerb this time Eric yelled, 'How much now?'

'Seven quid.'

'Can't stop. I've got to drop a patient off at Clatterbridge Hospital. I'll call in on the way back.'

At the end of the day Dad and I counted over twelve quid.

Dad was overjoyed at the amount, but cautioned that it was just curiosity that brought the locals in that day.

'Mustn't be disappointed when the takin's settle down.'

The takings never settled down. They continued to rise. Some weeks we even managed to give Mam ten quid out of the till.

We were grateful for the custom of shops closing on Wednesday afternoons, as we needed to use this time to source a variety of fancy goods as well as any new lines to sell.

The real treat for us was driving miles to the potteries in Stoke-on-Trent to buy up the seconds. On some of these buying sprees we got to fossick through the warehouses in Manchester for fancy goods. We were always excited at the prospect of arguing and bargaining with the spivs who seemed to have control over the Manchester fancy goods industry. We darted through the back streets into warehouses and wholesale showrooms – veritable Aladdin's caves full of tat. We bought up cheap table lamps, sewing stools, painted plaster ornaments, plastic lampshades, nodding-head dogs, cuddly toys, brightly coloured mop buckets, washing-up bowls and watering cans. The choice was endless. Much to the amusement of the spivs Richard learnt to do his own bartering, and never left without a battery-operated toy or a stuffed bear added to our bill.

To round off our contribution to the history of post-war commerce we always stopped on the journey home at the Little Chef transport café on East Lancashire Road for a big fry-up with mushy peas and a pot of tea.

Our little business grew very quickly. We were now supplying the bingo halls with a variety of prizes. The bingo craze was everywhere. Bored housewives, lonely pensioners and kids wagging school would spend hours mesmerized by the floating numbered balls. When the lucky winners shouted 'House' they were rewarded. Often the prize was an orange pedal bin with a pop-up lid, or a set of 'tasteful' plastic table-mats depicting the Mona Lisa.

Eric's mum was an angel of mercy to us during these hectic days when she brought us fried-egg sandwiches at lunchtime because we didn't get a proper lunch break. She sometimes took Richard with her to the pensioners club where she played the piano in the afternoons to entertain the oldies. Richard helped entertain them too. He became the star attraction with his rendition of our Georgie's version of Little Miss Muffet.

Little Miss Muffet sat on her tuffet
Her knickers all tattered and torn
It wasn't the spider that sat down beside her
It was Little Boy Blue with his horn.

He always came home with his pockets stuffed with pennies and sweets.

When Richard was nearly four, although delicate in stature, he was certainly not delicate by nature. He was spending too much time in the company of adults, often repeating very personal and private conversations – always at the wrong time. One day he announced, to a shop full of customers, 'My mummy can't 'ave any more children.'

That was news to me, so for the benefit of the gaping audience I challenged him. 'Why is that son?'

'Mummy you know why; 'cos we 'aven't got enough knives and forks.'

He was ready for school all right. He was inquisitive, he was bright, and he was a real pain in the arse. Maybe he was ready for an early start in a private school?

We thought that Mary Mount Convent School might suit Richard. Despite my own mixed feelings about the Catholic Church, we decided to interview the Mother Superior to see what benefits Richard would get for our money.

We soon discovered that we were the ones to be interviewed.

Fortunately we had parked our rattling old van outside the school grounds, as it was evident by the cars in the car park that this school was not taking in any old riff-raff. By the time the Mother Superior had finished giving us the third degree you would have thought we owned a chain of supermarkets and not a corner shop. Richard was duly accepted and enrolled within the month.

We watched him being escorted across the school playground on his first day, his tiny hand grasped firmly by an Amazon in flowing black garb, Sister Aquinas. All we could see of Richard was a head just visible over a huge satchel covering the whole of his back, with his skinny wobbly legs looking like bits of string hanging below. I cried all the way home, feeling like I'd put him down the mines.

By the end of Richard's first week, this outraged mother was up at the convent to rip Sister Aquinas's throat out for strapping my son. His crime it seemed was falling asleep at his desk during the afternoon, no less. Poor little bugger.

Not giving her a chance to get a word in, I faced the sister in an explosive rage. Trying hard not to swear, I challenged her about Richard's need for an afternoon nap. 'What about compassion? What about Christianity?' On and on I maligned her until I finally reached the end

211

of my tether. A gentle, serene smile crossed her saintly face.

She spoke in her soft Irish brogue. 'To be sure he is but a dear little wee mite, such a sweet boy. You are quite correct, he does tend to sleep through the afternoon break, and as always I put a pillow under his dear wee head for comfort.' With that she bent down and, holding Richard's face between her hands, kissed him softly on the cheek.

Now squeakless, I gave him a questioning glare. He looked straight back at me and gave me an enormous wide-eyed grin.

'So I lied.'

Still beaming he waited for my response. I was forced to control myself, smiling benignly, having recognized the Faulkner genes manifesting in my 'darling' son. Between gritted teeth, I vowed to respond in the privacy of our home.

There were many fund-raising weekends held at the convent, but we didn't get involved. Too busy, and apart from that, I wouldn't have been confident enough to mix with the affluent local families.

One particular fund-raising effort was a bottle drive.

Now that was simple, something I *could* participate in. We went into business right at the start of the new age of polishes, cleaners and aerosols. We coaxed our customers into giving up their old habits, such as using scrunched-up newspapers for cleaning their windows. We endorsed the rumour that dolly blues, ammonia, etc, were only used by the unenlightened and unsophisticated. (Well, there was no profit for us in *them*.)

I sent Richard to school with a bottle of bleach, a bottle of disinfectant, and a bottle of Ton Tar liquid soap, which we usually sold separately for a shilling a bottle or any three for half a crown.

'Hey Mummy, Sister Aquinas threw yer bottles in the rubbish bin today.'

More bloody lies from my two-faced little darling, I thought. 'So why do you think she would do that, son?'

'Dunno.'

When I collected Richard from school at three thirty I got chatty with one of the other mothers about the bottle collection. I told her of Richard's lies about the nuns throwing our donation of good cleaning gear in the rubbish bin.

She gave me a scathing glare before speaking. 'My dear woman, that would go without saying I should think.'

'Why? So what did you donate?' I asked.

'Champagne. Usually a decent label port or wine, even bath salts and perfume are acceptable – never bleach, I've never heard of anyone sending an assemblage of cleaning purgatives, that's the best yet. Wait until I tell the Parents' Committee.'

Toffee-nosed bitch!

I was pleasantly surprised to discover that two other shopkeepers on Brighton Street sent their children to Mary Mount Convent School. Before long we got chatting and set up a car pool. It was good to talk to someone with a bit more insight into private school etiquette, so I could learn what was expected of us. After a few brief conversations, we came to the conclusion that Eric and I should never enter the school gates with the old van when it was our turn to collect the children.

During the summer our turnover was less reliant on labour-intensive, low-profit lines like paraffin and fuel, so Eric and I had a bit more time and money. We could afford to visit friends, invite them to dinner, and even take in a few shows. We saw Shirley Bassey, Johnny Mathis, Emile Ford and the Checkmates and Norman Wisdom at the Liverpool Empire. Travelling a bit further afield was no problem since we had recently purchased a Standard Vanguard for a hundred quid – even if it too was a clapped-out old boneshaker.

213

One evening we had been to see Cliff Richard. On the way home we walked down Church Street with two drink containers filled with water from the washrooms, just enough to get our car through the Mersey Tunnel before the leaking radiator ran dry. We had just got through to the Birkenhead side when the number plate dropped off. When I got out of the car to pick it up, the wind caught the passenger door and blew away the lino that we used to replace the missing side windows. Then to top it off the engine died on us.

The bloody car wouldn't budge. Eric tried to crank it back into life without any success. After pushing the car into a side street, we faced the long walk home. The next day we rang a local wreckers' yard and told the boss we would let him have it for a steal – thirty quid. He rang back later that day and said our car was a sodding eyesore; he would tow it away and dump it if *we* gave *him* ten quid.

I learnt that, like us, Lillian and Ray from the greengrocer's shop were struggling financially to keep their children at the convent. Lillian worked long hard hours; whenever she got a rare few minutes' break she would nip into our shop for a cuppa and a moan. We became soulmates. She looked after my shop when I did the fuel deliveries, and I looked after her shop when she did the rounds of the streets dropping off bags of spuds and new-laid eggs to the gentry.

'Give us a lend of your boots will you, kiddo?' she said one rainy day. 'I've got deliveries to do and my shoes let in the water.'

I took my boots off and handed them to her.

'There's holes in the toes,' she shrieked. 'They're worse than mine! How come I never even noticed the holes in your boots when you wore them?'

'Well no, you wouldn't,' I laughed. 'I put shoe polish on my socks so yer can't tell there's any holes, unless you're down on yer bleedin' knees.'

'We've got no money but we do see life, hey kiddo?' she laughed.

We were losing stock, including rolls of Fablon and Contact vinyl off the display stand. At 3/9d a yard we didn't sell much, so we were puzzled about their disappearance. One night I remembered I had forgotten to switch the lights off in the storeroom, and returned to the shop to find several raggy-arsed kids lying on their bellies with one arm poked through the letter box at the bottom of the door. They were using an unravelled wire coat-hanger to hook the rolls of vinyl from the stand near the door and dragging them through the oversized letter box, plus anything else they hooked within range as a bonus.

So this was why hordes of the local schoolkids were walking around brandishing blue or pink gingham vinyl-covered exercise books. Compliments of Faulkner's, thank you very much!

Toilet rolls – now there was a funny thing. Through necessity I soon became expert at noticing what stock we bought more of than we sold, and toilet rolls were in that mystic category. Always disappearing without trace!

'Don't you think yer being a bit paranoid, love. I mean, who would nick bog paper?' my dad laughed.

Detective Cherry scanned every customer who hovered over the open basket of 6d toilet rolls at the entrance to the shop. Much to Dad's amusement I was unrelenting in my surveillance, watching for a clue.

Then I spotted him, the bog-roll thief. An old man in a big overcoat was hanging suspiciously round the basket. My heart was hammering in my chest as he slithered away – yes, the two pink ones, which I had strategically placed on top a few minutes earlier, were missing.

Like a robber's dog I legged it down the road in hot pursuit, yelling for him to stop. Cheeky bugger just kept walking. I was so outraged when I caught him outside Sayer's cake shop, I shoved him up against the shop window. He stood wide-eyed and open-mouthed while I frisked him, as a small crowd gathered to see what the commotion was.

Nothing, he had bloody nothing on him. I couldn't believe it. He'd taken nothing of ours. I felt a rush of blood to my face, realizing I had overreacted. This poor astonished old man was riveted to the spot, his bony Adam's apple jerking up and down his scraggy neck. Oh, no. My hands brushed at imaginary crumbs or some such, from the wide-eyed old man's coat. Attempting to tidy him up, I spluttered some sort of apology while patting his arm. 'I'm sorry mister, ever so sorry.'

I stumbled back to the shop and burst into tears.

'What the hell was all that about?' my dad questioned. 'I saw you doing a Roger Bannister down the road.'

I sobbed, 'I thought he nicked me bog rolls. Honestly Dad, we lose so many. I feel such a bloody fool, everyone gawkin' at me like that. It's a wonder he didn't 'ave me arrested. I think I'm goin' to be sick.'

I looked at my dad who was rubbing his hands across his face and grinning.

'So what's tickled yer fancy?' I snapped.

'Hang on love, I've got an idea,' he said, going out of the door.

He came back carrying two pink toilet rolls. I couldn't believe my eyes.

'Where did they come from? Don't tell me *you're* the phantom bog-roll nicker?'

'Course not. I thought to meself, what would I do if I nicked somethin' and some crazy madwoman was hot on me heels, screamin' after me?' He went on, 'Get rid of the evidence. And that's exactly what the crafty old swine did. He saw yer comin' in the reflection of the shop window and threw the bog rolls down the cellar steps at the side of the shop. Funny, that old swine must 'ave been doin' it for years. He always 'ad an 'abit of hangin'

216

around the specials at the front door. Never bought anythin' all the time me and yer mam 'ad the shop.'

I started to laugh through my tears, as I was still teary-eyed, outraged someone would steal from an honest person like me; well, almost honest.

Our little corner shop was bursting at the seams and we had given a lot of thought to employing someone who could help on the busy days, and also run the shop while we visited wholesalers and swag shops. Unfortunately I had a real problem with trusting strangers. So many bad experiences in life had taught me not to. Like many a dog that's been kicked, and will never trust again.

The shop was making enough to support the three of us, so I felt excited and apprehensive when Eric suggested he leave the Ambulance Service and we work together in the shop. But it didn't quite work out like that . . .

We were still trying to decide what to do when my sister Dolly told us of a shop coming empty near her house in Poulton Road. Only six pound a week including the flat above. We knew it would put a big strain on our finances to start with. And it would need a lot of takings to cover the overheads. But it would be just as easy to buy stock for two shops as for one.

We continued our board meeting in Flemming's fish and chip shop whilst waiting for our cod, chips and mushy peas. We were eighth in the queue so had ample time for discussion. The newspaper parcel containing our tea was slammed on the counter. 'Two and fourpence. Ta, queen.'

All in favour – motion carried.

'Ta,' I said, picking up the parcel while Eric fumbled for the money.

Two weeks of hard work and the doors of Eric's Hardware and Fancy Goods opened. Nearly every item of stock was taken from Faulkners, as we didn't have enough money to buy new stuff. Pots, pans, gardening equipment, fancy goods, cleaning materials, we halved

217

everything. If I had six tins of Kitekat, Eric's shop got three. If I had ten bottles of bleach, Eric's got five. There was a bit of a bun fight over my highly prized purple plastic lampshades but I did sacrifice a couple to Eric's shop in the end. However, I had no trouble parting with the seven-foot-tall teddy bear I had bought in a weak moment off a dishy salesman who looked like Tony Curtis. The bear was such an ugly brute it frightened the kids half to death. Nicknamed the bear from hell, for months on end it hung each day by its scraggy neck outside the shop door on a hook. Many an old codger made us laugh as they pushed past it saying, 'Excuse me.' But before long all the hairy-arsed dogs in the neighbour-hood assumed they had the right to pee all over it.

With the bare minimum of stock, an old table for a counter and a shoebox for a till, our business empire was established and under way. Every time Eric sold anything on that first day he would ring me.

'Just sold two packets of soap powder,' he boasted. We made a penny a packet on the soap powder; the phone call cost threepence.

Most shopkeepers closed their shops between twelve and one o'clock each day, and Eric followed suit. He always collected a meat pie and a custard square from the local bakery where Dolly now worked part-time. Then he met me over a cup of tea at Faulkner's in Brighton Street.

The new shop eventually compounded the problem of getting out to the wholesalers to source new stock. In no time the problem solved itself when we visited our friends Sue and her husband Jeff. Sue was bored at home and tried selling Avon cosmetics and catalogue clothes for pin money. We agreed she was flogging a dead horse with what she was doing, and working twenty or so hours a week for us would benefit everyone, besides, I knew she was someone I could trust totally.

We had settled into our respective shops very well and enjoyed the work, although ever-conscious of the burden of financial outgoings and overheads on a house and two shops and a shop van on the never-never.

Then came the blow. The monumental Co-op super-market next door to Faulkners was to close down at the end of the month.

It came as no surprise; the Co-op was losing customers because it had changed for the worse recently, by being modernized. Gone were the huge, welcoming wooden counters with a bacon-slicer each end, and the white-washed windows announcing the latest acquisitions, such as bacon bones and soup hocks at sixpence a pound, and Manx kippers or brown eggs. Cheeses, bacon and cold meats that were once selected and cut to suit your requirements were now pre-packaged. The personal touch and familiar odours – all now gone, along with the overhead cash system, the little tins suspended by sprung wires holding the money that were transported to and from the cash office by a catapult system. The money was checked and the receipt and any change returned on the overhead track to the shop assistant.

In days gone by the Co-op had been the snug local meeting place for several generations of local families, where all the latest gossip had been digested, regurgitated and redistributed at regular intervals, like the *Wallasey News*. Now, the uniformed ladies behind stainless steel and glass checkouts left you feeling like you were going through immigration. It seemed that you weren't a valued, long-time customer who had never before considered shopping elsewhere: like the merchandise, you were something to be processed.

Mam swore over her dead body that she would never be seduced into shopping at a supermarket. She preferred to shop somewhere where she would get personal service, not to mention the odd slice of ham or potted herring thrown in for luck from randy old Stan who always clamoured to serve the ladies. Of course that was until, like most other shoppers, she was seduced instead by

219

The Law of Green Shield Stamps. These huge national promotions finally lured her away to the supermarket, and after goodness knows how many years, the Faulkners gave up their family dividend number (14146). So, apparently, did thousands of others.

The friendly local Co-op grocers were doomed.

Like every speciality shop, we struggled to meet the overheads. So naturally Eric and I were very concerned that a new tenant in the Co-op could quite possibly jump on our bandwagon and stock similar lines to us. Almost scabby-eyed through worry and lack of sleep, we decided we had no option but to take on the huge Co-op premises ourselves and transfer Faulkner's little corner-shop stock to Faulkner's Supermarket.

By trial and error we had discovered the principle of loss leaders – desirable goods sold below cost, supposedly to bring in the punters. For the opening day of Faulkner's Supermarket, the 'Sale Specials' were dinner services for only twelve shillings and sixpence. We'd purchased over a hundred of these from the potteries at Stoke-on-Trent for the same price we were selling them at. Every penny we could beg and borrow went into this load of crockery; it meant the making or the breaking of us. Six cups and saucers, six side plates, six soup dishes, six dinner plates, teapot, sugar basin and milk jug: 12/6d. We'd excelled ourselves this time; no-one, but no-one, could compete with us. Both bay windows displayed mountains of dinner services in every imaginable colour, and we braced ourselves for the rush.

After the first week we had sold two sets (to family). We were desperate. What had gone wrong? We agonized over our haste in taking on the Co-op lease, let alone the wisdom of gambling everything we had on crockery.

'It's too cheap,' my dad said, wagging his finger at me. 'No-one these days buys an English dinner service for twelve and sixpence. The customers naturally think there's a catch or something wrong with them. Stick them

220

in the back room out of sight, and bring them out in a couple of months, a few at a time. And then double the price to twenty-five bob.'

Reluctantly we bowed to his better judgement – probably the eighty quid we still owed him swayed us.

The old bugger was right. We couldn't believe it – it worked. The customers came from miles around and we sold the lot. The shop was a success. Dad gave us the formula – not too cheap, not too dear, like the story of the Three Bears, just right!

Faulkner's original little corner shop remained empty for some time. We were reluctant to give up the lease in case of opposition; anyone with eyes could see we had the successful formula. But what to do with an empty shop was the problem. Funnily enough, once again the problem solved itself. As a favour to family and friends we agreed to store things on a temporary basis that weren't wanted but were too good to throw away. Good junk.

We put a notice on the shop door.

In case of emergency,
Owners now at the old Co-op.
(On opposite corner)

Before the week was out it started.

'Hey girl, how much for the wardrobe in the back of the junk shop?'

The wardrobe was a clapped-out monstrosity with woodworm that we retrieved from the local bonfire to use to make kindling that we intended selling at 9d a bundle.

'How much will yer give me?' I said.

'Five quid, OK girl?'

Naturally I showed reluctance to sell the item. Secretly I was well chuffed to be rid of it.

Eventually we cleared spyholes in the whitewash on the junk-shop windows, enabling punters to get a better look at the junk that 'supposedly' wasn't for sale. As time went by we were frequently asked to clear junk and furniture from old houses, the requests usually coming from the family of a recently departed loved one. Brass fenders, bedroom suites, old prams and suitcases were stacked in every cobwebby corner of the junk shop. Hoarding junk, once looked on as a favour to family and friends, became a very lucrative business, with sod-all effort. The old corner shop never officially reopened its doors, but as second-hand dealers we made good money. We spent some – we lent some.

All that fame without the customary three brass balls hanging over the door.

20

For over three years we had been in business; we only had four days off a year, Christmas Day, Boxing Day, Good Friday and Easter Monday. In the autumn of 1969 Eric and I were bone weary and irritable, when my old friend Marion swanned through the door looking like a film star as usual. She boasted that she had a new car and a new hardware shop, which, by the way, her *new husband* ran. She chattered on about how great life turned out and who would have thought it? I really was in no mood to chat. I felt shabbily exhausted and despondent.

Marion babbled on, seemingly never taking a breath, and then suddenly she stopped.

'Gosh Cherry, you look bloody awful. Are you all right, girl?'

'Oh I'm sorry love, I'm just tired. I'll feel better when we finish unloadin' the coal bricks and fillin' the paraffin cans, then I can go home and climb into a hot bath.'

She shadowed me as I went through the nightly drudgery, all the time yapping on. 'I've got it – you need a holiday.'

'You don't say.'

'Why didn't I think of it before? You remember our family has a holiday cottage at Loggerheads in Wales. We used it for years when we were young.'

'No.'

'Yes you do, I know I told you. So why don't you go and have yourself a holiday there? Just for a week, it will do you all the world of good, and you'd love it.'

'And who may I ask will look after the shop? Who will mind Richard? It's impossible.'

She wasn't taking no for an answer. She offered to mind the shop and said we could take her new car.

I protested, 'Really, we can't. But thanks all the same, love. I really mean it,' I said, touching her cheek.

'Why can't we?' Eric, who had been eavesdropping, interjected. 'It's over twenty years since you 'ad any sort of holiday and Lord knows we both need one. Go on love, let's give it a go.'

Eric thanked Marion and sorted out the details and directions there and then. I was too tired to argue or care. Late on Saturday afternoon we swapped instructions, and Marion generously handed Eric the keys to her new blue Triumph Herald sports car.

'Have a lovely time and don't worry about a thing. See you the end of next week. OK?'

We were too numb to talk much. Richard sat in the back of the car wearing a huge sunhat and nursing his red plastic bucket and spade, with his rubber ring already round his waist. He jabbered non-stop. A comical sight as the skies were grey and the weather overcast, plus we were still a long way away from the beach.

Before we got to Ellesmere Port, the car shuddered to a halt. Just our sodding rotten luck. I was already dreadfully worried about the responsibility of borrowing any car, let alone a new one. Eric switched off the engine. After kicking the tyres he gazed at the intricacies under the bonnet. Not at all mechanically enlightened, he went through the only motions he knew.

Radiator? Hell, drier than an Arab's jockstrap. It was lucky the engine didn't blow.

Battery? No water worth mentioning.

224

Oil? Didn't even register on the dipstick.

Typical of Marion, she probably never knew you had to attend to all these irritating inconveniences of owning a car. Luckily we were within easy walking distance of a garage.

Soon we were on our way once more.

Although the nights were drawing in, we figured we would arrive at the cottage in Loggerheads just before dark. We had taken all our food supplies and planned a big fry-up before unpacking all our gear. Then an early night in bed for all was planned.

I was familiar with the saying about the best-laid plans of mice, etc.

'This can't be number forty,' Eric muttered gloomily.

'That's what it said on the key and on the door, try it in the lock.'

It was pitch black and we had been driving round the area in circles, always ending back here next to the same shabby asbestos shack.

Someone flashed a torch in our faces. 'Yer won't stay there long I'll bet. Won't even last the night.'

We could just about make out the face of an old hag of a woman who was busying herself checking the contents of our car.

'Sorry, what did yer say?' asked Eric, politely.

'Yer won't stay there long, I'll stake me life on it.'

I watched her wide mouth open further to disclose a set of broken yellow teeth. Her grotesque face twisted like a squeezed lemon as she broke into a high-pitched laugh.

'Won't last long! Won't last long,' she chanted, disappearing.

Eric could see that the old hag had unnerved me. 'Looks as if Hallowe'en's come early this year,' he said, trying to make me laugh.

To our dismay the key fitted the lock. We entered the shack and stood motionless in disbelief. Most of the windows were filthy, cracked or broken, and the local furred and feathered population had claimed squatting rights. The wooden floors were littered with debris, and with no floor coverings over the bare timber, you could see the moss-covered foundations through the gaps.

The bed in the larger of the two bedrooms was buried under broken glass from the shattered window. The bed covers were sodden, wet through with rain. The place was musty and putrid. The whole scene would have won Alfred Hitchcock an Oscar. My face said it all. I was cold, my teeth were chattering and my stomach clenched.

'I can't stay here, I'm sorry. With the smell and the damp it could put Richard back in hospital for a month. Even I find it hard to breathe.'

'Sorry, love.' Eric put his arms round me, anxiety apparent in his sad eyes. 'How about I make a nice cup of tea, get the fire going then decide what to do next?'

He turned the tap on. Nothing came out except groans, rattles and shudders.

'Bring the torch and we will check the header tank for water. There must be a stopcock or something.'

When Eric lifted the lid the smell nearly knocked us over. I shone the torch onto the water. A crust had started to form on the top. Several congealed frogs and an assortment of disgusting decaying unmentionables surrounded a decomposed dead bird.

'I can't bear it,' I blubbered. 'I can't bear it. I can't stand any more. Please Eric, take me home. That old hag was right. Said we wouldn't stay. What was Marion thinking of? She never warned us we'd be ensnared by the *Gingerbread Cottage*.'

'Look love, let's make the best of this chance of a holiday and decide what to do tomorrer. Richard can sleep in the car where it's not so damp. We can snuggle up in the kitchen on the armchairs with blankets round us till the mornin'.'

I just couldn't be bothered arguing. We tucked Richard

up safely in the car with the sleeping bag, which was not an easy task as he refused to part with his rubber ring. Then we stationed ourselves in the cold kitchen in the dark with the blankets round us. I tucked my knees up before me and tried to sleep.

The scurrying fears of Littledale Road came flooding back.

'Eric,' I whispered, 'is that you?'

'What?'

'Is that you?'

'Is what me?'

'I thought I saw somethin' move. Listen, what's that noise, the scrapin' noise?'

'Sorry, I was asleep, I didn't hear any scrapin' noise.'

Bloody Eric could sleep in an aeroplane hangar.

'Where's the torch?'

'I'm sorry love, I left it with Richard in case he needs the loo – why do you need it?'

'Sshh. There it goes again. Listen – that shufflin' noise across the floor.' I sensed some unshapely things moving.

Instinctively I knew it was rats.

Eric tried to pacify me. He failed.

'What time can we leave?' I implored.

'We'll go at first light, but try and get some sleep now, you must be done in.'

It was difficult to contain my own screams of sheer fright. Why couldn't Eric understand my hysteria? Perhaps he felt that as he was here, he wouldn't let anything happen to me. I kept my feet elevated, using the hard tub chair as if it was an island. Any chance of sleep understandably eluded me. The first signs of light signalled for me the all clear. Time to escape this spooky place. I tentatively put my feet to the floor and focused my eyes.

'Good grief, what happened to the groceries?'

Eric was not yet with it. 'Cornflakes and toast will do.'

'What?'

'Cornflakes and toast, that'll do for breakfast. Don't want much.'

'I said, what happened to the groceries, dummy.'

We'd put the cardboard box of groceries on the floor. The contents were strewn everywhere. I thought I was going to faint. The rats had chewed right through the bag of sugar. The packets of butter were about four feet away from the box, and cornflakes like snowflakes were scattered everywhere. Rats. Rats. Rats. Would I ever be free from their persecution?

'Please Eric, I want to go home. Now!'

'Can we just fix breakfast first. I'm sure Richard is hungry.'

Eric went to wake Richard and give him the sad news that the place was a dead loss, and as we had no spare money for a proper holiday, returning home was our only option.

I could hear Eric calling, 'Richard, Rich, where are you, son? Don't play silly buggers at a time like this, we need to talk to you.'

Richard wasn't in the car. The strain showed as Eric tried to sound calm and attract Richard's attention from wherever he might have been hiding. We could always rely on him to do as he was told, so why would he disobey us now of all times?

'Coo-ee Mummy. Coo-ee Daddy, look, it's smashin' over here. I saw a real rabbit and I chased it. What's for breakfast, I'm starvin' hungry?'

Thank goodness for that. He was only hiding from us, the cheeky monkey. We could see his head and trunk just above a grassy bank in the distance, as he waved. Little sod had frightened the life out of us. We thought that he'd been kidnapped or something. We stood on tiptoes and waved back, noticing he still had his rubber ring round his waist. Couldn't wait to go in the water.

'I bet he slept in that rubber ring,' I laughed. 'Mind you, the sun isn't even up, the water must be freezin'.'

We walked towards him, but the closer we got the less we saw of him. My breath stalled in my throat, but not wanting to sound alarmed I quickened my pace, racing towards the water. I was now seeing even less of him, just his head and shoulders.

In a frenzy we both ran.

'Hold on Richard, don't move,' Eric shouted.

We ran over the ridge of the bank and Richard was in full view. What silly buggers we were, no water, no water at all, just sand dunes, Richard was happily playing in sand dunes. I dropped to my knees. Hell, what a laugh, such a relief as we sauntered towards him; our only serious concern now was how to break the bad news about our aborted holiday. The further we walked, the softer the sand became. Already up to my knees, just putting one foot in front of the other was almost impossible.

Suddenly Eric yelled at me, 'Go *back*! Go *back*!'

'Why are yer yellin' like that?'

'Do as yer bloody well told, woman, just for once. Go back.'

'Stop it, you're frightenin' me. What's up?'

I looked towards Richard. My God, our only child was in sinking sand, slowly being sucked downwards, now terrified and screaming.

'Don't move son, Daddy's here. Now listen carefully, you must stay absolutely still. Understand?'

I don't know how Eric got him out. I was in no state to make any mental notes. Eric's experience on the Fire and Ambulance Brigade, topped with his incredible ability to work through a crisis with a level head (coupled with the miraculous rubber swimming ring Richard had worn for the past twenty-four hours) had saved our son's life.

As we loaded up the car with what was left of the groceries, the hag reappeared.

I ignored her.

'Told yer yer wouldn't stay long. No-one ever does.'

With rigid fingers, I fumbled for the car door. I felt suddenly overcome by fatigue and dull despair. We struggled to make light of the situation for Richard's sake; another asthma attack brought on by stress would have been all we needed. We tried making a game of Wombles on the journey home, by creating a nest on the back seat of the car with cushions and rugs. Wretchedly, Richard, who would have none of it, climbed on top and stared dejectedly out of the rear window.

When we arrived home to our little palace, it looked cosy, inviting and clean. After a huge fry-up of bacon, eggs, sausage and chips we headed for the bedroom. Eric closed the curtains to block out the daylight, then placed Richard in the big double bed between us, where we slept for most of the day, huddled contentedly together.

I don't know why we played down our experiences of the past thirty-six hours when we arrived at the shop the next morning. Before we had a chance to open our mouths, Marion said, 'Well, it's no surprise to me you're back. Your mother said you wouldn't stay away long. What a pain in the arse. I hear you even came back from your honeymoon early.'

I didn't want a fight. She meant well, no doubt. We attempted to tell her of the dilapidated state of the so-called 'cosy cottage' at Loggerheads, but it went totally over her head. She suggested we try again after it had had its annual facelift in the summer.

'I always say everything looks better in the sun, don't you think?' With that, she pecked me on the cheek, gave us a quick summary of the business, removed her pink smock and rubber gloves and after completing her ablutions she announced, 'Now, don't forget, any time you're in need a holiday, you're more than welcome.'

With no more ado she climbed into her car and roared off.

*　　*　　*

Getting straight back into business mode, we ordered our stocks for winter: coal bricks, firewood, candles, paraffin etc. We had been offered part of a containerload of Christmas decorations and gift-wrapping from Super-foods. Most of the consignment was coming in from Hong Kong. On learning we'd be the only local shops to carry these new lines, we again hocked ourselves to the eye-balls and prayed that the early hint of snow in the air would encourage our customers to stock up early for Christmas. It cheered us up, the prospect of having more than the cold to look forward to during the lead-up to the festivities.

I had only just finished hanging out the day's Specials on the nails round the door and in front of the windows, when a benevolent voice behind me whispered, 'Sorry to hear about yer granddad, chuck.' She couldn't be talking to me, I didn't have a granddad. Still tagging behind me, 'Sorry to hear about yer granddad, chuck,' she repeated.

'Oh, sorry, I didn't see you there,' I lied, 'what can I do for you?'

'Don't want nothin', was just sayin' sorry to hear about yer granddad.'

'Not me. I 'aven't got a granddad. Never 'ad a grand-dad in fact.'

She was beginning to irritate me as she hotfooted behind me in and out of the shop while I loaded the trestles outside with pan scrubs and five-for-a-bob Brillo Pads.

'I was talkin' about the old gentleman who sits behind the counter sometimes. Thought he was yer granddad.'

I froze halfway to the door, my arms loaded with garden hoses.

'What about him? What 'ave yer heard?'

'I saw them takin' 'im, in an ambulance t'other day. I came to the shop to tell yer but I didn't recognize no faces.'

What could I do? Eric was at the wholesalers and

wouldn't be back for at least two hours. I slammed the shop door and left the stock adorning the pavement. Once in the street, my shaking legs impeded my running. I ran and ran, so fast I thought my lungs would burst. When I reached the house I was fully expecting bad news. Mam as usual was sitting amongst the knitted cushions smoking her Woodbines, her sorry gaze fixed on his empty chair.

'Where's me dad? What's happened?'

'He's at the hospital. His waterworks again probably.'

She was occupied in extracting some knitting from the corner of the chair.

'What's happened? How long will he be there? Is he OK?'

'I don't know. The ambulance men didn't say. Dolly has offered to take me to see him this afternoon. Not keen though, yer never get out of them places once they get you inside.'

Mesmerized now by her knitting, Mam continued clattering her needles without casting her eyes in my direction.

Frustrated, I did what any dutiful daughter would do. 'Can I make yer a cuppa or somethin', Mam? I'll stay with yer. Would you like Eric to take you in the car to see Dad or do any runnin' round?'

'No, love, thanks.' Her needles were still clicking, now more rapidly as the cigarettte ash dropped all down her front.

'Well, what about me dad? Does he need anythin'?'

'No love, thanks.'

She lapsed into another preoccupied silence. After some time, feeling like a spare prick at a wedding, I spoke. 'Well if yer sure yer don't need me, I'd best get back to the shop and check if I've got any stock left. I'll call back later when the shop's shut. OK?'

She gave a bewildered nod and carried on knitting her bloody squares.

I phoned Dolly when I got back to the shop.

'What's wrong with me dad? Why doesn't Mam know?'

'She does know. She's in shock. Just refuses to accept there's any real problem with Dad's waterworks.'

'What's wrong with his waterworks?'

'Just a blockage I think. They're puttin' in a catheter to ease the discomfort. Should be home in a couple of days. They can't operate 'cos of his heart.'

'His heart? What's wrong with his heart?'

'Well, his heart combined with his weak chest – too dangerous you see, love.'

'His chest? What's wrong with his chest?'

She didn't answer. I was still 'the baby'. Once again the grown-ups seemed to be taking control. They were sparing me the anxiety, so they thought. Unfortunately it only left my imagination to run amok.

True to Dolly's word, Dad was home within a couple of days. He didn't look too sick, just weary and watered-down.

21

In the winter of 1970 the relentless biting cold weather boosted our sales of paraffin, coal bricks and firewood. We laboured long and hard for a huge turnover but bugger-all profit, taking comfort in the fact that if we did enough turnover during the winter months it would cover our mounting overheads. By working from daybreak to dark, buying, selling, humping and hauling coal bricks, coke and coal, we supplied the filthy, grimy commodities that were much needed for the survival of many of our customers.

Most of our customers bought 'on the slate', which meant that we found it extremely hard to replace stock with so much debt outstanding. It was impossible to turn our backs on the pleadings for fuel from the young mothers, or the frail and elderly spending their last few coppers trying to keep warm. The slate got bigger and bigger while we got broker and broker, watching once-loyal customers passing on the other side of the road to avoid us in case we pressed for the outstanding account to be settled.

We decided to try and boost the business by offering free fuel delivery.

'Bloody daft idea if you ask me. Besides, yer making a rod for yer own backs,' my dad warned. Who needed to ask him? We were after all self-employed.

We learnt the hard way, after months of lugging back-breaking drums of paraffin around the streets along with bags of firewood and coal. Once again my dad was proved right. We were twice as busy and physically exhausted, but we were not making any more money.

The relationship between the Government and trade unions deteriorated. The country became gripped by endless industrial strikes. Finally, the national coal-miners' strike reduced British industry to a three-day working week. The precious bags of coal we stocked became nicknamed 'black diamonds' (probably by some greedy wholesalers). Sadly, we couldn't rely on the petrol companies to deliver paraffin regularly, which threatened our key bread-and-butter line. Out went the fashionable glass display cabinets; in came a huge paraffin holding tank.

During that endless bitter winter, Eric and I became overburdened from long hours in the shop and the effects of the perishing cold, both indoors and out. Our spirits deadened to see our previously well-laid-out shop, as fancy goods now sat on the shelves covered with a shroud of black coal dust. The buzz had gone out of the business. Simply existing became a day-to-day struggle for us and so many others like us. The Christmas club we initiated at Easter was doomed; anyone who had any credit spent the money on fuel to keep warm.

The country fell victim to the Hong Kong flu. Like the Black Plague, Hong Kong flu was not selective when killing loved ones and friends. Wretched survivors had to stand in sprawling queues outside the town hall to register recent deaths. There were rumours that the local produce markets with their huge meat and vegetable chillers were now storing endless dead bodies, as the undertakers were rushed off their feet, their latest clientele having died before they had dealt with the previous unfortunates. The ambulance men whose job it was to deliver the bodies to the undertakers were moonlighting for a quid a time on their days off. Some took the place of the professional pall bearers who couldn't keep up with the demand.

Merseyside was bleak. The whole country was bleak, bringing all the emergency services to breaking point. There were many tragic reports of young and old found dead, huddled together for warmth. The Hong Kong flu epidemic was out of control, causing loss of work, loss of income, and, worst of all, loss of loved ones. Fortunately Eric and I didn't have the problem of being cold. We were so knackered when we got home we usually climbed into a sleeping bag in bed and fell asleep as soon as our heads hit the pillows. Weakly we staggered round like a couple of drunks in our increasingly grubby shops that now resembled something left over from the Blitz.

'Blimey, me back's killing me,' I complained. 'I've just staggered to the old dear from Sandon Road with her five-gallon delivery of paraffin and she never answered the door this time.'

Brassed off, we accepted this as a regular occurrence with some customers, particularly if they hadn't paid for the previous delivery. They hoped you would leave the heavy drum rather than lug it back to the shop. Unfortunately we could no longer afford to do that.

'It's not like her, she's a sweet old duck. Give it to me. I'll go.'

You could have been forgiven for laughing at Eric's grumpy, lifeless appearance if it wasn't so pathetic. He was fortified against the cold with more skins on than an onion, wearing his knitted gloves with the fingers cut out so that his stiff, cramped hands could feel the loose change, and a thick woollen scarf wrapped round his neck and chest to relieve his barking cough.

With his shoulders slouched and his head down, Eric picked up the heavy drum and left the shop in the cold, driving rain. We had been treated so badly by so many indebted customers, yet Eric, who was a real softie, was still concerned for others less fortunate. At the best of times it was depressing going to the scruffy old flat in Sandon Road with the regular delivery. It was so heart-breaking to see yet another poverty-stricken old lady struggling just to get through the winter. Her room was always dark, cold and squalid. The only form of lighting was half a candle in a saucer. Perhaps the lighting was only a token or habit, as I doubted that her vacant milky eyes could see much. They certainly hadn't seen the dead mouse that had long since dehydrated and now lay looking flat and brittle in her fireplace. Probably it had starved to death.

A while later, Eric came lumbering back dragging the heavy drum.

'I told yer she was out.'

Eric didn't answer.

'What will she do for heatin'?' I asked. 'I suppose we should 'ave been more charitable and left the paraffin for her one more time.'

'She doesn't need it.'

'Why not?'

'She's dead. I found her frozen in the chair.'

A dull misery settled over us like a fog.

She was amongst the four hundred that died that day in the Hong Kong flu epidemic, which hit the north-west of England the hardest by far. Nationwide, there were 2,850 reported deaths in one weekend. Strange how the age of the Swinging Sixties and early Seventies was now grinding to such a tragic end.

Short of breath for our labouring lungs and coughing frequently, we worked from daybreak to dark humping coal bricks, coke and coal. We hardly spoke a word to each other as we pulled our aching bodies out of bed each day. Everything hurt, inside and out. One day I returned from the wholesalers to find a queue of drab, hunched customers standing with empty paraffin tins, waiting for their half-a-crown refill.

'Where's Eric?' I asked the woman in front.

'Gone for a pee I think. Takin' his soddin' time. Perhaps 'e's got trouble findin' it with cold 'ands.' She attempted a laugh at her own joke.

Thinking to myself that it was a bloody wonder we had anything left in the till with this lot hanging round, I grabbed the first tin ungraciously, begruding the effort involved in even the most minimal of tasks.

'Oh Lord,' I cried. 'Quick, someone phone for the ambulance.'

I don't know how long Eric had lain behind the paraffin tank, collapsed. Judging by the queue, some time.

Eric was taken to Emergency at St Catherine's Hospital. I followed behind in the shop van. He was still unconscious when I arrived and the doctor was waiting to do a lumbar puncture to confirm his diagnosis of pleurisy and bronchial pneumonia. I sat on the orange plastic chair in the waiting room with my arms folded across my chest, steeling myself against further bad news. After several hours I was told, 'Go home, lass. We've made your husband comfortable. He's in good hands.' As anyone who has had anything to do with overcrowded hospitals knows, that means 'no-one really can say anything much yet.'

I returned to the shop, cashed up. Then I put a notice on the door, 'Closed due to sickness'. After arranging for Richard to stay with Eric's family I drove home and crawled into my sleeping bag. I gasped, trying to restrain frustrated fearful tears, knowing I didn't have the strength to revisit the hospital or even to look after our son.

With just a week till Christmas I was haunted by visions of our overstocked shop, bulging at the seams with cartons of unsold brightly coloured Christmas decorations and novelties, still not paid for. I drifted in and out of delirium for three days and nights. I had always been prone to nightmares; even now I clearly remember dreaming of grappling my way through hollow-eyed naked corpses hanging like skinned animal carcasses from meat hooks in the market chillers, and hoping against hope not to find the face of a loved one.

When I emerged from my delirium I had lost eleven pounds in weight. The bad news, apart from us almost being bankrupt, was my perspiration had stained our new spring interior mattress.

I tried to ignore the ruckus at the front door. 'Yoo-hoo. Yoo-hoo, it's me.' I peered through the letter box – it was Joyce from next door. She had come to see how Eric was, and, 'if you would like some nice hot nourishing soup.'

I told her 'No thanks,' through the letter box and that I had no idea how Eric was. I was going to visit him at lunchtime.

'You won't be able to do that. There's no visiting at lunchtime except on the weekends.'

'Why, what day is it?' I asked, opening the door.

'Tuesday.'

'Bloody hell! It can't be Tuesday!'

'Afraid so. Well, if there's anything you need don't be afraid to ask.'

'Ta.'

Within the hour I was next door taking her up on her offer of help.

'Sorry Joyce, do you think your Ken could get our car started? It's been out of action for a while with me bein' laid up. I've taken the newspapers and old coats off the engine and poured warm water on the windscreen like Eric showed me: the engine must be still frozen and I don't know what to do next.'

Ken the cop towed our cumbersome old Rover 90 up and down the road for nearly an hour, his patience wearing thin. After telling me to take off the handbrake and put the car into third gear, he then told me to hold my foot on the clutch. He cussed and yelled but when he saw I was getting frantic he calmed down.

'Look, I'll drop you off at the hospital. It will be quicker,' he said. 'You ring me when you want to come home. Meanwhile I'll give the car a look over. Can't be much wrong.'

'They're sendin' me home for Chrissy. They need the beds.' Eric smiled weakly as I sat holding his hand.

'Surely yer not well enough to come home?'

'Look love, they're dying all round me like flies and they're so desperate for beds. I'm on antibiotics. They can't do much more. I'm better at home. Besides it's over an hour's drive for you to travel here in the big old Rover with all the treacherous ice on the roads.'

'Ken from next door brought me,' I smiled.

'That was very good of him. Why did he do that?'

'Couldn't get the car started.'

'It's probably only the battery. He should 'ave tried towin' you, that would 'ave done the trick.'

'He did tow me, up and down the soddin' road for nearly an hour. Nearly pulled the bumper off.'

'Can't understand it. After fifteen to twenty yards when you took yer foot off the clutch it should 'ave started.'

'But I never took me foot off the clutch.'

'After twenty yards you mean?'

'No, I never took me foot off the clutch at all, no-one told me to.'

Eric's mouth dropped open. 'Hey love, do me a favour, don't ever tell the new Assistant Chief Constable of Wallasey Police that he has been towin' you up and down the road and you 'ad yer bloody foot planted on the clutch all that time.'

Eric started to laugh, laugh, gasp and cough, as he gripped his chest. Exhausted, he fell back and closed his eyes.

He coughed so much a stroppy nurse came and fluffed up his pillows and told me I should go now; I was tiring my husband.

Eric was brought home in the ambulance on Christmas Eve. I still hadn't been near the shop. I was too depressed, weak and exhausted.

There had been 790 deaths nationwide in the previous two days.

Usually at Christmas I went overboard with decorations and goodies to create lots of atmosphere and Christmas cheer. But not this year. Christmas Day we sat like bookends in our dressing gowns as we huddled each side of the fireplace, watching Richard engrossed in his giant-sized box of Lego.

'Ho, ho, ho. Happy Christmas and why aren't you dressed? It's two o'clock.' Eric's best friend Billy Davies greeted us from the doorway. He and Eric both worked the Cunard ships from the time they were fifteen; they'd ended up on the *Britannic* together.

Eric brightened up. 'Hiya, come in pal.'

Katie, our Scottie dog, reluctantly got to her feet and crossed the room for a sniff of recognition, before leaping enthusiastically and weaving round his legs until Billy had stroked her head. Then she returned to the rug in front of the fire to fill the room with the pong of singeing hair.

'Oh, Billy, happy Christmas. It's great to see you. Sit down. Would you like a drink?'

'Beer, ta. Hey, I can't smell the dinner cooking. Are we eating late?'

Eric and I looked at each other for some clue as to what his friend Billy was talking about.

'Well, bugger me,' Billy said. 'You've forgotten, haven't you? You invited me for Christmas dinner – remember?'

With all the drama we forgot that we had invited him to dinner so that he wouldn't be on his own at Christmas, as his bitch of a wife had just left him. Oh, Lord! We told

Billy of the past couple of weeks and this being Eric's first day out of hospital.

'Don't you worry kid, I'll cook your dinner. Egg and chips all round OK?'

I loved having Billy come to visit. He was a great talker, painting colourful pictures of countries he and Eric had visited: of being shot at by Puerto Ricans in New York. He talked of rifle-firing competitions against the Israeli police (Eric was awarded a prize as the top shot); of soccer games against Farouk's armed soldiers who played barefoot (and won); of the many celebrities they had had personal contact with: Gracie Fields, Archbishop Makarios and Lilly Syncere (a famous stripper). I revelled in each new story, as Eric had never discussed his overseas trips other than simply saying they were 'OK'.

'One day I would like to take Cherry round the Greek Islands. She's never been out of the UK. She would love it,' Eric was now telling his friend.

'No,' said Billy, excitedly, 'Egypt's best, with so much to see. Hell, I miss the old *Britannic*. They were happy days.'

'It'd be good right now to be anywhere away from the bloody cold. I can't take this cold. Another winter like this will kill us.' Eric waited for me to make some comment. I couldn't think of anything to say. Then he added, 'We should emigrate to a warmer country.'

'Australia,' I piped up, enthusiastically.

'No, Canada would be great. I've a cousin in Canada,' said Billy.

'If I was to go anywhere,' said Eric, 'it would be somewhere I would never feel the cold again. Probably somewhere like New Zealand. Cherry's got a book on New Zealand somewhere. Looks a great place, and it's not icy like Canada. One day when the dog snuffs it we may emigrate to New Zealand.'

'Why do we 'ave to wait for the dog to die?' I asked, most puzzled.

'Because we couldn't afford to fly Katie out and leave her in quarantine for six months. That's the regulation and I know you wouldn't leave her behind. So, if we're not too old when the dog dies we may give New Zealand a go.'

Katie, now sprawled at our feet, just sighed and laid her head in the comfort of her paws, while blind devotion bordering on reverence for Eric shone out of her soulful eyes. Eric started to laugh while clutching at his chest and rasping.

'What's tickled you?' I asked.

'Only you, yer daft bitch. I've tried takin' you away from Wallasey not once but twice. Forty bloody miles at the most and each time we were back, at breakneck speed. You? You wouldn't last any time in New Zealand.'

A sore point.

'Would you like a proper drink, Billy, maybe a whisky or somethin'? We're not very good hosts, are we?'

'No love, honestly. You both look done in. Why don't you get back to bed? I'll go now and pop by again later.'

Even I got a hearty handshake instead of the usual goodbye kiss from Billy.

'Sorry kid, germs you know. See you soon, ta rar.' He closed the door quietly and left.

'Yer know, Eric,' I said, 'it would serve them all right, if we emigrated. We've been sick for weeks and neither of our families has visited the house or the shop to see how we were managin'. It's certainly food for thought.'

We both turned our eyes on the dog that was happily demolishing the bottom row of chocolate Christmas decorations dangling from the tree.

22

January 16th, Richard's sixth birthday. The nation-wide death toll from the Hong Kong flu had been reported at four thousand for the week. If we were to believe everything the media said the whole country was over the worst – with the exception of the north of England.

Our lives seemed to have slipped back into the familiar pattern at the shop. We managed to arrange a bank loan to pay for the unsold Christmas stock and to bring the rent on the three shops up to date. Then my mam, of all people, had this brilliant idea.

'Have you thought of sellin' Eric's shop? Yer've got it going nicely. You could pay off yer debts, build up the big shop, and then you could work together and not get so tired. Another episode like the last one on yer hands could be the end of you both.'

'I don't know what the shop's worth. Besides we wouldn't 'ave a clue how to go about sellin' a business. What do you think?' I asked her.

'Dunno. Stick a price on you would be happy with, and who knows? Why not put an advertisement in the *Liverpool Echo*? It'll only cost a few bob. No harm done by tryin'.'

The advert was placed in Friday's *Liverpool Echo* under businesses for sale.

**Hardware and Fancy Goods
Business for sale.**

**Easily run. Long Lease.
Suit married couple.
£750 o.n.o.
Apply Box No. 118,
*Liverpoool Echo.***

Amazingly, the shop was sold for cash on the following Monday. The couple that bought it had been looking for a similar business for a long time. They bought ours because they liked the name over the door, 'Eric's', that just happened to be the husband's name. After only a week of our nurturing, Eric and his wife went on to flourish on their own.

Poor Mam, she didn't know at the time that she had started a chain reaction. The money from the sale of Eric's shop not only paid our debts, but with the pressure off we had more leisure time to ourselves. We started going out more and having parties. Shipwreck parties, fancy dress parties, and dinner parties. Friday night became girls' night out. Now I could drive, Eric said I could go along only on the strict understanding I didn't drink. 'Yes dear, fine dear, get stuffed dear,' I thought. I was going through my rebellious, overdue teens, ten years late, but who was I to miss out on anything?

In the Seventies, with a bouffant hairdo, false eye-lashes, micro-miniskirt and ankle chain, I danced to the music of Billy J. Kramer, the Beatles, the Rolling Stones and Marianne Faithfull. Cocky as hell, with my friends Sue, Marion, and Liz (who was now my brother Teddy's wife) and her friends, we met at the Golden Guinea nightclub in New Brighton every week. The trendy black cave vibrated with noise and flashing lights. For five bob we could buy scampi and chips or prawn salad, served in a basket. We ate on the dance floor, as we didn't want to waste too much good dancing time on eating. Squandering our sixteen bob a week family benefit, we drank brandy and Babycham at five and sixpence a throw. We danced with each other; we danced alone; we danced with a never-ending supply of very attentive guys – even me. This was a new 'little Cherry Faulkner' who was not only getting lots of dances but choosing her partners from the multitude of gawking blokes.

My wardrobe was rapidly changing. I no longer picked out cheap and cheerful garments from C & A or the market, I preferred choosing my clothes from the fashionable boutiques. I had the desire to be slim and healthy, so the six of us girls lined the walls of the sauna parlour on a Saturday afternoon, detoxifying from the previous night's booze-up and hoping to lose weight. This was not a success story for me. And Liz's resolve, like mine, went out the window when we bought fish, chips and a bottle of pop on the way home.

I was seeing a lot of Liz, and we had become very close, although Eric and I were seeing much less of Ted. We heard from Liz that he thought that he had been cheated out of his inheritance; he thought Mam and Dad gave us the shop. I had tried to explain our parents' desperation when we bought the shop off them and the way we had struggled to pay it off, but he wasn't interested in the why or wherefore.

I tried hard not to dwell on the depression still shadowing the country, but working in the shop was a constant reminder of the never-ending strikes, blackouts, power cuts and more fuel and food shortages. When would it all end?

It hardly seemed worth opening the shop some days during the miners' strikes when coal bricks, firewood and paraffin were all so scarce. Candles were like gold, no longer twelve for half a crown, but five bob each and the price still soaring. During the blackouts we heard stories of them being a pound each in some shops. Naturally, the so-called 'greedy' shopkeepers were blamed for profiteering. The local butcher was even selling dripping at twice the price, and demonstrated how, with either that or lard and a piece of string, you could make your own candles. The newspapers carried many, many reported cases of children and old people severely burnt through misuse of candles and kerosene lamps.

We heard of a source of candles, torches and batteries smuggled in from France, and we had the opportunity of buying some. No questions asked – we readily accepted. This very expensive and precious stock was kept for preferential customers (usually the paying ones). Unfortunately, I made the mistake of giving our very good neighbours, Joyce and Ken, a box of precious candles in return for the kindness they had shown to us during Eric's illness.

Being who he was, Ken the cop was quick to comment that the candles were made in France. The next day Ken sent down two plain-clothes detectives, who arrived at the shop and introduced themselves. The thin man with grey hair gripped my wrist and leant forward across the counter towards me. Nose to nose and eyeball to eyeball he whispered conspiratorially, 'We've come to search the shop for stolen contraband.'

Legs like jelly, I thought I would faint, but hard-faced I brazened it out.

'What are you on about?'

His partner, the fat-bellied one, seemed intent on watching my every move. He tapped the side of his nose with his finger. 'You fell for that one, didn't you?' He laughed, adding, 'Hey kid, I hear you've got some candles. Couldn't let us have a packet each, could you? We're happy to pay the full price. We know they're not cheap. We've tried everywhere. By the way, love, what about batteries? Have you got any batteries? I'm sure you could manage to find some for a couple of handsome blokes like us.' Adding, 'Maybe if you looked hard enough,' he winked.

With their shared laughter echoing through the shop, I laughed, too. Possibly too loud and too easily. *They* probably thought I was laughing with them at the prank of being set up. *I* was laughing with relief. I steered them away from the counter where I had hidden a case of knocked-off whisky and twelve hot Sting Ray remote-controlled cars, as well as some fibreglass curtains and mirrors that had 'just happened' to have fallen off the back of a truck. I had no conscience. Taking occasional hot goodies from weasel-faced characters that offered their plunder seemed only natural. Straight-faced as you like, I sold the coppers some candles – made 200 per cent profit. Best of all, I managed to get the last laugh over Ken when I sold him the knocked-off curtains from under the counter. Poor Ken; we'd told him we'd got them from a cancelled order from our warehouse supplier. The curtains took pride of place in the windows of his front parlour for all the world to admire.

With winter behind us, we started stocking bedding plants, seeds and garden furniture, so much easier and more profitable than fuel. With more leisure time and more money in our pockets, our thoughts turned to the possibility of adopting a child. The memories of my own childhood were still very strong. I knew we could give some unfortunate child the love and comfort I had once craved. Now Richard was six, we didn't want to let the gap between siblings get too great. I hadn't fallen pregnant again, so without telling the family for fear of speculation, we made our application through the Social Welfare Services at the town hall. Surprisingly, we had a visit from them within a month, even though we had been told at the initial interview that there was a nine-year waiting list for babies.

On hearing the welfare officer was coming on Tuesday, Eric and I spent all weekend cleaning the house. It was scrubbed, polished and hoovered. The silver, brass and copper were shining. We wanted to make a good impression but somehow the rooms looked barren to me, and, much against Eric's better judgement, I borrowed some more luxurious items from friends and neighbours. An onyx table lighter with matching lamp, a leather *Radio Times* binder, sheepskin floor rugs and brass coffee tables were loaned to us, together with odds and sods from the shop, which we thought gave the house the middle-class look I was hoping to achieve.

Nervously, we sat waiting. I kept smoothing the cushions and emptying the ashtray Eric kept filling. The minute the woman from the town hall arrived, we were off to a bad start. She entered the house clinging to the walls. 'Does that dog bite?' she sniped, frowning at Katie, who had decided to make the starchy woman the subject of fervent scrutiny.

'No, but she can give you a nasty suck,' I said, stupidly trying to make her feel at ease. I failed – adding anxiously, 'Would you like a cup of tea?' This was a chance to show off our neighbour's real silver-plated tray and teapot.

'Thank you,' she said as she walked through to the kitchen. The dog seemingly lost interest and jumped up on the best sofa to sulk.

'Sugar? Milk?'

'Just milk please.'

Bloody hell, she started poking through our knife and fork drawer. I could have knocked her block off.

'What's the idea of that?' I smiled benignly.

'A cutlery drawer is an indication of character,' she said. 'A tidy drawer, a tidy mind.'

'Didn't do too well on that score, did I?' I laughed nervously.

Ignoring Eric, she addressed me. 'Actually, I have to

249

tell you that you have little or no chance of being selected as adoptive parents. Mr Simmonds is what? Turned thirty? In say, nine years when you could be considered for a child, he will be over forty and that's too old.'

She didn't get any of our iced animal biscuits with her tea – old bag. The interview was short and not sweet before she condescended to shake our hands, then left. I saw a whisk of a black tail stick out from under the sofa. 'Katie! Get in yer basket,' I screamed at the dog, which I swear had been farting during the tragic interview. (It was either that or the old bag from the town hall.)

'Don't take it out on the dog, it's not her fault.' Eric, being his usual kind considerate self, bent and stroked her ears by way of apologizing for my tantrum. Being a Scottish terrier, a stubborn, short-legged creature with a huge capacity for love, she gazed in adoration at Eric, just the way dogs look at their masters. She leapt enthusiastically onto his knee, putting her forepaws on his chest, and started licking his eyes until he laughed.

We immediately returned all the borrowed trappings of temporary middle-class. The next day Eric was at home, making time to wash and clip the dog. There was a knock at the door. Leaving Katie on the kitchen table surrounded by fur and clipped nails, he answered it to find our frosty-faced woman from the town hall.

'Silly me, I've left my glasses on the coffee table I think, I hope it's not too much trouble, do you mind?'

'No love, come in, you know where they are, help yerself.'

When I got home, boy did he get an earful!

'How could you? How bloody stupid! How could you let her in? One minute the house lookin' middle-class and spotless with all the good gear, the next day like Paddy's bleedin' market. How could you do that? 'Ad you forgotten we returned all the posh gear to the neighbours?'

'Sorry love, I never gave it a thought.'

250

And that was the end of the adoption saga – for the time being.

We were looking forward to the weekend when we would join Sue and Jeff for dinner along with their friends Gordon and Jan, who had returned to Merseyside from New Zealand because they were homesick. It seemed to us that they were already regretting their decision to leave New Zealand. We were fascinated to hear that the kids over there didn't wear shoes. I wondered how they avoided the dog muck, but was too polite at this stage in the relationship to ask.

We learnt that you could buy a new house in New Zealand very reasonably, and even have some say as to how it was built. Now fancy that. Looking at the photos, the sea in New Zealand was blue, the sand yellow, and the grass green. Everything seemed so clean, clear and fresh – no smog. Oh, how I envied them. I just couldn't understand anyone leaving all that behind and coming back to live in England. They told us about the chorus of the night insects amongst the fruit trees; long summers with barbecues on the beach and short winters when they'd gone ski-ing on the snow-peaked mountains in the South Island. Sounded to us that Gordon and Jan had known what it felt like to live as film stars.

Eric and I totally monopolized their time, hanging onto every word, hoping to hear some bad news – news that would kill this creeping dissatisfaction with our lifestyle; willing them to reassure us we were better off where we were. It never came. The settling words just never came.

In the early hours of the morning we drove home in silence, each having our own private thoughts, each afraid to address the possibility of living in New Zealand, each terrified of a rash decision that could be made in our present state of dissatisfaction.

We got home and I put the milk on for Horlicks, knowing that we would need something to help us sleep.

251

I carried the mugs back to the table where Eric had my school geography-prize book on New Zealand. It was open at a picture of Nelson in the South Island. Explosions of colour filled the pages of sunshine and beauty.

'If we ever go to New Zealand we'll live in Nelson. What do you think chuck, do you like the look of Nelson?'

'Yep,' I said, recognizing that Eric's growing appetite for a new life equalled my own.

We didn't discuss it any more than that at the time.

Dad was now a regular patient at Central Hospital with his ongoing waterworks problem. As always the problem was minimized, not only by the rest of the family but also by Dad, who seemed more embarrassed than sick. His weakening chest was still causing concern to the doctors. I once read that if there was asthma in a family, the male passed it down to the next-generation female, who passed it on to the next-generation male, and so on. Even if it was an old wives' tale it certainly had credence in our family.

Dad's stays in hospital were short and at the time I was discouraged from visiting him. In the face of adversity my dad said, 'Keep yer pecker up.' Well, seems his pecker became subjected to many embarrassing and painful processes in the hope of bladder relief. It was doubtful if his pecker would ever be up again.

Another Job's comforter settled with her elbows on the front counter for a gossip.

'Saw the bobbies at yer mam's 'ouse this mornin', everythin' OK, chuck? Them lads of hers still mis-behavin'?'

'Probably their neighbours havin' another domestic. Bobbies 'ave their work cut out with that lot,' I mused, unconcerned, while I stacked tins of Jellymeat.

'No, it's yer mam's 'ouse all right 'cos I saw the bobbies go in.'

As I drove up the road I pleaded once again with God to spare my dad this time. I was becoming a regular God-botherer although I hadn't much to bargain with as I'd already given up smoking. Perhaps I could try cutting out swearing. Oh bugger it – that was too unrealistic. I was still working on a compromise when I pulled up outside the door without finishing the one-sided bargaining.

'Hello lovey,' Dad greeted me, with his finger pressed against his lips.

'Where's me mam?'

'Hush, careful what yer say – yer mam's in shock,' Dad whispered as he walked me up the hall with his arms wrapped around my shoulders. Dad was alive and well. Oh, thank you God! I thanked him too soon.

'What the . . . ? Who the hell did this? When . . . ?' I stared in disbelief at the mayhem.

Mam looked lost as she sat bravely marooned in her now cushionless chair, staring unseeingly over a sea of wreckage. They'd been burgled and vandalized. Cushions, ornaments and tablecloths had been ransacked from the cupboards and drawers. Mirrors hung lopsided on the walls and even her prized electric fire had the plastic imitiation-log effect discarded and smashed.

I tried to hug Mam to comfort her as she sat traumatized. It was like hugging a wooden chair until suddenly the sobs she had been stifling racked her body.

'Why us? What 'ave we done to anyone? We 'aven't got much, only a few bits I'd been savin' for me layin'-out.'

I gave Dad a questioning look. He pulled her gently to him, his face against her hair, his eyes closed, as he caressed her face.

'The bastards 'ave been upstairs and got her good funeral linen she's been savin' for years. Been through the drawers, taken the bloody lot.'

I started to pick up and tidy the shambles.

'Leave it. Leave it where it is, I don't want any of it,' Mam yelled.

'Leave it be, love. Yer can see yer mam's very upset and doesn't want to deal with it, not yet. Give her time.'

The burglary had taken place the previous night. Mam hadn't been to bed and had sat amongst the carnage since then, shocked to the core, not allowing anyone to touch her broken, shattered memories that lay defiled and scattered before her.

Patty and Dolly were marvellous. Knew how to handle Mam so much better than me in a crisis, much more practical. They spent hours with Mam and Dad. Cooked and cleaned, sat through endless cups of tea, cheered Mam with juicy tales of other people's problems. The boys, on the other hand, simply wanted revenge. Heaven help the bastards who did this to Mam and Dad if the boys ever got their hands on them.

It was after several days and much coaxing that she allowed anyone to attempt a tidy-up. Not until then was the full extent of the burglary assessed. The precious gold necklace Joey had bought Mam out of his very first pay packet had gone, together with trinkets and presents given to her by the family over the years.

The sudden realization that her anniversary clock with the brass balls was missing from the mantelpiece brought a fresh deluge of tears from Mam.

Her chin quivered. 'One hundred and three soddin' books of cigarette stamps I 'ad to fill to get that. I even 'ad to smoke Embassy and I don't bloody like Embassy.'

I turned away sharpish, trying to stifle a laugh. Always laughing at the wrong time was my bloody downfall. She looked like she was about to cry again when she noticed the smirk on my face, then with the realization of what she'd just said, she started to laugh. I laughed and Dad joined in until finally we were all convulsed with laughter.

'Sod the bloody clock, I will get you a better one from

the Manchester spivs,' I said, squeezing her hand. 'Anyway it didn't work properly. Always sounded a bit sick if you ask me.'

'Sick? Oh no, that was just yer dad's fault – he stuck an Elastoplast on the donger, said the constant ding-dong got on his nerves. It was our Jacky who told him how to fix it, by bendin' the hammer thing. But oh no, yer dad, he would 'ave none of it; 'ad to do it his own way, so we had to put up with the bloody donk, donk, donk.'

23

It was gone lunchtime. I had just heard the one o'clock
gun on the docks near the Liver Buildings echo across the
River Mersey, and Eric was late getting back from
the wholesalers. The arse was boiling out of the kettle
in the storeroom. I went to switch it off. Thinking I
heard the shop door I squinted across the centre aisle,
through the strategically placed mirrors. I spied a regular
customer, who had become a good friend, putting a tin of
paint in her shopping bag and quietly sneaking out again.
I was dumbstruck; said and did nothing other than attack
Eric as soon as he came through the door.

'Where 'ave you been till now? Don't tell me; let me
guess, to get another pie and custard? Three and a half
years of pies and custards for lunch. You've bought
enough custard squares to tile the backyard; can't you
think of anythin' else? I can't face another soddin' pie.'

'You're upset that I'm late, sorry love, Duke Street
Bridge was up again. You should 'ave said you were sick
of pies, that, or shoot me.' Eric smiled weakly.

'Oh, I'm sorry love, it's this place, it gets me down.'

'OK, out with it, what's really getting you down?'

'Everythin'. The shop, Merseyside, the sickness, the
cold and that bitch Mrs Bradley has just nicked a tin of
paint.'

'Not our Mrs Bradley?'

'Yes, our Mrs Bradley and like a bloody big puddin' I was riveted to the spot – did nothin'.'

'Well I can fix Mrs Bradley but I can't change the weather for you, much as I'd like to. When the dog dies we can think of a warmer climate.'

'If we sold this shop we could pay for the dog's quarantine, couldn't we?'

'No, not unless we won the Pools as well. Besides, I don't know what the shop is worth. Anyway who would want a business that demands as much of you as this one? Everyone wants a chip shop or a laundromat, somethin' easy. Put the kettle on, love. By the way, do you want this pie or not?'

'Shove it.'

The takings for the day totalled less than eleven quid. A pretty lousy day all round. I would be glad to get home and put my feet up. The afternoon had been quiet and time had dragged. It was getting dark as we finished bringing in the mops and brushes from around the outside of the shop. A car stopped in front of the doorway.

'Excuse me ol' boy, do you sell mousetraps?' the posh driver called without even getting out of his car.

'Sure mate, what sort do you want?' Eric yelled back.

The driver switched off the ignition and followed Eric through the door. He looked familiar – that ruddy complexion and flourishing moustache.

'Don't I know you, m'dear?' he asked me.

'I was about to ask the same thing. Where was it now? Do you go to the Golden Guinea nightclub?'

'Certainly not,' he said indignantly. 'I live in Hoylake.'

It had come back to me. 'That's it, Sue and Jeff live in Hoylake. We met you at Sue and Jeff's fancy dress. You were the one dressed like a cavalier. Reg, isn't it?' I answered my own question. 'Yes, of course, Reg, that's it.'

'Small world,' he said. 'Hey, ol' boy, how about this place, terrific isn't it? Have you worked here long?'

'We own it,' Eric said impatiently, waiting to lock up.

'You're lucky, old chap, I would give my eye-teeth to have an emporium like this. I've just packed up my job in advertising. I could just see myself with a business of my own. This quaint little place would suit me down to the ground. Well, if you ever fancy selling it, let's have first crack.'

Eric slammed the mousetrap on the counter.

'How much?' said Reg, fumbling for his wallet.

'Twelve hundred quid.'

'What?'

'Twelve hundred quid, includin' stock.'

'No ol' boy, the jolly mousetrap, how much?'

'One and six. No, forget it, 'ave it on the house. We've cashed up.'

Reg walked around the shop browsing, taking it all in, commenting on the condition of the floor, examining the stock, the displays, etc.

'What's in the back room?' he asked.

'We use it for a storeroom and sometimes we hide in there and watch the shoplifters entertain us while we eat our meat pies and custard squares.'

The sarcasm was lost on Reg.

'Twelve hundred pounds you say? Hmm . . . OK, I'll take it.' He reached over the counter and gave Eric a vigorous handshake, picked up his mousetrap and left. As he put the key into his ignition he yelled, 'I'll be in touch, ol' boy.'

'Pompous sod. Wonder if he'll remember anythin' when he sobers up,' Eric laughed.

Sunday mornings were wonderful, lazy, sleepy and warm. We sometimes managed a lie-in if Richard didn't demand our undivided attention. The sudden ring of the phone put an end to all that.

'Oh no. Don't answer the phone Richard,' Eric shouted.

258

Too late. Probably someone had run out of dog biscuits or birdseed and expected us to open the shop.

'Daddy it's for you,' Richard yelled up the stairs.

I could hear snatches of what Eric was saying, 'Yes, yes of course I remember. You couldn't make it a bit later, could you? Say twelve o'clock our place. That's it, Mosslands Drive. Great! See yer then.' He put the receiver down, ran back upstairs and jumped on the bed.

'Come on you lazy faggot, out of bed, good old Reg is comin' round at twelve o'clock with his solicitor. Got the deposit and the contract for the shop. Good ol' chap,' Eric said, mimicking Reg.

'No. No, yer kiddin' me, on a Sunday? Hell, he's keen,' I laughed.

It was nearly two o'clock in the afternoon. Eric and I sat at the kitchen table drinking coffee and recapping all that had taken place in the last couple of hours.

'I wonder if I could get the dole,' Eric said.

'Why the dole?'

Suddenly we were laughing and he grabbed me up and swung me round and plonked me on the table, saying, 'Because, young lady, soon we will both be out of work, now that we've sold our little emporium. Remember?'

It hadn't sunk in. It had happened in a whirlwind. Did we sell it too cheaply? What would our folks say? Where were we going to work? It was too hard to take it all in so we all went back to bed with a tray of chocolate biscuits and a jug of cocoa.

'How would you fancy livin' in New Zealand, Richard?'

'Don't tease the poor kid,' I said.

'I'm not teasin' him. We can think about it, can't we?'

'I'll go to New Zealand if I can 'ave a little brother,' Richard coolly answered.

We couldn't see the connection. Why a little brother – what did that have to do with anything?

On Monday morning I was looking round the shop

with new eyes. In the long run it had been good to us, that little business. We'd met lots of people, made lots of friends, and seen hard times and good times. Mondays were always quiet, so with renewed vigour I had a big tidy round. I never heard the one o'clock gun, but there was Eric sheepishly standing in front of me with another meat pie and a custard square.

'This is one thing I won't miss. If there's one thing I can't stand it's the routine. I think that gets to me more than anythin', the miserable bloody routine, apart from yer friggin' meat pies.'

He laughed. Punching me lightly in the arm, Eric said, 'Well, we are going to break the routine for once.'

'Why? Don't tell me we're goin' to 'ave a fish pie for a change?'

'No, cheeky. Get yer gear. We're lockin' up the shop, and goin' to London.'

'London? Why London?'

'New Zealand House is there. We'll settle it once and for all. Find out first-hand if it's possible for us to go to New Zealand.'

'I really don't think we can afford it, and what about the dog? We can't go without her.'

'But where's the harm with making a few enquiries?'

The next twenty-four hours were spent getting to and going through New Zealand House, the Charter Travel Boat Company, and various shipping agents in London. We learnt that there was a boat sailing to New Zealand in the first week in April. Just over a thousand pounds would pay for the three of us, all of our possessions and a car, to travel by sea to New Zealand (without the dog).

'Greensleeves', that nauseating chiming 'Greensleeves' from the Mr Whippy ice cream van. It's the middle of the winter – when will the bloke give us a rest?

'Mummy, Mummy, quick, I may miss him. Can I 'ave a

260

cone with a Milk Flake? P-l-e-a-s-e? Hurry before I miss him.' Richard was pulling on my arm.

I handed him two bob. 'Make the most of it, kid, it'll be yer last this time of year. It's getting too cold for ice cream. Now mind how you cross the road.'

I got up to close the front door to stop the wind blowing the leaves and old papers into the vestibule. My heart did somersaults as I heard the screech of brakes and a child scream.

'Greensleeves' played on.

I heard the cries and shouts from the neighbours as I stumbled from our house. Everyone was running to see if they could help. Fearing the worst for Richard, I tried to make another deal with God as I ran.

Too late!

Richard was already under the Mr Whippy van. A splattered ice cream cone lay on the road. Eric was on his knees, surrounded by rivulets of blood running into the gutter carrying cigarette butts and toffee papers through the slits in the grid. Eyes brimming, I panicked – running in the opposite direction, to anywhere that took me away from the sight of the Mr Whippy man crouched over clutching at Eric's elbow, pleading his apologies.

'Not my fault, mate. Not my fault.'

I ran back into the house shaking uncontrollably. My mind was whirling. I couldn't shut out the horror.

'Greensleeves' continued to drone on, regardless.

Within minutes the front door was kicked open and Eric was carrying the limp body of our beloved dog in his arms.

'I think it's too late. Get me a blanket and the car keys out of me jacket pocket. I'll try the vet.'

I stood frozen in confusion.

'The wheels went straight over her. I don't hold much hope,' said Eric, shaking his head.

'What about Richard? Where's Richard? Who's got him?' I yelled.

'A neighbour's taken him in. Poor kid saw it happen. He's very upset. Blames himself because Katie followed him across the road.'

'But I saw Richard under the truck, isn't he hurt?' My eyes and nose were both running now.

'No, thank God. He was tryin' to get the dog out after she'd been run over. Now where's me bloody keys?'

I was not sure now where I stood with God. I had never thought to bargain for our Katie.

Three hours dragged by before Eric returned from the vet's without Katie. He rushed past me on the stairs and went to the bedroom without speaking. I sat and waited on the edge of the bed as Eric sat with his joined hands between his knees and rocked to and fro.

'The vet couldn't do anythin'. Too much damage. The flesh had been torn from her frame. He had no choice but to put her to sleep. I'm so sorry, I know how you an' Richard loved her.'

'It's OK,' I said faintly, 'I was terrified it 'ad been Richard. I really thought it was when I saw his legs stickin' out from under the truck.' I struggled to stay in control but that image kept coming back into focus. Eric remained silent.

'I'll tell Richard, shall I? I'll tell him Katie's in doggy heaven. Maybe we should tell him we will take him to the RSPCA to choose a puppy, before he gets too fretful and brings on the asthma,' I waffled on.

I could see the fury start to well up in Eric, almost choking him. 'No we won't. I've 'ad a bloody gutsful of everythin'.' He thumped his fist into his palm. 'We are going to New Zealand.'

That was it.

We booked on the Russian ship, the *Shota Rustaveli*, leaving on 4th April 1972. It was a charter ship weighing 23,000 tons. Eric felt that the month travelling would serve as a much-needed holiday that would do us all the world of good. Besides, flying would mean starting a new life before we had got adjusted to the idea of leaving.

Now . . . how to break the news to the family?

We tried with Eric's sister first to get a reaction. Rehearsing the long lead-up speech had been futile as Eric blurted, 'Hi Dotty, what do you think? We're selling everythin' up and we're movin' to New Zealand.'

She was shocked into silence. I thought she was about to cry as she and Eric were very close, being the two youngest in the family. After she thought for a moment she got her voice back and chipped in without stopping for breath. 'You lucky buggers. I wish we could come with you but we can't leave Colin's mother, she's too sick. Hey, what about the 'ouse, 'ave you sold it? Hell, you know what? We'd love to buy it and we could buy some of yer furniture, save you the hassle of sellin' it. I'll talk to Colin tonight. Oh, gosh, 'ave you told Mum and Dad? 'Ave you thought about how upset they will be?'

In turn our various other brothers and sisters gave their stamp of disapproval, but oddly, their spouses during the next few months acknowledged we were lucky but also very brave.

We chose to be alone when we told our respective parents. I don't know what Eric's parents said as Eric wouldn't tell me any negative stuff, except that they were very upset with me. They blamed me for plotting and scheming 'just like all the Faulkners'.

Mam and Dad heard my news in silence as expected. It appeared to have about as much impact on my mam as if I had said I was buying a new hat. She stared dry-eyed into vacancy, just like my dad's times in hospital. If you can close your mind to it, then it can't be happening. That always seemed to be Mam's way of thinking.

By coincidence our new friends Gordon and Jan had also resolved to return to New Zealand and decided to travel with us. We started to get really excited once we heard that piece of news. Gordon and Jan were about our age, and their son Paul would be good company for Richard.

It seemed we were destined to go. Everything was fitting into place quite nicely; even the owner of the print shop next door said he would take the shop van off our hands and carry on with the hire-purchase payments. Dorothy and Colin agreed on a price for the house with Eric. Now, with only the remaining few bits of furniture to dispose of, the way was clear.

It was hard watching the last of our possessions being picked over by prospective bargain-hunters. Part of our life was going out of the door, including all our bottom-drawer items and all the overseas presents Eric had bought for me when we were engaged. With a gulp of hysteria I watched helplessly until my much loved and cherished rubber plant was being loaded onto a pushchair by the old girl with the purple candyfloss hair. It was then that the implications of our move hit me.

'How much do yer want for this, queen?'

'What? Oh, sorry, it's not for sale,' I said, making a grab for the plant.

She continued to struggle through the front door with the pushchair, laughing and refusing to hand the plant back. 'No bloody good to you in New Zealand. Won't fit in yer case. Two quid! Hey, what do you say to two quid?'

I was losing the tug of war, and resorted to shouting. 'It's not for sale, understand? It was a Christmas present.'

Eric intervened. 'Sorry love, it's not for sale.' He lifted the rubber plant back to safety. 'Promised it to her mam yer see, sorry. If yer see anythin' else that takes yer fancy I'll knock a few bob off.'

'Suit yerself.'

He turned to me. 'Now, what was that all about?'

'Oh Eric, it's all happened so fast, we don't 'ave anythin' left. No dog, no house, shop, car, furniture, nothin'. What will we do if we don't like New Zealand?'

264

'Course we will. You'll love it, you'll see. Just imagine what it feels like to breathe in fresh air and be warm.'

With all our possessions gone, I wanted to spend our last few days in England with Mam and Dad. Eric wasn't keen but he was agreeable to anything at that stage, as I was getting panicky. Deep down I knew it would be hard on everyone just getting through the next few days.

Dad and Mam continued to ignore the subject of our imminent departure to New Zealand until I asked Mam, 'Can we spend what's left of the time with you before we leave? I thought it would be confortin' to 'ave some time with you and Dad.'

With a false smile that was full of unhappiness, Mam simply said, 'That would be nice chuck.'

We moved in with the minimum of fuss while Mam, without comment, continued to knit, seemingly more vigorously than ever.

It had only just dawned on us how thin and old Dad looked. The sight of him pained me as he sat in his big overstuffed chair dozing his life away, his Jim Reeves records playing in the background.

I lay in bed beside Eric in the dark shadowy room that flashed images of the past, a room that had been mine in childhood. A room that I had once shared with my best friend, my sister Patty. The walls had long since been papered in black contemporary wallpaper when Teddy commandeered the room after he was demobbed. Mam said she wasn't keen on black wallpaper but Teddy insisted, joking, you couldn't see the squishy marks left by the crushed cockroaches.

Now as our collective breath steamed up the windows on the cold March night I turned on my back and stared up at the ceiling, yellow with the stains of endless winters of burst water pipes.

I couldn't sleep properly – I kept wondering what sort

265

of future was waiting for us on the other side of the world. I went to the window and stood with my arms crossed over my breast, hugging myself for reassurance as I stared down into the neighbours' backyard, littered with old prams, rusting dustbins and pigeon coops long-vacated.

Dad's own sad-looking back garden appeared derelict and abandoned with the remnants of last year's tomatoes, and broken stakes marking areas where flowers previously flourished. A few stunted plants still struggled for their share of warmth and sunlight between the heaps of broken bricks and rubble that had once marked the pathways.

As I surveyed my childhood kingdom, all the memories came flooding back to me, memories of being buried in this miserable place. I shivered, perhaps from cold, maybe not. Climbing back into the old familiar sagging bed, I snuggled into Eric's sleeping back. We lay like spoons in a drawer, and I felt his closeness and warmth.

I had never imagined that I would voluntarily spend another night here in this house in Littledale Road.

On the Friday before we left Merseyside, Patty and the family were having a few drinks at Mam's to celebrate their twentieth wedding anniversary. We were invited to join them, when we got home from visiting friends, to make it a farewell drink. We stayed out as long as we could, as I was dreading any further upset at that late stage.

'Look love, it's gettin' late. You don't want to miss them. Let's get back to Littledale Road and get it over with,' Eric encouraged me.

We entered the house to find it throbbing with all my family and loved ones. They had put on a special supper and farewell do. Dolly, Patty, Jacky, Teddy and Georgie all under one roof. I was thrilled, as it usually took a funeral or a crisis to clan them together; they were constantly at war with each other. Soon I discovered why Dad had recently been given the nickname Alan Whicker. He had a recording machine and was recording the party, the messages and blessings from family and friends, to be edited later along with the miles of tapes he had been collecting from customers and neighbours for the past month, all the time pretending not to acknowledge our impending departure.

The tape was never finished.

We were touched when my brother Jacky, not known for his generosity, made a speech that he ended by offering Eric his business card, stating that the money would be made available to come home if we didn't like New Zealand. He added, 'By way of a loan, naturally.'

Next, Georgie punched me playfully. 'Well, who would 'ave thought it eh?' Then he made a nervous little announcement about me not being such a bad kid, a real pain in the arse, but OK he supposed for a girl, all things being considered.

Teddy, on the other hand, seemed quite emotional as he wished us all the very best with the promise of writing regularly. And who knows, perhaps one day we might see him and his family living with us in New Zealand.

All the time, the sight of my sisters keeping busy hanging round the kitchen sink swam before my eyes. Patty attempted a few funny remarks to ease the tension before stumbling from the room mid-sentence. Dolly wiped her eyes on the spare tea towel before leaning her elbows on the sink and dropping her head in her hands.

I stood motionless amid the strained chatter before laughing falsely and saying, 'For goodness sake, it's only for two years,' all the time fighting to avoid eye contact with my mother as I tried to make the lie sound convincing.

24

March 31st 1972 – Good Friday. I refused to call it Black Friday any more. I vowed it would always be Good Friday from now on. It was our tenth wedding anniversary, although no-one else (including Eric) had remembered. Not surprising with all the drama.

Eric's mum was still convinced that the whole idea of us 'abandoning our families' was my entire fault. But Eric's eldest sister Lillian was trying to keep the lid on things with her mother by arranging for the Simmonds family to go for a farewell drink in New Brighton of all places. Eric's brother George and his wife Kathy gave us a lift in their car to the New Brighton Football Club Social Rooms.

It was a cold, blustery night. The entrance to the building was badly lit and the wind whistled and swirled down the alleyway, carrying with it old newsprint, bus tickets and empty sweetpapers into a vortex of rubbish. We were all doing our best to seem jolly. I thought that George and Kathy, both being just token drinkers, must be dreading the next couple of hours. Not surprising, even Eric and I were having to pretend to be happy at the prospect of having a few farewell drinks, particularly in some run-down hall at the arse end of nowhere.

Eric whispered, 'Ten o'clock, Cherry, ten o'clock remember, we agreed? A quick drink and home by ten o'clock. In fact, if we can get away before then, we will. I'll shout a couple of rounds and that should do it.'

George was first through the doors and after blowing on his frozen fingers, fumbled for the light.

'Hurry up lad, I'm colder than Christmas,' Eric complained.

We stepped into a dimly lit room to a chorus of 'Surprise! Surprise!'

Eric and I stood in shocked silence as all the lights went on simultaneously. The band started up and the whole place came to life as we were whisked into the gaily decorated hall, buzzing with the Simmonds crowd, various friends and a few of our shop customers and club members. All there to wish us a fond farewell. Eric's mother gave me a peck on the cheek and told me in no uncertain terms that if anything happened to make her son unhappy she would hold me responsible. 'Have you got that quite clear?' she whispered, smiling benignly for the flashing cameras.

I simply nodded.

Just before midnight the compère invited Eric and me on stage and presented us with an enormous cake while he made a very emotional speech, wishing us a heartfelt Bon Voyage. With a self-satisfied smirk, Eric took over the mike and announced it was our tenth wedding anniversary. He gave me a reassuring cuddle as he announced to all and sundry that he loved me. We were cheered onto the dance floor while Wayne Fontana and the Mindbenders struck up the 'Anniversary Waltz' followed by 'For They Are Jolly Good Fellows'.

Legless and happy we laughed and joked with everyone into the small hours of the morning, until sobered with the music of 'Now Is The Hour' and 'Auld Lang Syne' and finally the National Anthem.

There wasn't a dry eye in the place.

I thought my heart would break.

*　　*　　*

April 1st – Easter Saturday, April Fool's Day.

No practical jokes today.

Mam hadn't eaten for days. Her eyes had taken on that long-familiar faraway look as she gauged our every move. I tried in vain to read anything from her face, thinking what would I do if she begged me not to go? Why did I torture myself like that when there was little or no chance that she would – in fact would anyone actually miss me if I never came back? The tension in the air hung around to the point that my poor father spent most of the time on the toilet. He had an upset stomach, so Mam said.

April 2nd – Easter Sunday. After squeezing shut our suitcases, cursing each other's attempts to help, we'd completed the final details and were ready to go, tired, trying to think if there was anything left undone and putting off the dreaded moment of agonizing goodbyes.

Mam watched the clock. Dad sat in silence watching Mam watching the clock. He stood and began to pace. Finally he was the first to speak as he clutched both my hands between both of his, squeezing reassuringly. Eventually letting go he stammered, 'Me and yer mam love you, little Topsy.' His words faltered as tears rained down his cheek. He struggled for composure. 'We both want the best for you. We want you and Eric and Richard to be happy.'

'Oh, Dad . . .'

'Ssh, I'm not finished. What I want . . . we want to say is don't stay there if yer not happy. Let us know and we'll find some way to get you home somehow; and if you do like New Zealand, don't come runnin' back if me or yer mam get sick. If it's nothin' serious it will be a waste of money, and if it is serious, we'll probably be dead and buried before you make it home.'

Although he was no longer the strong man he used to be, he was crushing me as he held me, looking over my shoulder at the tortured face of my mother who was

270

still in the cold turkey state of suffering I had come to recognize over the years. My mam's silent crying became silent no longer; she wailed like a woman in childbirth. I wrenched myself from Dad's grip and threw myself at her.

'Oh, Mam, I love you, don't you love me?'

'Of course I love you, you silly bitch,' she said, obviously shaken that I would ask such a question. 'I've always loved you. Probably too much, 'cos you were my baby. How could you even think I didn't love you?'

I heard myself crying, great, tearing, deafening sobs.

'All I've ever wanted was for you to tell me that you loved me. All my life I've lived without ever hearin' you say it. Why, oh God why?'

I fell to my knees and sank my head into her lap. She gently toyed with the strands of my loose hair before carefully placing them behind my ear. I closed my eyes as her words finally came tumbling out.

'Look love, it's hard for you to understand. Yer've always been a sensitive gifted child, pickin' up on the unspoken – you've become a mirror of what was goin' on inside me. I used to think I wasn't lovable, that everythin' was my fault. You were a change-of-life baby at a time I thought I'd finished with babies. The war was on. Yer father was always goin' away tryin' to get work just to keep a roof over our 'eads. The bombs were relentless durin' the blitz on Merseyside and I was alone and terrified, tryin' to keep the rest of the family safe.'

She paused, struggling for control. 'You must know I chose to 'ave you; didn't 'ave to, I could 'ave done away with you like a lot did in them days, the days of the war, and unwanted babies, if you know what I mean; heart-breakin' hard times. We were livin' in Buchannan Road at the time in just a couple of rooms with a few sticks of furniture, and when I couldn't pay the rent, the buggers threw us all into the street with nowhere to go. If it 'adn't been for us being evacuated to Neston and a brigadier

271

and his good lady wife takin' us in, God knows what would 'ave happened to us.'

Her voice took on a brighter tone. 'That's why you were called Cherry, after his beautiful daughter, an only child. She was a famous ballet dancer, you know. Couldn't christen you Cherry though. The Catholic Church wouldn't accept it as there isn't a Saint Cherry, so we called you Veronica Cherry instead.'

'I didn't know that. I always thought me name was Cherry Veronica.'

Like slow torture, cutting sharp and jagged, she continued as I closed my eyes, grappling with these painful revelations.

'When you were first born you wanted for nothin'. The brigadier saw to that. He and his wife took a special interest in you. It was he that first started callin' you "the baby", because soon after you were born his daughter was killed in an air raid. He couldn't bring himself to utter the name Cherry.'

Unable to bite my tongue, I blurted out, 'So, why was it that you and the rest of the family cursed me?'

She snapped, 'I never, I never cursed you, I only said that I cursed the day you were born. Can't you see, that's different?'

'No! Anyway why did you 'ave to curse the day I was born? Why? Why did you stop lovin' me, didn't you like me?' I begged, as I grasped her hand.

'After you were born you were a very sick baby and we nearly lost you several times with asthma. The doctor said it would be a miracle if you reached yer second birthday and at one stage yer dad and me were called to the hospital with the priest. They thought you wouldn't see the night out. Really poorly you were. I 'ad already lost two babies before you, who didn't make it to their second birthday either. I couldn't go through that again. The guilt – it was all too much to bear, I simply gave up.'

'Guilt? You couldn't help it that I had asthma.'

272

'Maybe yer right. I don't know. The doctor warned me that some babies born to older women 'ave a fair chance of being mongoloid, asthmatic, or 'ave some other serious birth defects when they're born. Well, that's where the choice came in. I took a gamble on him being wrong. He wasn't. You've suffered all yer life with asthma, and now yer son – God forgive me. I've never stopped feelin' guilty.'

She broke down.

With fresh tears of frustration and anger, I cried, 'Well I didn't bloody die, did I? Did I?'

'Just goes to show,' she whispered. 'I made a choice, gamblin' for a miracle that you wouldn't die like my other two babies did. And miracles can happen even for someone like me who doesn't deserve them – after all who am I? I'm nowt special, nobody in particular.'

The simple act of Mam reaching for a box of tissues and blowing her nose shattered the moment. Mechanically, she passed the box to me.

'Thanks.' I pulled out a handful, wiped my eyes, and stood up. Blindly grabbing some dishes from the table, I stumbled from the room into the kitchen. I tried to brace myself, gripping the edge of the kitchen sink, but I couldn't hold back the scalding tears.

Oh Lord, I had not been prepared for this revelation . . . what now?

I knew I was breaking their tired old hearts with our decision to emigrate and start a new life so far away. Could it be I wanted to teach them all a lesson – show them all I didn't need them? Was that the real reason behind moving thirteen thousand miles away? Please God, I hope not.

I'd have to pull myself together. Have to.

'We'll never see you again, we know that,' said my father wanly.

'Please Dad. Please don't say that. We'll be back in two years. Better still, we can even send for you some time,

273

then you can have the holiday of a lifetime.' I rambled on, knowing that they were both in their seventies and never had a day's holiday in their lives. What I didn't know was my precious dad was dying of cancer. The cocktail of pills he swallowed daily did little to ease his suffering other than help him sleep his remaining days away.

Eric hovered in the doorway. 'Look love, I'm sorry to rush you but we're runnin' out of time and we still 'ave my family to face. We really need to be gettin' on. Richard, give Nanna and Granddad a big love. And did you thank them for yer Easter eggs?'

'I love you Nanna, I love you Granddad. Mummy please don't cry.'

'Quickly Richard, get into the car,' said Eric, who had already checked our belongings and loaded cases on the back seat. Wretchedly, Richard followed us and waited.

'Sorry Mam, real sorry. You take good care of yerselves. Don't worry about Cherry, urm . . . Topsy, I'll take the best of care of her for you,' Eric said as he embraced them.

Mam and Dad clung to each other on the doorstep as they watched our farewell wave. My eyes lingered on them a moment longer before we pulled away from the kerb. I swear that she mouthed the words, 'I love you, Cherry.'

Eric patted my hand. 'Hold on, lovey, nearly there. After my farewell committee of family to face we'll be on our way.'

His parents' house was only fifteen doors away. I knew Eric would be upset at the prospect of struggling through another half-hour similar to the last. He was going through his own private hell. We entered number 51 Littledale Road to find Eric's brothers and sisters, their husbands and wives, his nieces and nephews had gathered. The mood was slightly different from that at 29 Littledale Road, as the Simmonds family obviously supported each other on such occasions. The atmosphere was highly charged and the eyes of the womenfolk were swollen and tender.

Eric's mother hugged me and wished me all the very best, then added woodenly, 'Like I've said before, I don't want to spoil things for you, but hope yer've thought this through properly. I hope to goodness yer doin' the right thing.'

Eric, after strained polite banter with his siblings, targeted his dad, no words, just hugs and silent tears. Eric showed a quiet courage until Lillian started openly crying, which was a trigger for the rest of the family. This left Eric heartbroken, bereft of all words other than 'Sorry. Sorry.'

It was Dotty who took control. 'Haven't you got to 'ave the car in Southampton by six? If so, you'd better be off.'

We were quick to take her cue. The hugging and tears ended abruptly. Sitting in the car Eric tried to compose himself before putting the keys in the ignition – all the time his family was on the step waving and smiling and crying, while numbness settled over me.

His hands seemed welded to the steering wheel. 'Please Eric, hurry. Start the car before I change me mind.'

As we drove out of Littledale Road I looked back one final time, hoping in vain to catch one last glimpse of Mam and Dad before we turned the corner. Then I recalled something Dad once told me he had read some-where. 'Pain is inevitable, but misery is optional.'

Fancy me remembering that now.

25

The clock on the Liver Building struck two as we left Wallasey. The fog began to settle into a downright drizzle and as usual, the north had more than its share of heavy traffic as we crawled along behind a car transporter through streets I'd known all my life. I was lost in thought, wondering how I would ever pull myself together, when I saw the familiar red lights flash and the untimely warning of the Duke Street Bridge being raised. The bridge that had plagued me during my years of working in Birkenhead, and during many dashes to hospital with Richard, would once again stop us dead in our tracks.

'Do you think this is a sign to turn back?' I mumbled.

Eric didn't reply, just looked blankly at me.

'Stop. Stop Daddy,' Richard cried out. 'You 'ave to turn the car round. I 'ave got to go back.'

Thinking Richard was overcome with the same feeling of despair, we tried to comfort his agitation. 'We will see everyone again one day, son, when we come for a holiday.'

'No, you don't understand. We just 'ave to get back now. I've left me Easter eggs at Nanna's.'

We both shuddered at the thought of an action replay. 'I'm sorry son, we can't go back. We'll buy you another Easter egg.'

'I 'ad twelve.' Richard sank down into his seat sulking. 'I've never 'ad twelve Easter eggs in the very whole of my life.' He continued to whine about the bum deal he thought he was getting.

'Sorry, son,' Eric said, 'but twelve Easter eggs is a small price to pay for the chance of a new life in a clean, warm country where you can breathe properly in the fresh air.'

As Eric spoke he put the car into gear and took a detour round to the Penny Bridge, now with a renewed determination to get under way. For him it seemed a relief to concentrate on the driving.

We gazed out of the car window at the charmless, miserable landscape that edged the busy roads, saddened by the dying smokestack industries in the distance belching pollution. Factory hooters heralded the workmen who were armed with their lunch boxes, their trousers clipped around their ankles, heads down and pedalling their bikes. Once on the motorway we could see the wet grey streets of Birkenhead with the hobbling women laden with shopping.

The noise of the car radio could not drown out the sounds and family voices reverberating in my head as the local news announced that there were now over a million out of work nationwide. The Merseyside dockers were on strike again, and Enoch Powell was predicting doom regarding the one and a half million immigrants expected to come flooding in from all over the Common-wealth. My thoughts continued to wander. Strange, this wasn't my news any more. I was somehow detached already. Eric broke into my thoughts. 'Well, we've done our bit.'

'What?'

'We've just made room for three more.'

We drove on for another hour in a melancholy silence.

'Please, love, can we stop at a transport café on the motorway?' I asked.

'Already? What for now?'

'To get Richard twelve Easter eggs. At least that will make one of us happy.'

The drive to Southampton took six hours. Our eyes were gritty and strained with staring out of the window. We had forty-eight hours to get the car dealt with. The Ministry of Agriculture vehicle inspection had to be faced, then steam-cleaning, followed by a special coating of wax to protect it from the sea air. And finally the Customs documents had to be completed.

'You wait in the hotel lobby while I phone a few people and organize tomorrer's timetable. I'll be back soon,' Eric said.

Gordon and Jan, and their son Paul, were travelling down to join us later that evening. That would help calm our shattered nerves. They had been through all this before and survived. It was all very exciting, as we had never stayed in a proper hotel. I was beginning to unwind at the prospect of the next four weeks. A holiday on a luxury liner, being waited on hand and foot and nothing to think about except sleeping, eating and having a raging good time.

Another family had arrived to check into the hotel. The thought struck me: what a healthy, good-looking family, nice and tanned. Five young children I counted, the eldest no more than ten. Then I heard them mention the *Shota Rustaveli*, the ship we were sailing on. What a coincidence, them staying at the same hotel.

Richard, with melted chocolate running down his chin, offered to share his Easter eggs with the other apparently Cadbury-starved children. They thought it was terribly generous but he was thoroughly sick of the taste after his first flush of chocolate had been satisfied.

'Hi,' I said, 'I couldn't help overhearin' that yer all goin' to New Zealand on the *Shota Rustaveli*, same as us. We can't wait. We certainly need a holiday. It's been a long cold winter. Yet you look like yer've just had a holiday.'

278

'Don't talk to me about bloody New Zealand,' the father said, putting in his two penn'orth. 'We've just disembarked from that bloody communist ship and glad to be back on terra firma. And you can stick New Zealand. We spent our life savings taking the family over there, hoping for a fresh start, and now we are left stony broke but at least we are back in good old Blighty.'

'What was wrong? Didn't you like it?' I asked, dreading the answer.

'Not like it? That's a bloody understatement. I feel sorry for anyone contemplating travelling all that way. I just hope you have the fare to come back, that's all. We've left friends stranded over there without any hope of getting back until they can save enough money for the fare. What a backward bloody place it is. You wait. You wait and see.' With that he got in the lift and left his wife and children staring at me.

'Oh, dear, I don't know what to do,' I said, 'Eric's just gone to phone the shippin' agents.'

'Look, love,' said the woman, indicating for me to sit down with her, 'you may like New Zealand but my husband's a true blue, dyed-in-the-wool Pom. I loved it, but Sidney, my husband, hated the ice cream and the sausages. They can't make sausages like us, you know – and no decent television to watch, it's all rugby and other foreign stuff. We travelled the length and breadth of New Zealand but we never had a decent sausage the whole of the time we were there.'

'Oh, is that all?' I laughed, relieved.

'No,' she bristled indignantly. 'Fish and chips. Wait until you taste the fish and chips. My kids will tell you. Fiona, you tell this lady, what were the fish and chips like?' Fiona didn't answer. The woman continued, 'They're all the same, these foreign countries. We even tried Australia at one stage. That was worse with their damn flies.'

I didn't know if I should laugh or cry.

279

Gordon and Jan arrived about eight o'clock. After a brief greeting, we agreed to meet in the bar later that evening after we got the children settled. I was dying to tell them of the family of seven that didn't like New Zealand sausages.

At nearly ten o'clock, when they hadn't appeared, we decided to take a bottle of wine to their room and join them for a nightcap. We were about to knock on the door when we heard it – the arguing, fighting, recriminations, and cupboard doors banging.

'I don't want to go. I don't want to leave my family again. It's your idea. You go if you want to. There's nothing there for me.' Jan seemed to be getting very worked up – her voice was getting louder and shriller.

We sneaked back to our room, the room next door to our seemingly reluctant travelling companions. The bottle of wine remained unopened as we lay in bed too troubled to sleep.

'Sorry we didn't make it last night,' Gordon blithely announced the following morning at breakfast. 'We were so tired after the drive down we had an early night.'

For the next forty-eight hours our friends continued to communicate happily with us but made no effort to talk to each other. I felt melancholy for the rest of the day, probably because it was weird feeling that we had left everything we knew and understood behind, yet we were still in England. I was homesick already.

Eric hesitated and then he opened the largest of the suitcases and handed me a parcel wrapped in brown paper and tied with string.

'I was told not to give yer this till we got to New Zealand but it might help to cheer you up.'

My hands were shaking as I fought with the stubborn knots. I knew, I just knew what it was. I sat tearless for the moment, my head bent against my chest. Then I heard myself crying great tearing, deafening sobs as I held Mam's knitted patchwork blanket against my cheek to once more savour the familiar, smoky yesterdays.

The note that fell to the floor simply said 'Love Mam'.

'Please, I need to phone me mam,' I pleaded with Eric.

'Don't think that's such a good idea love, do you?'

'I don't care what you think, I just want to talk to me mam.' Now I was getting agitated.

'Oh, do as you like, you will anyway, so why bother to ask me?' Eric said offhandedly, slamming the door to show his disapproval. The memories of past door-slamming made me even more homesick. So I phoned.

'Well what did they say?' Eric asked as he came back into the room. 'I expect you upset them all over again.'

'I couldn't get through, there was no answer.'

Eric looked at his watch. 'Eight o'clock, what do you expect, they'll be in the Brighton by now.'

Of course!

Two anxious Merseyside families silently lumbered on board the *Shota Rustaveli*. When I gazed at the ship I was surprised at the smallness of her. 'Twenty-three thousand tons, with stabilizers,' Eric kept repeating. It meant nothing to me, except it didn't look like the magnificent ships of the Cunard Line that tied up in Liverpool.

I watched, grinning, as a Russian sailor struggled, throwing my extra-large suitcase ungraciously onto the bottom bunk in the cabin. Then followed the broken handle.

'I expected that to happen. What the hell 'ave you got in there Cherry, the kitchen sink? It weighs a ton,' Eric laughed.

He would never in a million years have believed what I'd packed after I was informed by a jealous well-wisher that New Zealand was so backward. Apart from a spare suspension unit for our car, I had a couple of dozen torch batteries, twelve mop heads, twelve rolls of Sellotape, hair lacquer, spray starch, one gross of pan scrubs, coat-hangers, Elastoplast, Brasso, shoe polish, brush handles, safety pins, candles, and an endless supply of essential medicines and first-aid kits. These were last-minute items that wouldn't fit in the tea chests that went ahead of us. When Dad saw me packing the cases he said, 'Yer've been watchin' too much of *Gilligan's Island*, me girl.' What a comical old bugger he was, and oh, how I missed them both already.

The cabin that we would be living in for the next four weeks was small and sparse, not like the brochure showed, but we decided as we would only be sleeping there we could make do. That is until more suitcases were thrown on the bottom bunk opposite. We tried to explain to the cabin steward that there was some mistake – they weren't our suitcases. The Russian either didn't understand or didn't want to understand. We were still trying to explain the mistake when Gordon and Jan arrived.

'Looks like we will be sharing a cabin with you,' Gordon said in a monotone.

Like hell! This wasn't a good start to our new life. Jan was as upset as I was because we had paid for separate cabins. Eric and Gordon decided there and then to sort it out with the Purser – they would come off better than fighting it out with Jan and me. Apparently they were convincing; the spare luggage was removed after Gordon and Jan were allocated another cabin. We were all exhausted by the emotion of the past weeks, and nerves were a little close to the surface.

Everyone agreed to meet on deck in half an hour to show the children the ship leaving the berth and being piloted out to sea.

Our little family of three was hanging over the top of the rails, observing groups of fellow passengers, and the frantic activity below. Endless cases being loaded, last-minute taxis arriving, reluctant families and mobs of tearful children, all pushing and shoving to get on board.

It was a bit of a contrast to the Hollywood clichés – television's *Island Princess* or the *Titanic*, come to that, with champagne-drinking, fun-loving passengers, streamers and balloons cascading from upper decks, kisses blown, cuddles and laughter and surprise gifts of fruit and flowers in the cabins.

Instead, it was a bleak, overcast, rain-filled day as we peered into the murky water reflecting the lights from Southampton. The wonderful familiar smell, like our own Liverpool docks, teased our nostrils, while cold drops of rain stung my face, as my hair stuck to my cold wet cheeks. I felt my flesh grow goose-pimply with the wind on my throat. The tugs tooted and the ship blasted its reply. As the ship moved away from the dock Eric reached for my trembling hand.

Too late now – there was no turning back. My feeling of relief was equal to my feeling of guilt. Blinking through the rain, I stared at the misty outlines of the buildings, wondering if we would ever return. Wondering if we had made the right decision, choosing a life so far away, so different yet so full of promise.

Defiantly I shook my head. Then a familiar voice invaded my thoughts, it was my mam's. Her parting words echoed in my mind. 'I made a choice – gambling for a miracle and miracles can happen – even for someone like me who doesn't deserve them.'

Even for nobody in particular?

Farewell

TEN THOUSAND SORROWS
by Elizabeth Kim

'Magnificent . . . Elizabeth Kim writes with clarity, honesty and power about the enduring longing for a mother's love'
Dave Pelzer, author of *A Child Called 'It'*

I don't know how old I was when I watched my mother's murder, nor do I know how old I am today.

The illegitimate daughter of a Korean peasant and an American GI, Elizabeth spent her early years as an outcast. Ostracized by her family and their village, she and her mother were regularly pelted with stones on their way home from the rice fields. Yet because of her mother's love and calm acceptance of their fate, inspired by her deep Buddhist faith, there was a tranquillity in their intense bond – until the day Elizabeth's grandfather and uncle came to punish her mother for the dishonour she had brought the family, and hanged her in front of her daughter's eyes.

Elizabeth was dumped in an orphanage in Seoul where the orphans were neglected, deprived of all affection, and abused. After some time, she was adopted by an American couple. Brought to America, she was surrounded by fanaticism and prejudice: her strict Christian Fundamentalist parents forbade her to recall the traumas of her past, and she suffered racial discrimination at school. At eighteen she was married off to a man who turned out to be a paranoid schizophrenic. After her own daughter was born she ran away and lived in poverty and isolation with her, thus mirroring her past life in Korea. Eventually she made a career in journalism, but after her daughter grew up and left home, Elizabeth returned to Korea to exorcize the demons of the past.

'It is astonishing that Kim has survived . . . All one wants for this exceptional woman is that she be granted ten thousand joys to expunge all the sorrows that have been her life's companion'
The Times

'Elizabeth Kim's remarkable life is tragic . . . More harrowing than any novel'
Arthur Golden, author of *Memiors of a Geisha*

A Bantam Paperback
0 553 81264 5

THE WILDERNESS FAMILY
At home with Africa's wildlife
by Kobie Krüger

'A beautiful, tenderly written book by someone with a heart that
embraces all living things'
Virginia McKenna

When Kobie Krüger, her game-ranger husband, Kobus, and
their three young daughters moved to one of the most isolated
corners of the world – a romote ranger station in the Mahlangeni
region of South Africa's vast Kruger National Park – she might
have worried that she would become engulfed in loneliness and
boredom. Yet the seventeen years spent in this spectacularly
beautiful park proved to be the most magical – and occasionally
the most hair-raising – of their lives.

Kobie recounts their enchanting adventures in this vast reserve –
a place where, bathed in golden sunlight, hippos basked in the
waters of the Letabi River, storks and herons perched along
the shoreline, and fruit bats hung in the sausage trees. But not all
was peace and harmony. The Krügers soon became accustomed
to the sneaky hyenas who stole blankets and cooking pots, the
sinister-looking pythons that slithered into the house, and the
usually placid elephants who grew foul-tempered in the violent
heat of summer. And one terrible day, a lion attacked Kobus in
the bush and nearly killed him.

Yet nothing prepared the Krügers for their greatest adventure of
all, the raising of a lion cub, who, when they found him, was only a
few days old and on the verge of death. It is the rearing of this
orphaned prince, and their moving endeavours to teach him to
become a 'real' lion who could survive with his own kind in the
wild, that lie at the heart of this endearing memoir. It is a memoir
of a magical place and time that can never be recaptured.

'There are some nail-biting encounters in the bush, and myriad
touching tales'
Choice

'An exquisite book'
The Express

A Bantam Paperback
0 553 81334 X

ZOO TAILS
by Oliver Graham-Jones
Foreword by Desmond Morris

One puff adder
One antelope
One crocodile

This was the list of sick animals presented to Oliver Graham-Jones on his first day as veterinary officer at London Zoo.

It was 1951, and the care of wild animals in zoos was in its infancy. Previously, sick animals had been placed in the hands of their keepers and kept from public view. But Oliver Graham-Jones was to change all this. A pioneer of many of the techniques now used by vets around the world, he was instrumental in building the first animal hospital and in moving London Zoo away from its Victorian past into the high-tech world of modern veterinary medicine.

If a dangerous animal escaped or required urgent medical attention, Oliver was always on hand, ready for any eventuality. In *Zoo Tails*, he tells us about some of the extraordinary animals he looked after: how he anaesthetized, and was chased by, a gorilla; captured an angry polar bear in thick fog; performed a colostomy on a python; and fitted a raven in the Tower of London with a wooden leg.

'This delightful book, written by Britain's most distinguished vet, reminds us that animals think and feel, that they experience loyalty, friendship, sadness and sorrow, and it is a comfort to know there are dedicated people like Graham-Jones who treat them with love and enormous compassion'
Val Hennessy, *Daily Mail*

A Bantam Paperback
0 553 81342 0

BEST FOOT FORWARD
From La Rochelle to Lake Geneva – the Misadventures
of a Walking Woman
by Suie Kelly

Why would an unfit, fifty-something Englishwoman embark on a solo walk across France from La Rochelle on the west coast to Lake Geneva over the Swiss border?

And why would a total stranger from San Antonio, Texas come to live in her crumbling French farmhouse to house-sit for a multitude of boisterous and unpredicatable animals?

With no experience of hiking or camping, not to mention using a compass, Susie Kelly found out the hard way that it is possible to be overloaded and ill-prepared at the same time. Scorching days, glacial nights, perpetual blisters, inaccurate maps, a leaking tent and an inappropriate sleeping bag were daily vexations, but as she hobbled eastwards, the glory of the French landscape revealed its magic and the kindness of strangers repaid her discomfort in spades.

Best Foot Forward is an hilarious and heart-warming tale of English eccentricity, the American pioneering spirit, and two woman old enough to know better.

A Bantam Paperback
0 553 81490 7

A SELECTION OF NON-FICTION TITLES
AVAILABLE FROM BANTAM AND CORGI BOOKS

81341 2	**LIFE IN A POSTCARD**	*Rosemary Bailey*	£7.99
99065 5	**THE PAST IS MYSELF**	*Christabel Bielenberg*	£7.99
14093 7	**OUR KATE**	*Catherine Cookson*	£5.99
15027 4	**THE GOD SQUAD**	*Paddy Doyle*	£6.99
12833 3	**THE HOUSE BY THE DVINA**	*Eugenie Fraser*	£8.99
81529 6	**IF ONLY . . .**	*Geri Halliwell*	£6.99
81363 3	**AT THE MERCY OF THE WINDS**		
		David Hempleman-Adams	£8.99
14185 2	**FINDING PEGGY: A GLASGOW CHILDHOOD**		
		Meg Henderson	£7.99
14164 X	**EMPTY CRADLES**	*Margaret Humphreys*	£7.99
50696 X	**NEVER MIND THE MOON**	*Jeremy Isaacs*	£9.99
81342 0	**ZOO TAILS**	*Oliver Graham-Jones*	£5.99
81490 7	**BEST FOOT FORWARD**	*Susie Kelly*	£6.99
81264 5	**TEN THOUSAND SORROWS**	*Elizabeth Kim*	£6.99
81334 X	**THE WILDERNESS FAMILY**	*Kobie Krüger*	£7.99
14050 3	**I'M A STRANGER HERE MYSELF**	*Dedric Longden*	£5.99
13356 6	**NOT WITHOUT MY DAUGHTER**	*Betty Mahmoody*	£6.99
40936 0	**THE HIDDEN CHILDREN**	*Jane Marks*	£7.99
14288 3	**BRIDGE ACROSS MY SORROWS**	*Christina Noble*	£6.99
81302 1	**LA PRISONNIERE**	*Malika Oufkir*	£6.99
81195 9	**SORROW MOUNTAIN**		
		Ani Pachen and Adelaide Donnelley	£6.99
81240 8	**SIBERIAN DREAM**	*Irina Pantaeva*	£6.99
50491 6	**JENNY PITMAN AUTOBIOGRAPHY**	*Jenny Pitman*	£7.99
81269 6	**T'RIFIC**	*Mike Reid*	£6.99
81465 6	**BITTER ALMONDS**		
		Mary Taylor Simeti & Maria Grammatico	£6.99